Paul Pellicoro on Tango

Among the places Paul Pellicoro's work can be found are:

On Film:

Autumn in New York
Flawless
Summer of Sam
The Object of My Affection

Let It Be Me
Scent of a Woman
A River Runs Through It
Straight Talk

On Stage:

Midsummer Night Swing
(Lincoln Center)

Saturday Night Fever
(Broadway)

TangoFest
(Town Hall)

Copa Cabana
(Night Club)

On Television & Video:

The Vicki Show
Conan O'Brien
Nine Broadcast Plaza

Good Day New York
Today Show
All My Children

Celebrity Clients Include:

Kim Alexis
Jennifer Aniston
Gabrielle Anwar
Sidney Biddle Barrows
Helen Gurley Brown
Steve Buscemi
Brian Cox
Robert De Niro
Matt Dillon
Richard Gere
Sally Kirkland
Vicky Lawrence

John Leguizamo
Conan O'Brien
Al Pacino
Aidan Quinn
Daphne Rubin-Vega
Paul Rudd
Winona Ryder
Mira Sorvino
Lara Spenser
Stanley Tucci
Paula Zahn

Paul Pellicoro on
Tango

Souvenir Press

First Published in USA by Barricade Books Inc. 2002

This edition published 2002 by
Souvenir Press Ltd.,
43 Great Russell Street, London WC1B 3PA

ISBN: 0 285 63654 5

Manufactured in Canada

Table of Contents

A special thanks is owed to my partner and friend, Eleny Fotinos who took over the running of DanceSport while I was involved in writing this book. Without her help there would be no book. In fact, without her there would be a lot less of everything in my life.

Foreword

T he book you have in your hands evolved from a novice's first tentative tango lessons given by one of the world's best-known tango teachers, Paul Pellicoro. It grew into an entertaining full-blown "everything" book about the world's most intriguing dance—Argentine tango.

There was no question that I would choose Paul Pellicoro as my teacher. He had, after all, taught Al Pacino and choreographed Pacino's famous tango scene in *Scent of a Woman*. Indeed, he earned the name "Teacher of the Stars" because, when their films had a dance scene, celebrities like Robert De Niro, Richard Gere, Winona Ryder, among others, selected Paul to coach them.

I was hooked from my first lesson. Soon I was taking as many lessons as I could, signing up for workshops and joining a group of students who traveled with Paul's studio, DanceSport, to Buenos Aires, to experience tango in its hometown. That first trip was followed by a second, then a third, and, well, who knows where it will lead?

Eventually, I convinced Paul that he had a gift that should be shared with a wider audience than his New York studio could reach. A book would accomplish that.

What you will find in these pages is not the usual how-to-dance-tango book. Oh, it is that, too. But it is much more, and it will introduce you to the complete tango experience.

Using the talents of a number of writers, you are offered the expertise and impressions of a variety of people. There is an excellent illustrated section created by Paul Pellicoro on the basic, introducto-

Gabrielle Anwar and Al Pacino in *Scent of a Woman*

ry steps of Argentine tango. It also includes essays on the history of the dance, from its lower-class beginnings to the stages of the world's best-known theaters by writer Katharine Jones.

Paul tells about his journey from being a hustle dancer in the New York clubs to becoming an internationally known tango expert. He also speaks of his influence on tango and his role in popularizing it. He introduces biographies of some of the biggest stars in tango, both past and present. And his partner in dance and business, Eleny Fotinos, reveals her experiences that led her from classical ballet to tango. She also talks about Paul as only she can.

Noted musician Pablo Aslan writes about tango music in depth and Carlos Quiroga, publisher of *ReporTango* magazine and DJ extraordinaire, presents a suggested list of music for you to get started with. There is also Keith Elshaw's ToTango.net website for on-line music commentary.

There are personal experiences about getting into tango from Marilyn Cole Lownes, *Playboy* magazine's only British Playmate of the Year. I describe what to expect at the milongas (dance clubs) of Buenos Aires. Pamela Saichann, contributing editor of *ReporTango* magazine, writes about tango on Broadway.

There is the insight of a true "milonguero," Carlos Funes, one of those Argentine gentlemen who has had a lifetime of dancing in salons and shares his thoughts with us.

You will also learn general etiquette and what to wear both on your feet and on your body. And if you want to practice your Spanish, we include a glossary of tango terms.

Finally, because tango is becoming a universal passion, there is an extensive directory of tango clubs all over the world, provided by Paul Lange and Michiko Okazakiof Britain's *El Once* magazine.

Paul Pellicoro on Tango is designed to give you the fullest tango experience possible. We hope you will enjoy it. And if it inspires you to get out on the dance floor and learn this fascinating dance, the book in your hands may just change your life!

—Carole Stuart
Barricade Books

A Brief History of Tango

Katharine Jones

Today tango is nearly synonymous with passion and romance. It calls to mind romantic lovers, enticing women in elegant gowns and glittering ballrooms filled with the suave and graceful. This was certainly not the case in turn-of-the- century Buenos Aires, where tango began as a crude, even obscene, expression of low-class street culture.

Tango was born during a time of great change in Argentina. In the 1880s, Europe was in near economic ruin, and many looked to Argentina as the promised land, full of opportunity. Seeking a better life, hundreds of thousands of Europeans left behind their homes, families and lovers and headed to Buenos Aires with the dream of "striking it rich in America." For most, this dream was merely an illusion that was soon replaced with a harsh life of abusive labor, poverty, loneliness and despair.

The European immigrants settled just outside Buenos Aires in the suburban slums of an area called the *Orillas* (literally, outskirts). Here Italians, Irish, Germans and Greeks mixed with the population of native Indians, African immigrants, peasant Argentines, gauchos and criminals. From sunrise to sunset, they worked in packing houses on the Uruguayan border and on the docks of the Rio de la Plata only to return home to *conventillos* (boarding houses for immigrants and workers), where they slept five or six to a room. At night the men would gather on the streets and in bars, where violence was common, to drink away their sadness and sing love songs for the women they left behind. As women were scarce in this harsh, frontier-like society, men often went to the brothels for which the Orillas became known.

From these gatherings, a new music that would become tango emerged. The first tangos were played with flutes, violins, guitars and (in the brothels) piano. Later, the German bandoneon entered in, and its distinctive, haunting sound came to characterize the music. As the Orillas had blended together so many cultures, this music fused together rhythms as disparate as the Pampas' milonga, the African candombe, the Spanish fandango and the Cuban habanera. More than just a mixture of various origins, this new music expressed the sentiments of a growing outcast society. In its rhythms and in the mournful sounds of the bandoneon are heard the longings, frustrations and sorrows of the people from whose souls it came. It became the blues of Buenos Aires.

Like the music, the dance of tango was also born from these street-corner gatherings and in brothels' salons. It originated as a dance of the underworld—a way for local pimps to showcase their girls and to entice customers. The close, often breathless, embrace, the concentration of movement from the waist down, the sensual intertwining and scissor-like flicking of legs, were all symbolic of the skills and pleasure the prostitute had to offer, if you were her lucky man. First and foremost, tango was a sexual choreography—what would later be politely referred to by some as "the vertical expression of a horizontal desire."

The seductive moves of tango were not only captivating but challenging; soon the pimps began teaching the men to dance. First men danced as a way to pass time on the streets or in the brothels' salons, and with the tango, the brothels began evolving from a place where one waited his turn with a woman to a kind of seedy social club. As there were few women to dance with, men often danced with men to practice and perfect the steps. In this incarnation, tango often took on the role of a battle. A man's mastery of tango became, in fact, a means of impressing women and even a duel-like way for men to compete with one another for a woman's affection. Rather than a dance of romance and frustrated love, in its original form, tango spoke of lust, longing, conflict and violence. "Tango is an argument that you dance," Hector Orezzoli* said, "and that argument isn't just about who will go home with whom. It broadens to take in destiny."

The earliest tango music also bespoke these themes. Though most of the early songs had no lyrics, those that did were usually obscene or told stories of the street violence of the *compadrones*. Most songs were untitled, but those with titles usually referred to some famed character in the world of prostitution. And, like the dance itself, the first tango lyrics were also improvised.

Though respectable families in the Orilla first looked down on tango, little by little the dance and its music found their way into the neighborhood's cafes and dance halls, and finally into family celebrations. The middle- and upper-class Argentines, however, wanted nothing to do with it. But in the early 1900s when, in search of bordellos and adventure, the mischievous sons of the Argentine elite started visiting the Orilla, they discovered tango and became hooked. When they arrived in Paris later that year—where the wealthy young men were commonly sent to study—they began teaching this dance to their upper-class Parisian friends. This was in 1907, and within a year tango took Paris by storm and become all the rage. At the most elegant upper-class parties and in the finest dance halls throughout the city, people were dancing tango. By 1910, tango classes were even being taught in Parisian dance schools.

In its fine new European home, tango was changing. Though the form stayed essentially the same, the movements became more modest and refined. The Parisians were dancing their own tame version of the original, but it was tango all the same. The dress had gone from rouge to refined; the rough and sleazy wardrobes of the prostitute, pimp and dock worker were replaced by the elegant gowns and tuxedos of refined Europeans.

Tango quickly spread to the rest of Europe as well and was immediately embraced by the general population—so much so that

*Hector Orezzoli is the cocreator of *Tango Argentino*.

photo: Katherine Jones

Scene from a typical milonga

it became a political issue. In 1914, Kaiser Wilhelm II of Germany banned tango throughout Germany, condemning its "immodesty." Even the Pope spoke out against it, referring to it as "a shameless pagan dance that is an attack on family and social life." But it was too late for an official decree. Tango had taken hold, and all of Europe was dancing.

Having been legitimized and made fashionable by the Europeans, tango was enthusiastically welcomed back to Argentina and even embraced by its high society. This new acceptance was also encouraged by Argentina's passing of the Universal Suffrage law in 1912, which gave the lower class the right to vote. More than simply granting political power, this law effectively brought the lower class into the larger society from which it had been formerly cut off. Once the people were accepted, their music and dance followed.

Before long, tango was soon being showcased in the Buenos Aires cabarets and theaters, where the rich went to be entertained. This was in part because in 1919 the brothels had been outlawed, and with their closing a whole subculture was displaced. Writing tango lyrics, which had formerly been mere vulgar improvisation, was suddenly a trend. Though the themes were no longer obscene, they were still themes of the people; most often they spoke of a lover's betrayal and loyalty to one's family and social class. Tango singers and musicians, such as Carlos Gardel, Enrique Delfano, and Osvaldo Fresedo, rose to fame as the first tango celebrities. And during that time, tango was taking its place in America as well. In 1921, Rudolf Valentino danced tango in the film *The Four Horses of the Apocalypse*, bringing tango to the forefront and creating an image of romance and passion that would be forever associated with the dance.

While tango had risen to great heights in the first three decades of the century, during much of the 1930s it was pushed to the side in Argentina. The 1930 military coup ended the people's right to vote and with that the tango, "the voice of the people," fell silent. By the end of the thirties, the working class regained certain political freedoms and tango was again revived—this time with the greatest zeal ever.

From the late 1930s to the 1950s tango was in its heyday. These years came to be known as "The Golden Age." Throughout Argentina, tango became symbolic of the solidarity of the masses and became a living, breathing part of the society. Tango was in movies, on the radios and in salons. It was back in the nightclubs and cabarets, but more importantly, tango was in the social clubs, dance halls and even in elegant tea and coffee houses, where dancing in the afternoon was commonplace. In short, tango had become a significant part of the Argentine culture and was also beginning to define the character of the nation.

Milongas (the gatherings for tango dancers) at social clubs became elegant weekly events, where the young and old alike gathered to dance. This was a different, more refined world than that of the nightclub or cabaret. Rather than just tango bands, social clubs often featured large orchestras that played not only tangos, but jazz and classical music as well. At these gatherings, etiquette was strict. Married women were escorted by their husbands, young women attended with parents or siblings, and women of age came with large groups of friends so that they were always in some sense chaperoned. Men and women dressed well and danced modestly; there were none of the leg lifts and dips or high-slit skirts so often popularized by show dancers today.

When Juan Domingo Peron rose to power in the 1940s, although himself a military dictator, tango reached its highest point. Both he and his wife, the now famous Eva, embraced the new popular tango culture and nearly held it up as a national treasure. Tango lyrics were no longer written in Lunfardo (the language of the Orilla and of thieves) but in Spanish, and by commoners and intellectuals alike. Having lost the class affiliation, the themes were now romantic and nostalgic, and imbued with pride and longing for a "lost society" that people had idealized. While it was nostalgic, tango was also a celebration of Argentina's present culture and status. It was a point of pride for a country that had become in those years one of the 10 richest countries in the world and the one that inspired the world to dance.

With the death of Eva in 1952 and the invasion of American rock and roll, tango lost its popular appeal and certainly its spotlight. Many tango dancers became rock and roll and swing dancers. In Europe and America as well, tango was pushed out of the dance halls and lounges and replaced with the new music and the dance that came with it.

In the 1960s, Juan Carlos Copes, the man credited with keeping the flame of tango alive during the years of harsh military rule in Argentina, brought tango to the New York stage in the Broadway production *New Faces of 1962*. He appeared on the *Ed Sullivan Show* three times in the early sixties to reacquaint America with this nearly forgotten dance. The New York studios saw these developments as an opportunity. Thinking they might be able to rekindle an interest in tango, they began offering tango classes that year, but their attempts failed. Ten years later, witnessing the hustle craze, the Arthur Murray Studios tried to start a dance hybrid, tango-hustle, but that, too, failed to catch any public interest.

In 1985, *Tango Argentino* came to Broadway and ignited a new passion for tango that swept through New York like wildfire. The stage had been set, in a sense, by the popularity of partner dancing that had started with disco and hustle in the seventies. But more than anything, it was something in tango itself that spoke to people. Dance studios started offering tango classes again, and this time the classes were in high demand. Tango performances suddenly appeared not only in Broadway shows, but in dinner clubs and nightclubs as well.

In essence, *Tango Argentino* started what became an international renaissance for tango. Similar to what had happened in the Paris of the twenties, New York's interest in tango brought tango back in fashion worldwide and once again in Buenos Aires. Today in every major city, from New York to Tokyo, people are once again fascinated with this dance. Tango shows like *Tango x 2, Forever Tango* and *Tango Pasión* travel from city to city performing for enraptured audiences. In cinema, tango has made a comeback as well and become the subject of films like *Naked Tango, The Tango Lesson, Tango!* and *Assassination Tango*. Musicians have also become inspired by the allure of tango music. In 1996, Julio Iglesias released the CD *Tango*, and in 1997 noted classical cellist Yo-Yo Ma recorded the music of Astor Piazzolla in his critically acclaimed *Soul of the Tango*.

Today, nearly every night of the week in every major city throughout the world, tango classes and milongas are filled, not just with dancers, but with ordinary people: students, lawyers and secretaries. Most often they are people who want to recapture some immediate sense of passion and romance in life and who find just that in the breathless pauses and subtle movements of the dance. Visiting Buenos Aires has become a common retreat among tango junkies who want to experience the real thing in its city of origin, and many dance schools now offer yearly "tango tours" to this city. And in Buenos Aires? Each night there are numerous tango shows, milongas, practicas, and even afternoon tango salons. Once again, the people in Buenos Aires are dancing until dawn. Whatever forces are at work, one thing is certain: Tango is back.

My Crusade for Tango

Paul Pellicoro

How did I wind up on a crusade for tango? Well, I have to go back to how it all started for me and give a little history.

In the mid-seventies, I found myself, along with other baby boomers, dancing in nightclubs to a style of music that had a simple beat that everyone could feel. The music became known as disco, and the slick rhythmical dance that grew out of this era set off a dance craze. The dance was appropriately called the hustle.

At the time, no one knew that this one dance would start a retro movement for dance and music. As nothing else in history, hustle whet the dance appetite for a new generation, creating an interest in the pleasure of partner dancing.

From the very start, my peers and I were pioneers in a dance that we learned and created on the dance floor, not in a dance school. That came later. I didn't know it back then, but we were what were known as "street dancers." At the time, this was a derogatory term if you were an aspiring professional. But it simply meant that you learned to dance by dancing in nightclubs and discos. If you were too young to go to a club, you would dance at house parties, in neighborhood parks or even on the streets. A dance school was not an option. Back then, dance schools were reserved for conservative zombies who didn't have a clue.

Fueled by youthful enthusiasm and musical inspiration, we all learned together through trial and error. Showing off and challenging friends to figure out your personal steps also played a part in this learning process. If you were lucky enough to dance with the better dancers, there was a good chance you'd learn faster. Whomever you danced with, learning required trusting your instincts, listening to the music and daring to experiment.

It was exciting to take part in the creation of the hustle trend, and I feel fortunate to have lived through this time in dance history. Hustle and "street dancing" is a part of my dance background that I will always cherish because I learned things as a street dancer that I could never have learned in a dance school or from any dance teacher. Most importantly, it taught me to trust my intuition and instincts, which have served me well, first as a dance student and even now as a teacher.

This informal way of learning to dance is, historically, the way most real social dancers learned, and this is especially true of tango

dancers from Argentina. But however you learn tango, either in a class, at a club or from a book, it's essential that you develop a feel for how to move with your partner. Learning to trust your instincts and to improvise movements to fit the music is the heart of real Argentine tango. This personal interpretation is what allows you to create your own individual style. Perhaps witnessing how different dancers expressed their individuality in this way is what drew me to tango in the first place.

While trusting my instincts as a dancer was important, and something I did easily as a beginner, somewhere early on, when I became a professional, these instincts became vague and things became unclear and confusing. It took about 10 years of searching before I was to put it all together again. In large part, it was through my experiences with Argentine tango that my intuitive spirit for dancing was reawakened. But let me explain.

Paul Pellicoro and partner Eleny Fotinos

In 1976, I began working at Arthur Murray's in New York, which was one of the popular franchised dance studios. The traditional ballroom and Latin studios were trying to get in on the disco-hustle craze, and I was recruited to teach because of my popularity in the disco clubs as a hustle or "street" dancer. I saw working in the studio as an opportunity to broaden my horizons by studying other ballroom and Latin dance styles. The international competitive style was highly regarded at the time, and it was also the most disciplined of all the techniques being taught. Thinking that the discipline of this technique would make me a real professional, as opposed to just a club dancer, that's the training I decided to concentrate on.

It wasn't long before I fell into what I know now is a common problem that many natural dancers experience when they turn professional. As a result of studying and analyzing technique to pass my professional exams, I began to lose my natural feeling for the movement.

In my rush to become the next rising star champion, I started working hard at dance, and that focus on "hard work" was the problem. If you are working hard at dance, rather than going with your instincts, you're doing it wrong. I fell into the pitfall of trying to force the technique rather than just letting it happen. Along those same lines, I was also prematurely concerned with having a winning competitive "look," as opposed to understanding that if I just felt the dance, soon enough the look would come. Again, my biggest mistake was thinking that hard work would compensate for inexperience.

In short, I forgot about the essence of good dancing, which actually has little to do with steps, and everything to do with feeling. I started paying more attention to mimicking patterns rather than trusting my instincts. That, coupled with the fact that the teachers and coaches I studied with often seemed to be contradicting each other, caused me to take many unnecessary detours in my quest to become a top dancer. Only after years of study and thousands of dollars in dance lessons did it all start to make simple sense once again.

The fact is, there are as many different approaches and concepts to teaching and learning to dance as there are dance teachers. I truly feel that the road to becoming a good dancer doesn't have to be long and painful. It doesn't even have to be expensive. In fact, with the right guidance, it should be a joyful process of discovery from day one.

My love of dance and my ambition to share what I have learned with others led me quite naturally to start my own school. In 1985, in the heart of New York City, I founded what is now DanceSport Ballroom and Latin Dance Studios.

While I have always enjoyed both teaching and dancing a wide range of different partner dances, in 1985 I saw the hit Broadway show *Tango Argentino* and became inspired by real tango. (By real tango, I mean the style of tango danced in Buenos Aires from the late 1930s to the end of the 1950s.) I was particularly attracted to the emotional embrace and the musicality of the tango. I was also inspired by the way the general public related to it as well. You could feel that they wanted to do this dance. The audience wasn't intimidated by it. In part, people felt encouraged by the fact that most of the dancers in the cast of *Tango Argentino* were well over 40 years old and looked like anyone's aunt or uncle or the folks next door. This was important because it made the average person in the audience feel that tango was something that even he or she could do —and it is!

Before long, some dancers from the cast started capitalizing on the tango renaissance that *Tango Argentino* had inspired by teaching their own classes. Hector Mayoral and his wife Elsa Maria, were the first to offer tango classes in New York, which they held during the day and also on their night off. The very first class was in a small studio in Queens.

This first class with Hector and Elsa Maria was quite memorable. They didn't speak a word of English, so one of the bilingual members of the class took on the role of interpreter. There were about 15 of us. Most were semi-professionals, and a few were professionals like me. None of us knew quite what to expect that day, but we were all caught up in the excitement of learning this new and captivating dance that was the talk of the town. It turned out to be unlike any dance class we had ever had.

The most notable aspect of their teaching was that they never taught any of the figures the same way twice. Instead, they showed us how the choreography and timing could be altered and improvised to the musical phrase playing at the immediate moment. They continually demonstrated how different music influences the steps one does.

Their way of teaching was completely different from the orthodox method, which is by rote and repetition. At first, this style of teaching was very frustrating and quite difficult for a room filled with analytical dance professionals. Our first impression, of course, was that Hector and Elsa Maria may have been great dancers and performers, but they weren't very good teachers.

By the end of the class on that historic afternoon, however, a sudden revelation occurred to all of us. We realized that our teachers weren't as inadequate as we thought. In fact, they were quite the opposite. In that first class they taught us an important lesson that many of us had all but forgotten: that dancing must be connected to a feeling inspired by the music.

At the end of the day, I felt transformed. The class had helped me see my role as a dance teacher in quite a different light. It reminded me of what I had always known as a "street" dancer, but as a professional teacher had quickly forgotten. Namely, that learning to dance was not just about repeating set steps to repetitive rhythms. It was about letting the rhythm of the music inspire and create the movement...and this is the true essence of tango!

Soon after Hector and Elsa Maria's class, other cast members also started teaching at different places in town. I took as many classes as I possibly could. I was fortunate to learn the different ideas and styles each one had to offer.

Paul and Eleny

It wasn't long before I added tango classes to the curriculum at my own dance school and started teaching the classes myself. Everything I learned from the lessons that I took with the cast during the day, I began teaching to my students later the same night. DanceSport was the first and only dance studio in New York to offer the Argentine tango, and as a result, our classes were instantly packed.

Word of tangomania spread through the city and soon the newspaper and television media began coming to the studio quite regularly. The tango scene just took off from there. To top it off, we were lucky enough to have the legendary Juan Carlos Copes, *Tango Argentino's* choreographer, teach exclusively at DanceSport. This was a really exciting time; tango was catching on like wildfire and sweeping through New York City and soon enough the rest of the world.

Around this time, I started dancing with a new partner, Eleny Fotinos, who is still my dance partner today and my partner in the studio as well. With DanceSport as our vehicle, we began our crusade for tango. Along with teaching classes and private lessons throughout the week, we also started a tango practice session on Wednesday nights.

Here, tango students could put their lessons to practical application with fellow students and professionals alike. This "practica" or "milonga," as it is known, was the first of its kind in the United States and is today the longest ongoing practica in the country.

We started recruiting other Argentine tango dancers to teach at the studio as well. It wasn't long before our students caught the fever and became as addicted and dedicated to this dance as we were. With all this enthusiasm, in the winter of 1986, DanceSport began taking students on the first tango tours to Buenos Aires, which have since become an annual event.

photo: Jeanette Jones

Club Gricel, a popular Buenos Aires milonga

Aside from all we did at the studio, Eleny and I were promoting tango around town as well. Wanting to fan the flames of interest that *Tango Argentino* had started, we began doing tango performances in nightclubs where the trendier crowds hung out. In 1988, Nell's was "the" chic celebrity hangout and the owner, nightclub impresario Keith McNally, hired me to create a tango night there. Tango was the thing, and everyone wanted to be connected to it. Accompanied by a live tango band we assembled from local Argentinian musicians, we also ran a milonga at Nell's, where we performed throughout the evening for famous personalities like, TV personality/musician Paul Shaffer, pop star Prince and fashion designer Carolina Herrera. That original New York tango orchestra included pianist Frank Valentine, bassist Pablo Alsan, guitarist Horacio Blanc, and bandoneonists Raul Jaurena and Alfredo Perdernera. These musicians have since become very established in the world tango circles, and some have gone on to produce their own CDs.

In the years since then, Eleny and I have continued to produce, create and perform in many tango shows and events. In 1997, launched the first "TangoFest" at New York's Symphony Space, which features some of the best tango dancers in the world. "TangoFest" has now become an annual spring event at New York's famed Town Hall. In 1997, we also brought tango to Lincoln Center's annual summer "Swing Nights Festival," which now features all types of music and dance. Clearly, tango inspires us and as a result we feel compelled to continue inspiring others!

While I am still involved in various tango productions, teaching and dancing tango remain my passion. This book is devoted to the goal of sharing that passion.

From Ballet to Tango

Eleny Fotinos

For the last 15 years, I have been lucky enough to dance with a partner who is one of the best women in tango today. This is not just my own biased opinion, but the general consensus of all those who know Eleny Fotinos and have seen her dance. She especially commands the respect of those who have had the "sensational" experience of actually dancing with her. When she follows, she is able to give men a feeling that fascinates them and leaves them wanting more. She has been a muse for many of today's greatest tangueros, such as Juan Carlos Copes and Carlos Gavito, to name but two. Often singing her praise, they consider Eleny's dancing to be nothing short of "inspirational."

Dancing with Eleny has been a humbling experience, especially because she started as my protégée. Years ago, when I first started dancing with her, my coach at the time, Walter Laird, put it this way: "As a partner she is almost impossible to equal. The only problem you'll have when dancing with Eleny is being able to dance up to the high level of talent and beauty that she possesses."

So this is what I have to contend with. On top of that, Eleny's own expectations of herself are nothing short of perfection. Unfortunately, I am far from perfect. So when dancing with her on the stage or in a performance, I can never escape the feeling of being dwarfed by her presence. She's a tough act to lead.

What follows is her story about how she started dancing as a young girl and how she became my professional partner. She also shares her feelings on what tango means to her and what attracts her to it.

—Paul

• • •

I always knew that I wanted to be a dancer. I don't really know where it came from, but one morning, when I was seven years old, I woke up and declared to my mother that I was going to be a prima ballerina in the New York City Ballet. I begged her to put me in classes and she finally did. So from age seven to 17, I started studying ballet full time, six hours a day. I danced at a studio in Astoria, Queens, which also had a small dance company. I danced there for a few years, and then was awarded scholarships to the Joffrey and Harkness ballet schools. I was very devoted and focused on making my dream a reality.

Along with ballet, however, my mother also enrolled me in weekend ballroom classes. She had been an amateur ballroom dancer, and she also used to compete. One year she had even won New York City's prestigious "Harvest Moon Ballroom Competition," which was held in the Felt Forum at Madison Square Garden. Though my heart was set on ballet, she wanted me to dance ballroom as well. So at seven years old, on weekends I was coerced into taking ballroom lessons with my 11-year-old partner, Andrew Jushenko, with whom I danced in numerous junior-level dance competitions. I was very shy back then, and though we danced together for nearly four years, we never once spoke!

I was 12 years old when I decided to stop taking ballroom classes and doing competitions because I wanted to devote all my time to ballet; again ballet was my dream.

In 1984, my mother, after taking a hiatus,

photo: Carole Stuart

Eleny and Paul in Buenos Aires

started dancing again at a well-known dance studio on East 85th Street. Her focus was on international style competition dancing, and her teacher happened to be Paul Pellicoro, who, at the time was a protégé of Bill Davies. Bill, the owner of the school, was the former U.S. international style ballroom champion, and his school had a strong reputation for its training in international style competition dancing. My mother kept encouraging me to come with her to the studio's dance parties. She was also anxious for me to meet Paul, her teacher. She mentioned that Paul was also the studio's specialist in disco-hustle. This was something that caught my interest because I always liked disco music. It was something that I could relate to. I was a seventies baby, and it was what I grew up with! The studio's hustle parties were held on Friday nights. At the parties, I would dance with different people, but I really looked forward to dancing with Paul because he had such a good lead and was really easy to follow. At times, while we were dancing, he would be nice enough to go out of his way to teach me. The next thing I knew, I was hooked. I liked it so much that I found myself going every week. Soon I was going to the studio on 85th Street every day after school.

As a present for my fifteenth birthday, my mother bought me a package of private lessons to study with Paul. The next thing I knew, I was entered to dance hustle with him in the Pro-Am division at one of the local dance competitions—and we won.

Paul was an all-around competitor in all the Ballroom and Latin-American dances, and here and there he began teaching me the other dances as well. Little by little, I became more and more involved with the world of partner dancing again. I guess it was my destiny.

A little while later, in 1985, Paul started his own school, DanceSport, on the Upper West Side of Manhattan. I came along as one of his students. Soon after that, Paul decided to train me to be his dance partner. In exchange for my training I worked the front desk and did other odd jobs around the studio as well. That year *Tango Argentino* was making its Broadway debut at the Mark Hellinger Theater. One of my first "scholarship" jobs was to hand out flyers in front of that theater promoting DanceSport tango classes.

At 16 I officially turned professional and started teaching full time at DanceSport. Paul and I have been dancing and working together ever since. I practically lived in the studio. It was typical for me to work 12 hours a day for six and sometimes seven days a week. Every day in the early afternoon, Paul and I would rehearse for three or four hours, and in the evening we would usually teach another five hours. But the day still wasn't over. After teaching classes we would then host our nightly practice parties from 9:30 PM to midnight.

We were really into the competition world. Though I was competing professionally I also partnered with students and competed in the Pro-Am divisions. In 1990, when I was 20 years old, the studio really took off, and I became Paul's partner in business as well as in dance.

Early on at DanceSport, promoting Argentine tango as the "new" trend in social dancing really helped our business by bringing a lot of people into the studio when it first opened. When Paul and I saw *Tango Argentino*, what we saw on the stage truly inspired us. Since Paul was my mentor, he was definitely the motivation behind my desire to learn tango. We were already proponents of more than 10 other styles of dance, but Paul's passion for tango was contagious. He related to it as being a "real street dance" like the hustle. The more I was exposed to tango, the more I felt connected to its style and character. I think it was in part because of my classical background. Not only was I attracted to tango's elegance and drama, but I have always been drawn to its moodiness and intensity.

As a professional performer, I could relate to the music, and taking on its emotion and character was easy for me. Something inside me connected naturally. As a performer who dances tango, I must admit that what I enjoy most in tango is experiencing the physicality and the dynamics of the movement.

Paul and Eleny teaching at DanceSport

I've always regarded dancing as the discipline of combining technique of the dance with the music's emotion. As a professional dancer, I am always trying to perfect the art of finding a balance between the two. Whether I am dancing socially or on a stage, I always challenge myself to reach the highest level I can. I always strive to be more sensitive to my partner and the music as well as being more aware of my lines. From partnering in tango, I have become more aware of my own balance as well as the balance of my partner and what he requires. My objective is to make the dancing feel effortless yet beautiful.

Social dance was always a part of my life growing up, and it remains the foundation of everything I do. I learned about the essence of tango through improvising in the practicas and milongas. I am inspired by the challenge tango poses for two bodies in such a close embrace to be able to dance in perfect harmony.

As I mentioned before, when Paul and I began dancing tango we also trained intensely in international competitive style dance as well as various authentic social dances. As a result of our experience with so many different types of dance, we've gained a unique understanding of the way in which all dance is connected by a few very important principles. The mechanics of the movement in tango and competitive ballroom, for instance, are almost identical. While the competitive style emphasizes an outward presentation through its wider frame, the Argentine tango stresses an intimacy through a more enclosed embrace. They both involve the same technique for creating the release of power and movement through the body and legs. You are always triggering weight from one leg to the other in the same way. The principles are the same because the options are limited when you have two bodies moving in a somewhat contained close embrace throughout the dance.

I feel that the close embrace of tango requires a great deal of sensitivity and develops a real understanding of the balance required for two bodies to move as one. There are other dances that are quicker and easier to learn and have fun with, but tango takes a little more sensitivity and patience for the beginner because it is much more refined. To improve in tango you must pursue it: Take classes and go out dancing every week. One hurdle that many people have to get over is that—like many things—it is frustrating in the beginning. If you are sincere about learning, other dancers will help you. They were beginners once, too.

Dancing at the milongas is a great way to learn and improve your tango because each person you dance with teaches you something. Each person has a different style, and it's a challenge to try to fit with your partner. I don't think I've ever danced with two men who dance the same way; each is really unique in what he focuses on, and each has different strengths. Sometimes you dance with a partner who brings something out of you that pleasantly surprises you. What's important is that you are really able to connect with the other person and dance together as one. I find that the most important thing I try to do when dancing is to give my partner a good feeling, and I hope to experience one in return, and I always try to learn from that.

For me, as a woman, the "perfect tango" happens when the person I'm dancing with is very much in control of what he's doing. To dance well, I feel that a man must be in touch with the music and in control of his movement, and he must be sensitive to the person he's dancing with. While it's true that the man leads and the woman follows, there is always room for the woman to embellish and move with her own personal quality, which the man in turn will have to follow. And, though a woman doesn't lead in tango, she can certainly inspire and invite her partner to go in a particular direction by the way that she dances.

One of the fascinating things that many people aren't aware of is that tango has many moods. There are passionate, sad, lonely and even happy tangos, and this is all heard in the music. Personally, I tend to be drawn to the more serious, heavy tangos as opposed to the happier, lighter tangos and milongas.

In New York today, there is definitely a thriving tango scene, but my hope is to see Argentine tango move to an even bigger public, and that is what Paul and I have always worked for. I would like to see tango shows become even more popular on Broadway and in theaters around the world. It would be great to see tango become a part of every culture.

Paul and I will, no doubt, continue our work with tango for years to come. And as for Paul, I have a great respect for him not only as a person but as a teacher. He has patience with students and a love for teaching that few people have. He makes teaching itself into a creative process. I feel fortunate to have him as a partner because of his passion and sensitivity. More than anyone I know, he has devoted his life to bringing dance to a larger public. His insight and vision in dance continue to guide and inspire me.

Cheek to Cheek

Paul Pellicoro

In Argentine tango today, there are many different ways of danc-ing in the milongas (the dance clubs). In fact, different styles are encouraged, as each has its own aesthetics and special appeal. People have given these styles names such as cayangue, salon, milonguero and fantasia, to name just a few. But when I invite a partner to dance with me in a tango salon, I don't have to think about what style of tango I'm dancing. I do what is comfortable and appropriate for me, and in particular, for my partner of the moment.

Whatever style of tango one dances, there are basically two ways to dance: open or close. Open style tango is considered the more classical, and schooled way to dance. In this style, tango partners move in a slightly more distant embrace, leaving space between their bodies. Here partners connect through three key points of contact: the hands, arms and the lady's back. Because the openness allows a couple to execute larger, more elaborate figures, this is often the style of tango danced in shows. But it is also often the way beginners dance, as the close tango embrace may seem too intimate and chal-lenging. Though it may at first be awkward as a beginner, it's best to master close style tango as soon as possible. Once that is accom-plished, a couple can dance more open, when needed, while still maintaining the balance and poise developed in their close dancing.

In close style tango, partners dance cheek-to-cheek in a close, intimate embrace with their upper bodies in constant contact. The man will lead his partner by the way he directs her upper body. Dancing close is something that I instinctively do with more experienced dancers. When dancing with an inexperienced woman, I can still dance close, but it is best to first build her confidence and gain her trust by starting at a distance where she feels comfortable.

As partners get accustomed to each other, an almost intuitive physical and social understanding develops between them, and then the option to dance close is something the man can invite quite easily. It could take a year to get to that point, or an instant. In the end, the lady always has the final say in how close the couple will dance, and an experienced man will always sense and respect this, regardless of the lady's level of experience. In reality, the more accomplished dancers become, the closer they tend to dance, but the line between dancing close and intruding on your partner's physical space should never be crossed.

Aside from the aesthetic appeal, there are many advantages to close dancing. Most importantly, the woman will find that it encourages a poise that makes following a lot easier, and a lot more natural. When done right, the woman's feet will naturally fall where they ought to, which also makes it easier for the man to lead. The reason this happens is simple. When the lady brings her head and chest close to the man's, it brings her weight forward of her feet. This creates what is called forward poise. And whether dancing open or close this forward poise is prerequisite in tango for both the man and the woman. Simply put, forward poise is created by shifting one's weight forward over the balls of their feet. This stance helps partners dance toward each other, regardless of whether they are dancing forward, back or to the side. While it takes some getting used to, especially when one of the partners has to go backward, maintaining this forward togetherness is a main priority for a couple dancing tango.

The forward poise reinforces the strong connection created in close dancing because partners begin to counterbalance each other. While maintaining control of their individual balance, both dancers lean slightly on one another so that each feels and shares the other's weight in a light and comfortable manner. This counterbalance requires trust, but it also creates more security and confidence in both leading and following. More than anything, this connection creates the partnership. As tango master Juan Carlos Copes once explained, "The center of weight of a solo dancer is not the same when one dances tango with a partner. In tango the center of weight is between you and your partner. Two become one."

Physical awareness and sensitivity—both to oneself and one's partner—are necessary for the subtle exchange of understanding that occurs as the center of balance moves from being in two separate individuals to existing between the couple. When the dancers have this awareness, they will truly dance "as one." Moving together in such an attached way may take a bit of getting used to, and doing it really well takes experience, concentration and experimentation. But it is this balance in the tango embrace that allows the natural responses and clear communication so necessary for a couple to truly dance as one. Once they can do this, the ease of communication between a skilled couple can appear telepathic to the unknowing observer.

Because dancing tango is really a creative and spontaneous response both to the music and to the situation on a crowded dance floor, a lot of emphasis is placed on the man's lead. To lead means not only to initiate and direct the woman's movement but then to follow her movement as well. While the more creative and experienced leaders dance from moment to moment, from one step to the next, beginning male dancers usually have to think ahead from one "set group" or combination of steps to another. As a leader becomes more experi-

Paul and Eleny performing

enced, he'll forget about set groups and learn to create and react from each single step to the next, or rather from foot to foot, moment to moment, beat to beat.

Doing the basic step in tango (or the "salida," as it is called) can be compared to doing bar exercises in ballet or the major scales in Western music. Within this basic tango figure lie the primary elements and positions that characterize the dance. This eight-count pattern contains many reference points to work from. Repeating and practicing the basic, as well as other standard combinations, is a necessary phase of learning that gives a new dancer a foundation to work from. Eventually, the beginner should break down these standardized teaching patterns and play with the smaller pieces as elements in themselves. Doing this will help a novice leader understand how to spontaneously fit his movement to the spirit of the music at any given moment within the dance. Dancing tango is not about executing set patterns but about creatively improvising with the pieces from which they're composed. With that in mind, one will find that the possibilities will effortlessly spring from the impulses and feelings inspired by the music. In short, the music will essentially be creating the choreography.

All of these variables influence how a tango takes shape and, consequently, no two tangos are ever exactly the same or should you want them to be. Each new tango is a unique experience. It's helpful to remember that at heart social dancing is a couple playing in an embrace to music. Many tangueros let that alone be their guide to dancing. In this way, the dance floor itself becomes the classroom, which is why there are so many excellent dancers who never learned to dance in dance schools. They just found their way to tango by dancing "cheek to cheek."

Technique aside, the most important thing in the quest to become a good tango dancer is to follow your instincts and surrender yourself both to the music and to your partner. To dance well, you must dance in the moment. The fundamentals taught in the basic steps are the guidelines through which to do this. Be patient! Once you have learned the standard figures I show you in this book, you'll be able to begin your tango journey immediately. All that you need to add are a little desire and practice, and you'll find that you will progress from a beginner to a confident improvisational tango dancer in no time!

The Different Styles of Tango

Paul Pellicoro

Once you become involved in the tango world, you'll start to hear a lot of talk about different styles of tango. If you find it a little confusing, don't panic. There's a reason you're confused: Not only are there different styles of tango, but there are also different styles within Argentine tango itself—styles within this style, so to speak. But not to worry, it's all a lot simpler than it sounds.

Due to tango's popularity in the early 1900s, Argentine tango (the mother of all tangos) was imported to other countries throughout the world. As a language might be spoken with an accent by a nonnative, or perhaps even turn into a dialect if taken far enough away from its place of origin, tango outside of Argentina likewise began to be danced differently. Each host country gave tango its own accent, in accordance with its own specific culture, and thus today we have many nationalized styles of tango: American tango, British tango, Parisian tango, Finnish tango and even Chinese tango. While in some countries, tango changed in only minor ways, in others the dance changed so dramatically that today they are considered entirely different dances that now share only the name "tango."

While there are numerous nationalities of tango, the most popular and most important ones to know about are the British (international competitive style), American style and the Argentine tango (the focus of this book). Although Argentine tango is the original tango, it is the British style that has become more popular worldwide than any other.

Primarily, its popularity is due to the fact that it is the style danced in the global network of international ballroom competitions, which the British pioneered. This style is distinguished most by the large frame it employs and its emphasis on power and presence. Although the couple does not dance in the more traditional close tango embrace, they do keep constant close contact between their torsos.

In British tango, the science of two bodies dancing together with maximum dynamic power is nearly perfected. Movement is used to emphasize presence and power rather than intimacy and passion. The efficient mechanics of the movement take priority over the emotional content of the dance. Unlike other styles, the aim of British competition tango is to make the couple stand out with an aristocratic kind of elegance. Another important distinction is that, unlike its Argentine predecessor, this style is rarely improvised.

While closer to British than Argentine tango, American style tango is again different. With more flare than its British counterpart, it is much more expressive and theatrical. Unlike the British style in which there is a strict code that bodies must stay in constant contact, in American tango (based on a "Fred and Ginger" dance style) the couple goes back and forth between dancing close and dancing apart—at moments connected by only an outstretched hand and sometimes even dancing solo. One of the benefits of this freedom is that it gives dancers greater possibilities to express a story through the dance. Perhaps the woman walks away, for instance, until the man pulls her (dramatically) back into his arms. It is certainly a style more suited to the drama of film and stage, where it often appears. In this way, it can be compared to the fantasia and stage versions of Argentine tango.

Although each of these tango styles has its virtues, what makes Argentine tango the more aesthetically pleasing and the most pleasurable to dance—in my opinion—is that it remains more connected to its roots and therefore more organic. Tango, as already described, was born as an expression (among other things) of longing, lust, passion, loneliness and conflict. Each of these emotions is archived in the basic Argentine tango movements and appears with alarming potency when tango is danced not for the praise of the spectator but for the enjoyment of the dancers themselves. This original tango remains more in touch with the universal humanity from which it was born. Its virtue is that it doesn't stray too far from its social roots. Of course, the technique of the other styles can be used in Argentine tango as well.

Having some knowledge of these different national styles of tango is helpful, but what is perhaps more important is knowing about the different styles within the Argentine tango itself. This style is quickly becoming dominant in most dance schools, salons, ballrooms and theaters around the world. In these places, you'll often hear tango aficionados make reference to milonguero, club, salon, confiteria, apilado and fantasia style tango. Understanding the differences between them will not only allow you to understand and participate in the many tango conversations and debates, but it will also encourage you to experiment with these styles and discover the way of dancing that you find most pleasurable.

What instantly defines the different styles of tango is the type of embrace each uses. This determines the amount of space partners keep between themselves while dancing. This is quite important because this space is what determines both the possibilities and limitations a couple has in terms of choreography. When a couple dances in a close style tango, for instance, where they keep their upper bodies in constant contact, often dancing cheek to cheek, the choreography available to them is limited to simpler, smaller figures. In an open style, however, where there is space between the bodies, dancers have the option to do more elaborate choreography.

Fantasia, a style of Argentine tango, which developed in the practicas of the 1940s, is the most popular of the open style tangos. Although it is considered an open style, in actuality, dancers move between an open and close embrace, using the "brazo elastico" ("elastic arms"), which creates the space needed for the figures they are using in that moment. Because this style is filled with many turns and figures, such as boleos, ganchos and sacadas, people often confuse fantasia with show style tango. According to Eduardo Arquimbau, however, they are not the same. For one thing, show tango was developed not only for the stage but also on the stage, whereas fantasia came directly from the dance floor. Furthermore, while fantasia uses many figures, they are always tango figures. Show tango, however, is much broader and includes jumps, lifts and movements from other kinds of dance such as modern, jazz and ballet.

Far different than fantasia, milonguero style tango is the closest, most intimate style of Argentine tango. Known also as club, confiteria and apilado, milonguero is considered by many to be the *true* Argentine style. In this "club" style, men and women dance in a very close, sensual embrace where the woman's arm is often draped entirely around the man's neck so that her hand falls on his left shoulder, and the man's right hand cups the woman's right shoulder blade. Unlike fantasia or show tango, milonguero does not typically involve complicated figures or elaborate choreography, but rather focuses on the connection between the two partners moving as one to the music. With this focused attention to one another, the simple tango walk can become mesmerizing—for spectator and dancer alike. Becoming the popular style in the 1950s, milonguero style is the one most seen today in the tango clubs in Buenos Aires. Aesthetics aside, on a crowded dance floor, this style (lacking large steps and tricks) is the most practical tango style, since it requires the least space.

Perhaps most important about milonguero style tango is that it is based on a relaxed intimacy and surrender both to the music and to one's partner. Also, while one can dance fantasia with or without set choreography, milonguero is always improvised. The connection that a couple feels in this dance, their awareness to their own and to one another's body, breath and weight, and their intimate connection to the music are what guide their movement. While fantasia may invite greater admiration from an audience, it is in milonguero style that one is most immersed in the essence of tango.

The Different Styles of Tango

Though the term salon style is often used as just another name for milonguero or club style, it is actually a bit different. While both are close style tangos, salon style concentrates more than milonguero on the simple tango walk and the elegance of vertical poise. Also, whereas milonguero style does include some figures off the floor, in salon, again according to Eduardo Arquimbau, everything is done on the floor. Another difference is that in salon style men and women often dance with the man's right cheek to the woman's left cheek, gazing toward the couple's outstretched arms. Though this option exists in milonguero, it is more typical to see the woman dance with her head facing directly over her partner's right shoulder (right cheek to right cheek), often with her eyes closed.

The more you dance, the easier it will become to understand the differences between these styles. You will, no doubt, eventually find the one that you feel most comfortable in and inspired by. The best advice I can give is to master the close style Argentine tango because in this style you will develop a solid tango technique that will carry over to any other style of tango you may ever want to try.

Tango Instruction

Paul Pellicoro

In this section I am going to teach the figures and elements that are the basis of Argentine tango. Always remember that tango is about creating and sharing pleasurable feelings with a partner in harmony with the music. That experience begins with our very first touch on the dance floor known in tango as "the embrace". Ideally, every couple will maintain sensitivity in their embrace regardless of what figure is being executed. A "sensitive embrace" in tango is much like a nice hug—consistent and comforting but not too confining. Dancing with an appreciation of the embrace is essential to experiencing the true spirit of tango.

Once you've come together in the embrace it's time to learn the basic tango step, the 8-count salida. This basic figure is comprised of key movements and positions that make it an essential starting point in learning to dance tango. When you are just beginning, learning this step is important because it will give you a framework and reference points from which to build and develop you choreography. I strongly recommend that this basic step be learned, practiced and mastered before going on to incorporate the other steps and elements in this section such as forward and backward Ochos, Balanceos, Cunita, and the Caminada.

When you feel comfortable dancing these figures it's time to go out dancing! And remember the true dance teacher is the dance floor itself!

The Embrace

Togetherness in the Dance

The allure of tango begins with the embrace. With each new partner the embrace will always be slightly different. The position of your hands and arms, for instance, will vary to accomodate each different partner's shape, height and posture.

While there will be as many variations in the embrace as there will be tango tango partners, there are certain key things that go into creating a good tango embrace with any partner. First, both dancers must keep their upper bodies poised forward, toward their partner, and over the balls of their feet. It is also essential to keep the embrace soft. It should be sensual and positive—but not forceful. Keep your shoulders relaxed and avoid bringing tension and rigidity into the hold. Remember: the tango embrace is a not-so-distant relative of the gentle hug—it should be comforting, not stiff.

Open Embrace

Often used in traditional "salon style," the open embrace is a good alternative for beginner dancers and it gives more choreographic options for advanced dancers.

*In the instance that the woman is significantly shorter than the man she may feel comfortable with her head turned to the right and with a slightly open body position.

Close Embrace

This is now a very popular style in the milongas of Buenos Aires and many cities around the world. It is more challenging than the open position. In it one finds the true essence of tango: two bodies moving as one, giving and accepting the sensual pleasure of being embraced.

Alternate Head Positions

The man's head position will always be turned slightly to the left, while the woman may position her head to the left, right, or straight on to the man's right cheek.

**In the open embrace the man's hand is placed just under the woman's left shoulder blade. In the close embrace it is just under the right.

Salida

The eight count basic

It may be helpful to know that the English translation for word salida is "to enter or to exit" (as on a road or highway). Similarly, the salida is used as an entry and an exit to many tango variations.

    The last step (position 8) becomes your starting position from where you can repeat this figure. The turning and timing can vary according to the situation and the inspiration on the dance floor!

> **KEY:**
> **RF**= Right Foot • **LF**= Left Foot •
> **OSP**= Outside Partner

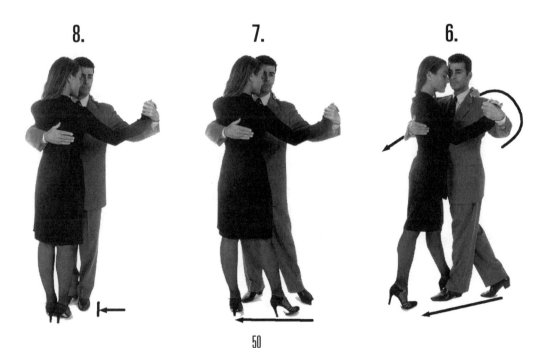

8.   7.   6.

SP. Starting position: feet together
1. Man: RF back (*woman in line*)
   Woman: LF forward
2. Man: LF side
   Woman: RF side
   Man prepares to step outside the woman
3. Man: RF forward (OSP)
   Woman: LF back
4. Man: LF forward
   Woman: RF back
   Man prepares to lead woman to cruzada
5. Man: close RF to LF
   Woman: cross LF in front of RF (*cruzada*)
   Man leads woman back in line
6. Man: LF forward
   Woman: RF back
   commence to turn left
7. Man: RF side
   Woman: LF side
   continue turning left
8. Man: close LF to RF w/weight
   Woman: close RF to LF w/weight
The couple is now in starting position (to repeat #1 of the salida)

SP.

1.

5.

4.

3.

2.

51

Salida

Solo breakdown and foot patterns (Man)

SP. Starting position: feet together
1. RF back
2. LF side
3. RF forward (OSP)
4. LF forward
5. Close RF to LF (w/ weight)
6. LF forward
   commence to turn left
7. RF side
   continue turning left
8. Close LF to RF
   returning to the start position

Salida

Solo breakdown and foot patterns
(Woman)

SP. Starting position: feet together
1. LF forward
2. RF side
3. LF back
4. RF back
5. Cross LF in front of RF (Cruzada)
6. RF back
   commence turning left
7. LF side
   continue turning left
8. Close RF to LF
   returning to the start position

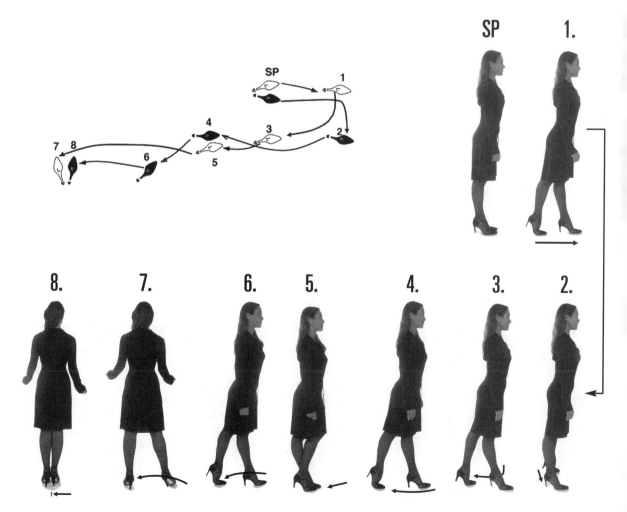

Ocho
Figure eight

The Ocho is a variation that the woman is often led into from step #5 (cruzada) of the salida. In this figure the man leads the woman into forward swiveling walks.

The name "Ocho" reflects the imaginary "figure 8" pattern created on the floor by the woman's curving footwork.

The Ocho can be used as a single figure or repeated consecutively. To exit from the Ocho return to steps 6, 7, and 8 of the salida.

8.   **7.**   **6.**   **B.**   **A.**

SP. Starting position: feet together
1. Man: RF back (woman in line)
   Woman: LF forward
2. Man: LF side
   Woman RF side
3. Man: RF forward (OSP)
   Woman: LF back
4. Man: LF forward
   Woman: RF back
5. Man: Close RF to LF
   Woman: Cross LF in front of RF (Cruzada)
   The starting position for the Ocho is with the man turning left and commencing to move backwards while leading the lady forward to his right side
A. Man: LF back and across, turning left
   Woman: Small swivel left on LF and step RF FW and across OSP
   Man leads lady w/ his right and to swivel and step forward into the ocho
B. Man: Close RF back to LF w/weight
   Woman: Swivel to the right on RF and step LF forward and across in front of man
   Man continues to lead lady to swivel and step forward with his right hand. Man finishes woman's Ocho by leading her to turn left on her LF to end facing him for the step to be in-line

6. Man: LF forward
   Lady: RF back
   Commence turning left into the resolution of the salida
7. Man: RF side
   Woman: LF side
   Continue turning left
8. Man: Close LF to RF
   Woman: Close RF to LF
   The couple is now in starting position to repeat #1 of the salida

SP   **1.**

5.   **4.**   **3.**   **2.**

Back Ocho

Like the forward ocho, the back ocho is a series of swiveling walks, done in reverse Itdiffers from the forward ocho primarily in that it begins after step two of the salida rather than after step five.

SP. Starting position (feet together)
1. Man: RF back (woman in line)
   Woman: LF Forward
2. Man: LF side
   Woman: RF side
A. Man: RF closes to LF w/weight
   Woman: LF closes to RF w/o weight preparing to swivel on RF
B. Man: LF side
   Woman: Swivel to the right on RF and step back and across w/ LF
   Man leads lady by turning the shoulders to the left
C. Man: closes RF to LF w/o weight
   Woman: Swivels to the right on LF, brushing RF to LF w/o weight
   Man leads by turning shoulders to the right
D. Man: RF side
   Woman: continue swiveling to right on LF and step back and across w/ RF
   Man continues turning lady to step back and across

E. Man: close LF to RF w/weight
   Woman: swivel to the left on the RF to face the man. LF brushes to RF w/o weight
   Man stops lady's left turn to prepare for step #3 of the salida
3. Man: RF forward (OSP)
   Woman: LF back
   Continue with #3 to #8 of the salida
4. Man: LF forward
   Woman: RF back
5. Man: closes RF to LF
   Woman: cross LF in front of RF (cruzada)
6. Man: LF forward (commence to turn left)
   Woman: RF back
7. Man: RF side
   Woman: LF side (continue turning left)
8. Man: close LF to RF
   Woman: close RF to LF
   The couple is now in starting position (to repeat #1 of the salida)

8.   7.   6.   5.   4.

SP. **1.** **2.**

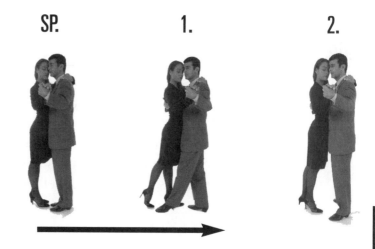

A.

*Note: In this figure, steps C and E requires the woman to let her feet pass closely while swiveling, therefore creating a **brushing action**.

3. **E.** **D.** **C.** **B.**

Other Elements That Can Be Incorporated Into the Salida

Side Balanceo

The side balanceo is a useful step to help the partners "feel" each other's weight. It is especially useful when first commencing to dance.

Step 2 of the salida serves as an entrance and/or exit from the side balanceos. In fact, one side balanceo (A) is commonly used by many dancers as an entrance into steps 3 through 8 of the salida. It can be repeated as necessary as well as combined with the forward and back balanceos.

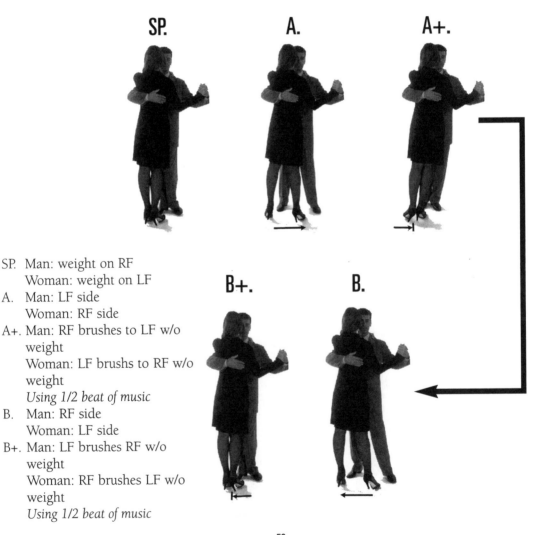

SP. Man: weight on RF
Woman: weight on LF
A. Man: LF side
Woman: RF side
A+. Man: RF brushes to LF w/o weight
Woman: LF brushs to RF w/o weight
Using 1/2 beat of music
B. Man: RF side
Woman: LF side
B+. Man: LF brushes RF w/o weight
Woman: RF brushes LF w/o weight
Using 1/2 beat of music

Balanceo: Forward & Back

This step is important when it's necessary to change direction in a crowded room. As an alternative, the man can also change direction starting with the balanceo with the forward (B) after step #5 of the salida. As an exit, step A is the same as step #1 of the salida.

This step can be reeated on the spot and turned as desired (as in the cunita). When dancing on a spot you can create different combinations of cunitas (forward and back as well as side to side) while playing with the rhythm of the music.

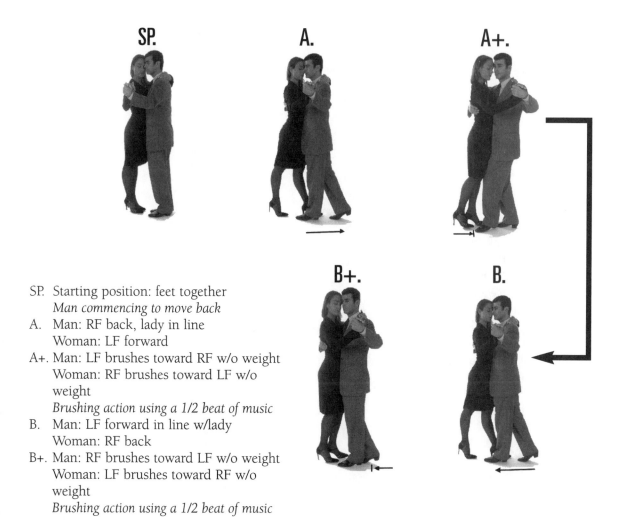

SP.   A.   A+.

B+.   B.

SP. Starting position: feet together
Man commencing to move back
A. Man: RF back, lady in line
Woman: LF forward
A+. Man: LF brushes toward RF w/o weight
Woman: RF brushes toward LF w/o weight
Brushing action using a 1/2 beat of music
B. Man: LF forward in line w/lady
Woman: RF back
B+. Man: RF brushes toward LF w/o weight
Woman: LF brushes toward RF w/o weight
Brushing action using a 1/2 beat of music

Cunita

A cunita is essentially a series of backward and forward balanceos turning left. It turns counter-clockwise throughout with a pivoting action on each step. It can be repeated as many times as desired with more or less turn.

To exit simply the man can use any back step (A, C, E) as an entrance into the salida. As an alternative, the man can also enter the cunita going forward (B) w/ the LF forward after step #5 (cruzada) of the salida.

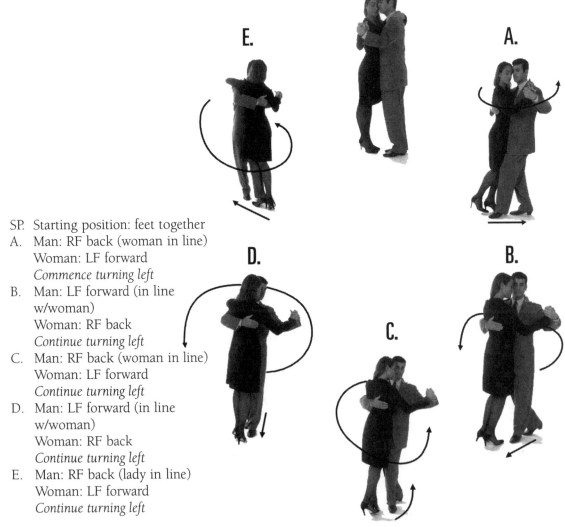

SP. Starting position: feet together
A. Man: RF back (woman in line)
    Woman: LF forward
    Commence turning left
B. Man: LF forward (in line w/woman)
    Woman: RF back
    Continue turning left
C. Man: RF back (woman in line)
    Woman: LF forward
    Continue turning left
D. Man: LF forward (in line w/woman)
    Woman: RF back
    Continue turning left
E. Man: RF back (lady in line)
    Woman: LF forward
    Continue turning left

Caminada

Walking steps

To walk tango is to dance tango. When done well this is the most revered step in tango. Though it seems simple the caminada actually requires perfect poise and confidence when there is a partner in front of you.

The walking steps can be done in repetition, forward or back, and they can curve either to the left or right if desired. The rhythm should be walked on each down-beat. If syncopated it becomes a "Corrida" or a run.

In this example we are commencing it from step #5 of the salida, but the walk can be commenced from almost any position.

A good ending is a balanceo forward or #6, #7, #8 of the salida.

B+.   **B.**   **A+**   **A.**   **SP.**

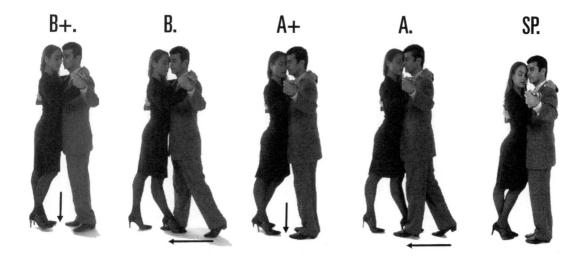

SP. Commence from step #5 of the salida (cruzada). The woman's LF is crossed in front of her RF

A. Man: LF forward (in line w/ woman)
Woman: RF back (in line w/man)

A+. Man: RF brushes the LF w/o weight
Woman: LF brushes to RF w/o weight

B. Man: RF forward (in line w/ woman)
Woman: LF back

B+. Man: LF brushes RF w/o weight
Woman: RF brushes LF w/o weight

Some Tips on Dancing the Argentine Tango

Dancing with the Music—Walking on the Beat

As far as dancing with the music, it may be interesting to know that the rhythm and tempo of tango music was inspired by the tempo of a medium paced walk. (See the Music section.) In essence there are two beats to each tango walk. A light upbeat and a stronger down-beat. When we dance "or walk" the tango we will commence to move early on the upbeat so that our free leg and foot swings out and catches our weight on the following downbeat.

So the walk in tango can also be broken down into a two part process to match the beats in the music. There is "commencement" to move followed by the resulting "step." In a simple analysis it's a fall and catch process. Sometimes I think of tango as elegant organized stumbling that is inspired by the music. While leading my partner through my embrace, I will first decide to move our head and bodies in a chosen direction and then as a natural reaction our four feet will follow!

Dancing Around the Room—The Line of Dance

It should be mentioned here that when dancing tango at a practica or a milonga dancers should make their way around the dance floor in a counterclockwise direction. This counterclockwise merry-go-round action in which the dancers move around the dance floor is commonly known as the "line-of-dance."

Dancing just the salida as it is first shown here is not always the most practical way to navigate around the room. In it's basic form the salida is not a very progressive figure, but with practice and by experimenting with different amounts of turn it can be. Navigating around the room will get even easier when you start combining other simple elements and figures such as turning rocks (cunita) and walking steps (caminada). An increased vocabulary of steps will allow you to have more versatility and mobility on the dance floor.

Traffic

On a crowded dance floor, space may not always be readily available. This is often a common reality when dancing tango in a popular venue, especially in the milongas of Buenos Aires. It should also be noted that on a crowded floor it is most impolite to collide and crash into other dancers. So being able to stop and change direction is very important. When confronted with these restrictive situations, the dancers should feel confident to simply pause momentarily. Always take your time! Many dancers will use a series of simple balanceos to dance on the spot while waiting for an open space to dance into. When a space finally does open up, be careful never to rush to fill it. Take note that good dancers will stay calm and avoid traffic whenever possible! With all of this in mind, after learning and practicing the popular figures taught in this section you should soon be able to maneuver around the floor quite easily with great confidence and style!

PRACTICE AND EXPERIENCE

There is no substitute for experience! By dancing at local practicas and milongas, the ability to navigate will soon come naturally, often out of sheer instinct and necessity. This book has a chapter in it that can help you find places where you can dance tango. If you don't have a place to dance tango in your city, then invite your friends over to your home, put on some music and start your own milonga. Later on try to find a local nightclub or available dance studio who might be interested in housing a "tango night." There is no better way to learn to dance than by putting your self out on a crowded dance floor with a partner letting your intuition be your guide. This is where fun and excitement begins.

To be quite truthful, in my professional opinion as a teacher and the owner of a very successful dance school, academic instruction will only take you so far as a dancer. Out on the dance floor you'll quickly find yourself doing many things naturally and spontaneously. Historically, this is how people learned to dance in the first place, before there were any dance schools. Most importantly remember that tango is not a job that has to be worked at. It is a fascinating game of communication that is played and shared between two people! It is an experience to be enjoyed!

Anyone Can Tango

Marilyn Cole Lownes

Tango is passion.

In tango, we dance our emotions rather than speak them. The dance floor becomes a canvas, and our hearts become palettes. Feet and bodies paint sensuous emotion in sweeping strokes. With a dab of desire here and shading of sorrow there, the tango comes to life.

We dance tango because we have secrets. Stoic expressions mask seething emotions, adding to the mystery of tango and the aura that make this the most captivating dance of them all.

Though tango originated in nineteenth century Buenos Aires, today tango is danced throughout the world. From the snowy peaks of the Rocky Mountains in Aspen to the Latvian Embassy in London, enthusiasts meet up at tango gatherings called "milongas."

While tango magic has spread to nearly every major city in the world, it is in New York that one man has cast his unique spell over the world of tango. Here Paul Pellicoro has realized his dream of teaching thousands of others to tango. At DanceSport, his school just off of Manhattan's Columbus Circle, students are introduced to tango in an ideal setting in a way that establishes a lifelong love of the dance.

Like the voyage of the tango itself, Paul Pellicoro's own journey has been quite remarkable. After majoring in dance and art in college, Paul found himself drawn to New York's music scene. To support himself, he bartended at clubs like CBGB's and Max's Kansas City, where punk and new wave music had their roots. On his nights off, he also ventured into the disco scene, where he became one of the most renowned hustle dancers in clubs around town. Then, as he puts it, "I saw an ad, 'Travel, Romance, Glamour: Learn To Be A Dance Instructor.' I knew I wanted to be both creative and physical. Maybe it's in the genes—people in my family were mostly athletes and artists. So, I went and auditioned for the job."

But there are also other benefits, too, Paul admits. "Being naturally shy, I found it a nice way to meet girls. And, I wanted to lead my life like a Fred Astaire movie," he says, "where I could gatecrash a glamorous party of society people, blending in by wearing the required top hat and tails, find my Ginger Rogers, and win her heart by dancing up a storm."

photo: Jeanette Jones

A young dancer trying a few steps

Paul may have fantasized about this new life but, realistically, dancing was a way to interact with people from all walks of life and his ability to do that has been a key factor in his amazing success. Join one of his classes and you'll find people that range in age from 17 to 70, and in social position from bohemian to socialite to celebrity. Through his love of dance, and their desire to learn, he reaches each of them with ease.

After teaching hustle, mambo and other ballroom and competitive style Latin dance for a decade, in 1985 Paul saw a dance show that changed the course of his life. "When I saw *Tango Argentino*, I was knocked out. First, by the dance itself. I thought it was so fascinating and exciting. But, more significantly, I was impressed by the fact that here was a partnered dance show that was not only a huge hit, but also it was a hit on Broadway. The dancers were all shapes and sizes and ages—it appeared anyone could do it. The tango had universal appeal."

Inspired by *Tango Argentino*, Paul's creative bent and business sense spurred him into bringing tango into his own studio. "We started offering tango classes and then milongas. We ran the first 'milongas' in New York City, actually. We put all our hard work and dedication into promoting them, as well. We were making a Manhattan tango scene where one did not exist. There weren't any websites for advertising such things back then, so we had to spend what little money we had to get it going. We took an ad in the *Playbill* program of *Tango Argentino*, advertising our 'milongas,' classes and private lessons. We stood outside the theater and handed out flyers, too. That way, we became the first studio in New York to teach tango and it quickly became very popular." Soon enough, he had succeeded in bringing the tango craze to New York.

Paul's unique approach to teaching tango lies in his simple and practical philosophy. "Anyone can dance," he tells me. "Tango is simply elegant stumbling to music. I make sure my students get the instruction they need to master the basic elements of the dance—not techniques and steps that they will never use in real life. Then I advise them to expose themselves to the tango scene—to get out there and watch the different styles being danced at the 'milongas.'"

About the same time that Paul discovered *Tango Argentino*, an even greater influence came into his life. Paul tells how he discovered the beautiful young dancer Eleny Fotinos. "I met Eleny while I was teaching her mother tango. Then, I taught Eleny, too, and immediately recognized her very special talent. I asked her to be my partner. As well as performing in shows as my partner, Eleny became one of our best instructors. We've been partners ever since, and now we run the studio together as well."

In the last 18 years, thousands have been coached at DanceSport, but perhaps screen star Al Pacino best underlines Paul's status as the foremost tango teacher in the U.S.A. Recruited by the producers of *Scent of a Woman*, Paul both taught the actors to tango and choreographed the film's now famous tango scene. "It's very flattering to be asked to teach celebrities," Paul admits. "I also taught Robert De Niro for his tango in the film *Flawless* and both Richard Gere and Winona Ryder for their waltz scene in *Autumn In New York*.

"You know," says Paul, "I respect Pacino and De Niro for their talent. It's nice that they both came to me with respect for my talent, too. It was a great experience. Actors are good students. They know how to stay focused. Al Pacino was particularly good. He really enjoyed the lessons. It's only when timing becomes a factor that signs of stress begin to show. It's one thing to learn to tango in your free time, but quite another when you have to do it while keeping to very tight production schedule with precious little time to learn (or teach) a whole routine. Nevertheless, trying as it was, it was a wonderful experience."

As for actresses he has coached, Paul remembers Gabrielle Anwar, who danced with Pacino in *Scent of a Woman*, perhaps best. "I remember at the first lesson I just took her hand, led her onto the floor and danced with her. She was spellbound. She said she felt as though she had been on a carousel," he recalls. "I told her to save that feeling…use it for her scene in the film."

Whether it's a famous actor or a reclusive writer, most people arrive at DanceSport with some trepidation. Paul treats them all the same. "My philosophy is that there are two basic emotions in life: love and fear. People come to the studio in a state of fear—deep-seated fear that they won't be able to do whatever is required to become a good dancer. My job is to take that fear away. I have to make people understand that they can probably dance well already. Dancing is, after all, just shifting your weight from foot to foot to the beat of the music. Students must move from a state of fear to a state of love: love for the dance and their own dancing ability."

"It helps to remember," Paul continues, "that historically dancing has always thrived amongst friends, families and communities. Dancing isn't passed on so much by telling people precisely where to place their feet as much as it is by generally transmitting feelings.

People embrace each other and move to the music. In the thirties and forties, people danced in halls and ballrooms all the time. Today, there are few venues of that sort, so people don't get to see live dancing in action; they don't really know how dancing is supposed to look."

In the end, Paul says that anyone who can walk can dance. "Dancing is all about walking paces—walking to music with a body in front of you. I get people to relax and let go of that phobic feeling that body movements are being obstructed. Once you move and your partner moves with you, you develop trust and faith, and you start to love the dance. You start to feel confident and self-assured, and soon the fear is gone."

And for those of you who claim you just can't dance? Paul thinks you can. "Most people don't have physical problems that prevent them from dancing," he tells me. "If there is resistance, it is a mental barrier that has to be broken down." And Paul Pellicoro is just the man to do it. As he says, "My own style of social dancing is all about harmony. Harmony between me and the music and the person I'm dancing with. Musical, harmonious and tasteful—that's the way I like people to think of my dance style and me."

Dancing the Night Away in Buenos Aires

Carole Stuart

They're doing it in Paris, Stockholm, New York and Berlin. They do it in Moscow. But nowhere do they dance the tango as they do in Buenos Aires, where it began as a dance men did with each other. When you visit a milonga, everybody is doing it.

Buenos Aires is *la corazon*, the heart, of tango. It embraces the city. They even have a twenty-four-hour television channel devoted to tango music and dance. They dance (for tourists) in the streets of San Telmo and La Boca. But the real dancing takes place at the *milongas*, the clubs.

Buenos Aires is a late city. That is, it comes to life in the hours when most people in the world are turning over in their beds. Dinner often begins at 10 PM or later. And, if you are going on afterwards to a dance club—one of the many milongas that dot the city—you will remind yourself not to eat onions or garlic because if you are dancing Argentine tango, you'll be in a close embrace. And you don't want to offend with bad breath. In fact, you might want to put a bit of perfume behind your right ear, since that is the side of your face that will be turned toward your partner.

Buenos Aires also has a number of magazines that list all the milongas and practicas. Or, if you prefer, you can easily find a network of people who will lead you to the hottest tango places.

Nino Bien, a longtime favorite, is still among the best. It's well established, and there you will see dancers whose years of experience are obvious as they glide along. Gricel is another popular tango hangout. Confiteria Ideal, made famous by Sally Potter's film *The Tango Lesson*, has afternoon dances, and La Estrella is a great night scene, as is Parakultural, where dress down is the fashion.

You may see the same faces from club to club, and add to the mix young girls and boys who are more familiar with salsa who have recently taken up the national passion. They don't dress up as their elders do in suits and dresses. Their choice of clothing may remind you more of grunge, but the lithe bodies still lean in toward their partners, repeating the steps and variations that have been handed down for generations.

While milongas outside of Argentina may not have rules, in BA there are still important codes to follow. In other words, ladies, if you're thinking of walking over to that good-looking fellow and asking him to dance, think again. There is a strict etiquette in Buenos Aires: A woman must wait to be invited. You learn to give him "the look," catching his eye and staring. If he looks away, he's not interested. If he returns your gaze and inquires with a lifted eyebrow, you nod, almost imperceptibly. He'll approach as you walk onto the dance floor, and then the dance begins.

A woman has options, too. She can look away if he asks her with his eyes for a dance. But if she sits at a table patiently waiting, she may miss the milonguero hanging out at the bar. It's perfectly acceptable to "work the room"—stand at the bar, walk up and down. Let them see the goods. Wear your most enticing dress. Let your shoes be good dancing shoes, and he'll know you are serious.

photo: Jeanette Jones

Afternoon milonga at Confiteria Ideal, made famous by the film *The Tango Lesson*

Once on the floor, you don't just start to dance. No, there's an unwritten rule of waiting for a few bars of music before you begin. You don't even have to look at each other, although a smile doesn't hurt. And then he walks toward you, holds out his arms. You meet him, accepting the invitation, and he then pulls you close. Your hand goes around his neck, and you are cheek to cheek, unless he prefers forehead to forehead (old-fashioned, but still seen) as a dance position.

There is another custom. A sequence of dances is played—several tangos, milongas, valses. And you are pretty much committed to dance the entire set. With each successive number, you tune in to your partner, and if he's good and you follow well, the two of you move in unison, with each dance becoming better and better. Don't anticipate the next step, because the man of experience may have some steps you haven't tried, or he may make something up on the spot. But not to worry. A good dancer will hold you close and lead you exactly where you are supposed to go.

Wait for the pressure of his hand, his torso, urging you to the left or right, backwards or forward. But not all men can lead well. It's quite a responsibility. You indicate your acceptance by moving in closer; putting your hand further around his neck. Is he moving too fast? Apply pressure with your hand, slowing him down. Or, if he's too close for comfort, pull away slightly.

If it's not good for you, you can thank him after a dance or two, make an excuse and walk away. But it is an insult, so it's best to hang in there and make the best of it. The delicacy of ego balance is up for grabs with each new partner. But don't expect the same partner to ask you at tomorrow night's milonga. You may take no notice of each other, no matter how good the previous night was. A puzzle, but there it is.

It may sound like there are a lot of codes to follow in Buenos Aires, but it can be wonderful. Often referred to as a three-minute love affair, tango is an exchange of mutual pleasure—sensual without intimacy. Your eyes close, you lean in, he guides you firmly and you are truly one. When it's good, it's great. When it's bad, it's awkward, unpleasant. Without a strong lead from the man, you flounder, unsure where your feet should go. But at the very least, the music is always terrific.

Unlike the strong, independent female role model of today's modern world, tango is a throwback to when a woman waits for a man's cue. So leave your ego at home along with your ideas of male/female interactions. You may be mistress of the boardroom, but in Buenos Aires, you're a tango junkie, hoping to be invited to dance.

The older milongueros, men who have danced the steps for a lifetime, dance with the young girls eager to learn. Tall dances with short, stout with thin. Great looks will only get you so far if you can't dance.

The cost for all this fun? Less than you might imagine. For about $10, you can dance until your feet hurt with no one pushing drinks at you. Often, the milongas will have a brief show, especially if, as often happens, professionals are in attendance. For the price of admission, you get terrific entertainment watching stars from shows like *Forever Tango* or *Tango Por Dos*, etc., perform, and then you can join them on the dance floor.

If you're looking for one of the best times you can have—dancing until dawn living and breathing one of the most fascinating and sensual of all dances—start planning for your trip to Buenos Aires, the city that started it all.

Tango On Broadway

Pamela Saichann

From Greek tragedies to musicals, Broadway shows have always attracted a wide audience. Perhaps we are drawn to theater not only because it immerses us in a world of fantasy, but because it also exposes us to a universe of inspiration.

In the afterglow of an exciting performance, which of us hasn't had the desire to belong to that otherworld of lights, drama, dressing rooms and applause? We leave the ballet reproaching our mothers for not having forced us to continue the ballet classes we abandoned when we were five years old....We leave the opera wondering whether the time has come to stop singing out of tune in the shower and start taking singing lessons postponed many years ago....We leave a play ready to find the nearest acting workshop. ...And we leave a tango show ready to discover within ourselves the passion we just saw onstage by joining the first dance school we can find.

Perhaps even more than other performances, tango shows inspire their audiences in lasting ways. Ninety-six percent of the non-Argentine dancers in the world were drawn to learn tango after seeing a performance. Many confess that until seeing their first tango show they could only relate tango to the image of Rudolf Valentino with his arms rigidly extended and a rose clenched in his teeth, pulling his partner in a straight line from one corner of the dance floor to the other in the rhythm of a monotonous "Cumparsita." But from the moment they left the theater, they were consumed by this new and passionate sensation that came in through their eyes and reached their deepest senses within minutes.

The worldwide resurgent interest in tango is due, for the most part, to tango shows that traveled around the world's stages—shows that carried a piece of Argentine culture to faraway horizons and ignited in spectators a flame that continues to grow with time.

These shows, big budget or small, began a movement that has given tango new energy and recognition in recent years, and all signs indicate that this interest will continue to grow.

We could not possible talk about every tango show touring the world and so we will limit this overview to a few outstanding productions.

"TANGO ARGENTINO"

Nearly everyone in tango agrees that the show most responsible for inspiring the public's love for tango is *Tango Argentino*. This project had been archived for almost 10 years, when the French festival De Otoño decided to help Claudio Segovia and Hector Orezzoli produce six days of performances in Paris in 1983. Almost immediately following the show's debut tickets were completely sold out and would-be audience members flocked to the streets, signs in hand, to demand more performance dates.

When *Tango Argentino* arrived in New York two years later, for a five-week run on Broadway, New York also exploded in a tango craze. Again people went into the streets, this time dressed in costumes that mimicked the show's characters.

Tango Argentino's cast was revered not only while onstage, but after the performances as well, by dance professionals and amateurs alike who waited outside theater exits to persuade the performers to teach improvised classes in dance halls outside Manhattan. With firuletes, ganchos, sacadas and boleos, tango was catching on in pure "Broadway" style. The tango being taught then was very different— both in style and form—from what we are now used to seeing in the daily New York milongas. At that time, the lessons responded to the needs of the spectators whose imaginations had been filled with show tango, rather than the social tango of the milonga scene—which had yet to be created in New York.

In 1991, Hector Orezzoli, one of *Tango Argentino's* creators, died, and the show disappeared for almost a decade. Then, in 1999, *Tango Argentino* triumphantly returned to the stage at the Gershwin Theater on Broadway. Though some of the same tango masters from the original cast reunited for this performance, this run did not awaken the public madness as the original had. Nonetheless, it still drew favorable reviews and well-deserved applause, and in the audience were some of the same faces, more wrinkled perhaps, that fell in love with the first tango show 15 years before. But there were also the new and different faces of those who, either due to chance or destiny, fell for the bewitching rhythm and the melancholy sounds of the bandoneon.

After the original success of *Tango Argentino* and the craze it inspired, it isn't difficult to understand how international demand for tango encouraged the development of new shows in Argentina. *Tango Argentino* had inspired a subculture throughout the world of people ready to line up for tickets and even take lessons, and the shows kept coming.

"TANGO x 2"

In 1988, Miguel Angel Zotto and Milena Plebs (who started working together in *Tango Argentino*), created the company *Tango x 2*. While *Tango Argentino* had gathered together the greatest tango dancers of its day to celebrate, in essence, tango's survival under the military rule that ended in 1983, it did so not with the tango of the social halls and milongas, but with fantasia, a show style of tango. Miguel and Milena's vision was somewhat different. They wanted to bring milonguero style tango—the style born in the social clubs and milongas—to the stage. This was something that had never been put on the stage before.

Based on excellent musical accompaniment, impeccable costumes and sublime choreographies, *Tango x 2* walked the audience through tango history from its beginnings. With this first show, these young artists enjoyed an unprecedented reception in Buenos Aires, the home of tango. Even during the difficult economic times, they achieved a record number of performances in the legendary Avenida Corrientes. Inevitably, the show began an international tour that, of course, included Broadway.

Today, over 13 years after its debut, this company—which has now toured in North America, Europe, Asia and Latin America as well—continues to create new works.

"FOREVER TANGO"

In 1997, almost 15 years after the success of *Tango Argentino*, an oversized image of a provocative couple ready to kiss appeared in the middle of Times Square, awakening the curious glance of the world below. After a long stay in San Francisco's Theatre on the Square, *Forever Tango* had arrived in New York.

Created and directed by Luis Bravo, *Forever Tango* was composed of a company of 26 dancers who were primarily younger dancers from the new generation of tango. Led by an impressive orchestra, directed by renowned bandoneonist Lisandro Adrover, this show brought more modern—theatrical and balletic—elements into tango. After a long season on Broadway, the show continued on a world tour that, except for a few impasses, is still going.

"TANGO PASIÓN"

Five years before *Forever Tango*, *Tango Pasión* was also presented on Broadway. Although it did not stay in New York for long, the show toured in other cities in the U.S. and Europe. Accompanied by the acclaimed Sexteto Mayor orchestra from Argentina, *Tango Pasión* offered something completely different. This time there was no strict tango chronicle. Rather than presenting a narrative to tell a detailed tango history, this show evoked times and memories of tango with an aesthetic similar to that one would encounter in reviewing an album of old photographs.

While there have been many tango shows since *Tango Argentino*," I feel that *Tango x 2, Forever Tango* and *Tango Pasión* are the most important ones to know about in order to understand the influence that tango shows have had on the global popularity of tango. From the great masters to the new generations of tango dancers who traveled over the world's stages, and the stages of Broadway, each left their mark, in their own style on the history of tango and in the thousands of audience members who they inspired to dance. *

---

* Adapted from an original article in *ReporTango, The New York Tango Magazine,* July 2001.

A Milonguero Speaks:

Reflections on a Life in Tango

Carlos Funes

A few words from Paul . . .

Long before *Tango Argentino* came to Broadway, there was an association in New York for the Argentine and South American community called "Amigos del Tango." Composed of a diverse mix of elegant, old-time tango dancers who lived in New York, they held dances around the metropolitan area, which most often included live music. In the mid-1980s, they ran a monthly dance at my studio.

Carlos Funes and his wife Cati stood out in this group as both excellent dancers and wonderful people. They have continued to support tango over the years, encouraging the non-Latin community to try this dance, through their love of tango and their inspirational personal interpretation of the dance.

Carlos and Cati have always been among the better milongueros in the New York dance scene, and even among their peers in Argentina, they are held in high esteem. The tango they do is not show tango, but social dancing at its best. Without fancy ganchos and boleos, even within a simple tango walk, this couple dances in a league of their own, using simple elegance and musical characterization as their sole means of expression.

When I first brought my annual "TangoFest" to the stage in New York City, my intention was to show the diversity of Argentine tango and to educate the audience about its roots as well as its contemporary developments.

Some of the performers were amateur dancers now in their seventies and far more comfortable as grandparents than as dancers on a stage. But as part of "TangoFest," they took their love of tango to a wider public and brought the audiences to their feet. Without rehearsals and with music as their only guide, they did what many seasoned professionals spend a lifetime aspiring to: They transferred the soul of tango to the audience.

Carlos Funes with his wife
and partner Cati

Carlos Funes on Tango . . .

To live in Argentina between 1930 and 1955 was to live in a celebration. Tango was everywhere, and dance was everything. Every Saturday and Sunday we would go to the soccer clubs and stadiums that had ballrooms or social halls for dance. There they had grand orchestras, and young and old alike would meet every weekend.

During the week, we went to other local clubs, downtown. The young guys would go out every night. The young girls (18 and under) would go at least three or four times a week, but always in big groups with all their friends. We would also go to the confiterias—the café-like restaurants in Argentina where people dance during the afternoon—nearly every day. Even on their lunch hours, people would go there to dance and then return to work. This was normal. Sometimes there was live music, sometimes not. But in those years, people loved tango, and they would dance at any time.

I was born in Argentina in 1931. It was in 1945, when I was 14 that I started going to the dances. That was during World War II, but the war didn't really affect us in Argentina; we weren't really involved. At that time, the United States was the dream to us; we were watching all the American movies and listening to the music.

When we went to a dance, we didn't just dance to tango music but to all kinds of music. At each milonga, they played a half hour of tango and then a half hour of American and swing music. But when we heard a tango at the milongas, it was something different; it gave us a sense of patriotism, of pride. Even today, tango touches a special place in my heart; tango always feels like home.

Back then the tango scene was a very different thing. There were rules of etiquette, and the dress codes were very strict. All the men wore ties and jackets when they went out dancing. The women dressed up, too, very sexy and very elegant, in dresses with a French and Italian influence. There were no skirts with slits up the sides in those days—this era of tango had nothing to do with pimps and prostitutes. It didn't matter if it was afternoon or evening, people always dressed well, even if you were poor. Today some kids dance tango with sneakers, but in my day, even if you were poor, you saved enough to buy a suit for the milonga. You might wear that suit for a year, but you wore a suit.

At that time, walking in the streets of Buenos Aires was like living and breathing tango. Life was beautiful with romance, friendship and family love. Hanging out in the barrios on the streets and plazas was common. People would play soccer and dance. The young kids often danced with the older boys so that the older ones could try new steps and practice. When I learned a new step, I would go home and teach it to my sister. Not everybody learned that way, but we did. And I learned to dance tango in the house with my sisters, too. Often we would dance on Sunday afternoons, when the radio played the big bands; my father wouldn't dance then, so they had me.

During carnival, which is summer time in Argentina, after midnight every little barrio had dancing in the street. Your neighbors were like family, and on Christmas and New Year's Eve, after midnight, there were milongas on the main streets of the barrios, and all the young people would go out dancing in a celebration with the music of tango. Life was a big party then. It was very good. Argentina was prospering, and it was a happy country.

In those days, what style of tango you danced depended on the neighborhood you were in. We had 50 neighborhoods in Buenos Aires, and each had its own style of tango. At the big dance halls, people from all the neighborhoods would come together, and it was wonderful to see the mixture of styles. I could dance with girls from all the different neighborhoods, and not because I was a good dancer, but because I was good looking. It was really about going out. If you danced very simple, very elegant, you were okay.

A popular barrio for tango was Avelaneda, a suburb outside of the city. This barrio had a special style, different from the way people danced in the center of the city. While people in the center danced in a more simple, elegant way, outside the codes were looser, and they didn't have as many restrictions in their clubs. Avelaneda people danced with more experimental choreography. Although they danced with ganchos and boleos and other such figures, they did it with elegance. It was the same when you went to some of the smaller clubs; nobody cared how you danced. At the bigger, more popular city clubs, it was too crowded to dance in this freer way because it could result in kicking people and getting kicked. The owners of the clubs didn't want the dance floor to seem like a soccer game, and they put you out of the club if you danced too wildly.

Today people are learning to dance in a very close embrace from the start, but back then you had to really know someone to dance so close. Today people call this close dancing "milonguero," and it seems to be a compliment to say that someone dances milonguero.

That may be what "milonguero" means now, but not back then. In my day, to call someone milonguero was an insult. It was what you called a person who didn't have a job and who just hung out in the clubs all the time, dancing and borrowing money. But for me, now that term refers to dancers of a specific time: those who went to the milongas between 1930 and 1950 and who are still dancing today. While older now, they still dance very elegantly, and very simply, which is characteristic of that Golden Age.

In those times, milongas also ran late—like now—until dawn. During the week or on weekends, it was the same. Going to work the next morning wasn't a problem because in Argentina we have three hours in the day for siesta, and that's still when people sleep if they've been up dancing all night.

From the time I was born, my country was happy—until Peron left. I left for the United States around then, so I was not living in Argentina during the military rule in the seventies. When I went back for a vacation, though, it was very different. There was no tango. I only found one place, and there weren't many milongueros there. Milongas were very rare.

But the military rule was not the only reason tango became less popular in Buenos Aires. When the young people got into rock and roll in the fifties, tango's popularity waned and the big tango clubs could no longer afford to hire the big bands. The music during the Golden Age was everything. When there was live music, everyone participated; and when the music stopped, the tango died.

EARLY TANGO IN NEW YORK . . .

When I got to New York around the time Peron left Argentina, we were dancing tango in basements. I used to organize dances on 34th and Broadway, and in the Crystal Room at the McCarthy Hotel. We had musicians and everything. I organized dances in New Jersey as well.

At that time, tango in Buenos Aires and tango in New York were very different. At clubs in Argentina, people didn't want to watch a competition; they wanted to dance. In New York on the other hand, they often used to have a champagne hour at the dances to draw people in. An MC would run the evening, and couples would dance in competitions, where the winner would be chosen based on the audience's applause; the winners would be given a bottle of champagne. But those weren't the places I went. I wanted to dance, not watch.

One day in 1958, however, I heard about the Harvest Moon competition. They were having a tango contest, and I went to dance. All the other men in the competition wore tuxedos, but I was just in regular clothing. The people there didn't know Argentine tango yet; they danced a different style. I gave them a tape of

Argentine music and I did an exhibition, and everyone went crazy. They didn't know what real tango looked like, but they liked it. Unfortunately, because they didn't understand this style, they couldn't judge it, so another couple won.

What was also different in New York is that here people went to particular places for the bands, just to listen to the music, and suddenly no one was dancing. Music was taking the forefront. One time Mariano Mores's orchestra came to the Waldorf-Astoria. It was $300 a dinner, and he played and put on a show—but nobody was dancing. I said to the people at my table, "If I'm going to pay $300 to listen to Mariano Mores, I want to dance." My wife and I got up and went into the hallway of the place and started to tango. Mariano stopped and said, "Looks like people want to dance....Okay, I'm going to play for dancing," and suddenly the floor was full of people dancing tango.

ON A GOOD PARTNER...

What I like is a dance partner who can move easily. I like a partner who will follow and who is light. The way people dance now, they stop and do a step, instead of dancing through it and just making it part of the dance. I still believe that one must do the gancho while dancing, while moving, not while stopped. In tango, you should never stop or look at the woman and her dancing, or at the floor. You must dance together with the woman. I never look at the floor and I never look at the woman to see what she's doing or where she's going. She's going to do what I lead her to do.

I always say that a woman is going to dance well if the man knows how to lead. You must give the woman time to do what she has to do—don't rush her—but do it together. And when the woman is doing something, you must be in a position to support her and to look elegant. You don't have to wait for her to make you look elegant.

My wife is a good dancer because she follows so well. I don't dance with anyone but her now, because nobody can dance the way she can. The way she turns...nobody can turn that way. She has a very special balance. Gavito—everybody—comes to dance with her because of her turns. Look at the finale of Town Hall, where she danced with Gavito: six turns in the same position, and she was 70 years old at that time. Each was done perfectly…it's incredible.

What makes dancing tango most pleasurable for me today is the music and my memories—I see my mother cooking and singing, my sisters, all my friends dancing. I met my wife in a tango club. I was 16, and she was 19. At the clubs, she always stayed together with her girlfriends, and I would stay together with the boys in the middle of the floor. Many times big dancers, like Roneta—he was the best milonga dancer in all of Buenos Aires—would come and ask my permission to dance with my wife (who was then my girl-friend), because she was a great dancer, one of the best at that time. (She was much better than me.) They would say "I want to dance with the most beautiful girl at the dance." But for over 60 years, I was dancing with the most beautiful girl.

For me now, tango is life coming backwards. When I hear tango music, it brings me back to being 17. I am 70 years old, but tango always takes me back. Again, in that music I am 17, and the only thing that makes me feel older when I dance is that my feet hurt. But my life goes through my eyes every time I dance tango. I'd like to dance another 20 years.

The Stars of Tango: An Introduction

There are good tango dancers, and there are great tango dancers— the artists, those who have truly added to and in some cases changed the course of this dance's history. In the 20 years I have been dancing, I have been fortunate to meet and work with many of them—from the legendary Juan Carlos Copes and Maria Nieves to the up-and-coming legends like Pablo Veron and Guillermina and Roberto.

In the following pages, these stars of tango share with us their best stories, and some of their thoughts on the dance that, for many, became their life.

JUAN CARLOS COPES and MARIA NIEVES

A few words from Paul...

I met Juan Carlo Copes in 1985 at one of the first tango classes he taught with Maria Nieves in New York City. I had seen them perform in *Tango Argentino*, and their dancing inspired me then, as it did so many others. But their classes were an even greater inspiration because there they danced without any set choreography.

Soon after our initial meeting, Copes became the first of the tango greats to make DanceSport his New York teaching base. Our studio was, in fact, the only place in New York where he would offer his workshops, and that was quite an honor. I think he liked being at my studio because it had, and still has, a lot of energy. We have always had a mixture of both young and old students.

Over the years, Copes has been very generous in teaching me and Eleny, as well as our staff and students. When *Tango Argentino* was still on Broadway, he would often invite us and our friends to meet him for dinner at the club La Milonga after his nightly shows. There, along with other members of the cast, we would dance and talk passionately about tango into the late hours of the night. This was at the beginning of the tango revival in New York City, and it was a memorable experience.

COPES'S LIFE IN TANGO...

Juan Carlos Copes

Just as tango singer Carlos Gardel is known as "The Voice of Tango," tango dancer Juan Carlos Copes is known as "The Legend of Tango" in the dance world. The Buenos Aires legislature even made this official when, by popular vote, they officially declared Copes "Dancer of the Century."

An innovator in tango, he was the first person to choreograph tango for the stage. Since the fifties, every major tango show has used Copes's choreographic hallmarks, so much so that they are now considered classic: men fighting with knives and being bested by a gun; milonga danced on a tiny table; immigrants dancing a folk dance that melts into a tango.

Copes was also the first Argentine tango dancer to achieve major recognition in the U.S. Not only did he perform on *The Ed Sullivan Show* (three times) in the early sixties, but he also achieved success on Broadway in *New Faces of 1962*. In 1985, he returned again to Broadway as the choreographer and star of *Tango Argentino*, the show credited with reigniting the public's passion for tango worldwide. Aside from performing at Carnegie Hall, in 1986 he was given his greatest U.S. recognition, when he was invited to the White House to perform for President Reagan and a select group of dignitaries on Reagan's birthday.

Copes has also participated in several movies. Most recently, he choreographed and played a leading role in the critically acclaimed *Tango*, which won the American Choreography Award for Best Feature in 2000.

Although Copes first danced in a brief partnership with Nata Nieves, it was with her young sister Maria that he made tango history. The first competition Copes and Nieves entered was at the famous Luna Park. At the end of the night, the judges picked the traditional winners, but when the crowd went wild in opposition, they retracted their original decisions and Copes and Nieves were awarded the top spot. From there they went on to perform and inspire audiences and dancers around the world. While it is primarily Juan Carlos Copes who is spoken of when one speaks of this legendary couple, the fact is that Copes would not have been Copes without tango's first lady, Maria Nieves.[1]

• • •

Nieves and Copes not only had a tremendously successful professional relationship but also one of a personal nature for many years. The professional relationship outlasted the personal one, and eventually the legendary partners had a difficult separation. Nieves never mentions her former partner by name, but Mr. Copes is clearly the one she alludes to.

MARIA NIEVES ON TANGO . . .

"Tango took everything away from me, and gave me everything."

I started going to milongas when I was eight years old, but not to dance. I went with my older sister, who was also young, and was already dancing. But I was a girl. I would go

Maria Nieves

---

1. This piece was adapted from ToTango.net.

for a little while; I'd watch and then I'd fall asleep. When I was 12 years old, I began getting interested in tango. But my sister wouldn't let me dance. She would call me names. She is six years older than I am and said dance was only for young ladies. Finally, at the Atlanta Club, I started dancing behind her back. They had a very large dance floor there, and when I would see my sister dance in one corner of the floor, I would take advantage and dance in another corner with a friend. And when I would see her come back, I would sit down and make a bored face. By that time, I had already danced my tanguito. By the time she found out I was dancing, well…at that point there was not much she could do.

After a while, my sister and I would go dancing together. Later she got married, and her husband made her quit dancing, but I continued and concentrated on tango as a profession. Now when we talk, she reproaches herself for not continuing with dance. "How stupid I was!" she tells me. That is how we women were in the past. Nowadays, girls are much more audacious, fortunately.

Nobody really taught me to tango. I learned by watching. But today I believe young people should find a good teacher to have a base, and then the best they can do is go dancing. Step on someone's feet, and have your feet stepped on. Dance with everybody and not simply with one partner.

One thing I notice that is so different now is that today, everybody dances the same. A couple of years ago, I went to a milonga and saw that all the women hung from the men's necks, pushed their behinds out, pressed themselves against their partner's chest and stayed so separated below that in between you could see a tramway. This style is today's fashion. I respect it, but it is not my taste. My time was a splendorous time for tango, because you wouldn't find two boys who danced the same. And back then, in the Atlanta club there were over 1,000 people on Saturdays and over 1,000 on Sundays. I would dance with 15 different men, and each one danced something different.

Back then, when we left the milongas we also practiced in the bus. We would come back at 4 AM (we took the bus because we were very poor), and my partner would say, "María, I have a great step on my mind" and we'd get off the bus, and right there we'd try it. And I'm still like that—creating. It happens to me when I'm giving a class—I come up with little steps. Back then we would both come up with steps...I don't want people to think he was the only one. It was 50/50...but you know what? Now I feel that for the most part, say 80 percent is the woman. The woman, when she has personality, fills everything.

A man can be a good dancer even if he doesn't let the woman shine. However, even if he is a great dancer, the focus is always more on the woman. The woman fills the stage and is admired as much by the men as by the women. Often they act as if we women are only company. What company? We are 80 percent of the dance. But one thing young women have to understand is that the man is the one who leads. Then, once you've learned the steps by heart... well...you know how many times I've saved my partner?

I got into tango as a profession because I was very much in love —that was my first motivation. I followed that man because of love. I said to myself, if I say no, he'll find a partner, travel the world, and one day he'll leave. So I followed him in tango. I gave up having children for this. Now my children are tango, my love is tango. I continued because it was the only thing I knew how to do.

One day my partner and I decided to leave Buenos Aires. Tango had to be shown in the world. We had perseverance. We had dreams. The real decision to travel came from my partner. He had the vision...that choreographer thing. He wanted to create dances. But nobody cared about this until the agent Carlos Petit. He encouraged us. In those days, we were 10 couples who did not know how to stand or to bow. But he saw our enthusiasm for showing people tango. It was quite a transition. The stage is not the milonga, you know. I used to go to the milonga without any makeup. After we started performing, we all started looking in mirrors, pushing the belly in, etc. But I don't think I realized I wasn't an amateur anymore until I separated from my partner. Then it "clicked."

When we began, the change from the milonga to the stage took a bit of time. We began in the milonga. Later they called us to participate in tango championships in different Buenos Aires neighborhoods. The championships lasted six months, and the organizers would make a lot of money and perhaps they'd give us a glass of wine and nothing else. Later they started calling us to do exhibitions. And at first they thought we were ballet dancers. I have never been a ballet dancer, however, since we could tango so perfectly, they couldn't believe we did not have formal ballet training. Then in '54 Carlos Petit, from Nelida Roca's vaudeville show, hired us and said: "These young kids are going to make a revolution." He gave us our first opportunity in the Nacional and Tavarís theaters, and that's where we started. But the dancer was always a minor figure then. We earned very little—enough to travel by bus and eat, but that was it. It wasn't like being a singer or a musician during that time. Now that has changed. After *Tango Argentino*, dancers came to be highly valued because they realized that, regardless of how big the orchestra is, without dancers, you have nothing. Dance is what entertains the public. We pour everything onto the stage. When people see a couple dance tango it stirs their imagination, and they come up with their own stories.

To become professionals, we had to pay our dues. We came to New York around 1958, and we ate a lot of spaghetti, cooked with borrowed oil. We did auditions. What we did makes me feel very proud…to know that we opened the way for all of those who started traveling afterwards. When we started, we didn't have a mirror to look at ourselves in. I didn't have a model of a female tango dancer that I could say: "Okay, I'll do that…" It was hard work.

I think that women today learn a lot from me. Whether they like my style or not, they learn. And I survive with that—it sustains me. The girls who mention me, who feel I'm their teacher…and not because I taught them, but because (as they say), "I'm a legend." So many years of dancing…I have a lot of love from the public. Calls from the people who love me sustain me: Robert Duvall, who called me for his new movie, *Assassination Tango*. In the movie, I play a very small role. Duvall wants authenticity. I speak, and I speak, and I curse. He wants me to talk about my life in the milonga. Truth is, I'm very happy. Duvall said that I am a great actress, but he must be making fun of me.

I don't look back and wonder what I would be now if I hadn't become a professional dancer. I certainly have a lot of nostalgia when I look back. How can you deny the heart a bit of nostalgia? But, if when we die there is another life, I would like to do the same! I had a very poor youth, but the worst punishment for me would have been if they would not have let me dance. I'm from a generation that fell madly in love with tango.

Before we started *Tango Argentino*, we had traveled almost the whole world. When we came to New York in '58, we came alone. Then we worked on Broadway in *New Faces of 1962*. After that, we were hired by all the American shows, from New York to Las Vegas. When we were in Buenos Aires, we did the best television shows. Back then, we were already well known; we were almost the only ones. So when Segovia and Orezzoli conceived *Tango Argentino*, they came to see us. My partner used to tell me: "These people are crazy, thinking they can hire the regular milongueros and the top singers the way one would hire professionals." But they did it. And it was an incredible success.

The first time we were in Paris with *Tango Argentino*, we could feel that it was something incredible. We were only there for 10 days, and the shows sold out. People who hadn't seen the show brought signs to the streets, asking us not to leave. And after that, we went to Broadway. *Tango Argentino* was, for me, the most beautiful tango show ever done…and everybody copied it.

In 1999, they made a remake of the original, and it was different because many of the people who originally did it were not there: Virulazo, for instance. Many couples didn't return. When you change the dancers, the attitude starts changing also. It was a strange phase.

Also, at that time of the remake, I had not danced for four years. It was very difficult to go back—to get in shape. But I managed, and I decided onstage to outdo my partner, and I did it. These are satisfactions that God gives you.

I have a special way of preparing before I go onstage. I shut everything off. I don't hear anything. The nervousness doesn't leave me, despite all the years of performing. But I like to concentrate. I don't like to be talked to. You cannot go onstage thinking of other things, or what you are going to do at night, or your problems. You have to give everything to the performance.

When I get onstage, it's mine. I feel it's mine. I want to die with tango, not giving classes, but onstage. I'm another person there. I teach, yes. But it is not my thing. I get tired. When you teach, you have to speak, repeat things. When I teach, I don't allow my students to call me "teacher." Because first of all, that makes me feel older, and second of all, I'm nobody's teacher. Do you know what I teach? My experiences, what I learned from 40 years onstage. I teach how to walk, to be elegant, to walk the tango. There's nothing prettier than walking the tango. It's not the acrobatics, but the walking that is the most difficult.

It makes me happy to see that so many young people are learning tango. I love the fact that places for young people have opened. This did not happen in my time. And I think that with so many people learning, we'll keep on seeing new talents emerging. The singers and the orchestras leave their recordings. But the day young people don't dance anymore, tango dancing dies. And I don't want that to happen. I hope tango goes far. Young people are the ones who decide. I hope it is not a fad. There always has to be somebody who fights the rhythms—like rock—that come from abroad. The Beatles killed tango.

I still like tango music,but now I'm more inclined to melodic music. I like Recuerdo from Pugliese. Among the singers I like Goyeneche, Floreal Ruíz, Raúl Berón, Fiorentino, and from the orchestras Pugliese, Troilo, Di Sarli, Caló and Tanturi. I don't like going to the milongas now. I go when I have to. I always lived at night, my whole life. Now I go to bed at 8:30 PM and I get up at 7 AM

Among my colleagues, there are many good dancers: Carlos and Alicia, Roberto and Guillermina, Roberto and Vanina, and Geraldine. I like them because they have many styles.

The way I want to be remembered is as a tango dancer who devoted over 50 years of her life to tango and as a simple person. And I think people see that when they see me onstage, and I want them to keep that memory.

One word to summarize my career in tango? Happy! Very happy!!! Because I did what I loved: tango. [2]

2. Adapted from an original interview in *ReporTango, The New York Tango Magazine,* August 2001.

EDUARDO and GLORIA

A few words from Paul…
In my opinion the history of tango would not be complete without the story of Eduardo and Gloria. They are legendary performers who have greatly influenced the last two generations of tango dancers.

Gloria and Eduardo Arquimbau

EDUARDO and GLORIA'S LIFE IN TANGO…

Gloria and Eduardo Arquimbau began working together as youngsters with Francisco Canaro on numerous musicals, and for nearly 40 years they have been one of the most popular tango couples in the world.

From 1985 to 1992, they performed with the critically acclaimed musical *Tango Argentino*. They were also the choreographers and featured performers in the original cast of *Forever Tango* in San Francisco from 1994 to 1995. With the wide appeal and success of their shows *Tango Tango* and *Corazon de Tango*, they paved the way for many shows that followed.

Today Eduardo is considered one of the great milongueros of his generation. He and Gloria are the only living masters of the Orillero style of tango. Though he can dance any style of tango his specialty is milonguero or club style, the most rhythmical and intimate style of tango. Eduardo is, in fact, one of the teachers most responsible for the worldwide popularity of milonguero style tango, which is the style of tango danced in most of the world today, and certainly the predominate style danced in the salons of Buenos Aires.

EDUARDO ON TANGO…

"The things of the tango are internal…"

Well…as I am older than Gloria, I first started dancing tango in the decade of the '40s, at the age of 13. After I began dancing tango (which was the first dance I tried), I fell in love with dancing, and I began studying other dances as well: modern, Spanish, folklore, tap, all the dances of that time.

I met Gloria when I started taking dance classes. We were both studying with the same teachers. I was 16 or 17, and Gloria was 11. We went to the same teachers for different dances. From the beginning, I was also doing tango on the side, but Gloria was too young to do tango. Later, when she was 13 years old, we began to do a little bit of tango. And when she was 14, we were already dancing professionally. In 1961, when Gloria was 15, we went to Japan with the orchestra of Francisco Canaro. At the time, a trip like that was almost like going to the moon today. I said farewell to my family because I didn't know if I would ever come back.

The way Gloria and I grew up, tango was always with us. Being born in Pompeya, the neighborhood where we were both born, was like being born into the tango itself. Gloria's father, for example, danced tango. Our brothers and our friends danced tango. Everything was tango, tango.

The fact that we were able to turn tango into a career is a miracle. A tango career simply did not exist. But in the fifties, television was introduced in Argentina, and we were youngsters who could dance. We had good teachers, and television made popular figures out of us, and we appeared on the most famous programs of Argentine television. Also, we were part of the first color television program to be broadcast in the world. We were artists of the television era.

Later, we were actors, too, and worked on the most important television programs. We danced with the majority of orchestras...the 20 most famous: Troilo, Pugliese, Canaro, Mariano Mores, Sassone, Jose Basso, De Angelis, Calo....We danced with all except Di Sarli, because Di Sarli got ill and later died.

At that time, we were on a program called "Yo te canto Buenos Aires" (I Sing to You Buenos Aires). We were the choreographers. We had a ballet in the program...a tango ballet. Pugliese worked on this program, too. Catulo Castillo wrote the script and the producer was the famous Julio Jorge Nelson. Then, they had Troilo. They had Di Angelis. They had Jose Basso...all the orchestras...D'Arienzo. We were dancing with Canaro in the theater, and each week we danced with a different orchestra in the TV program. And we were not only the choreographers, we did everything. We moved the singers around, the dancers, everything. We brought Piazzolla so he could work. Piazzolla worked with our ballet! All the artists did; the most famous tango artists. The most famous personalities of Argentina—from Borges to Castellini, painters and writers—all appeared on the show.

Later, we choreographed another show produced by Vergara Neuman. The most famous artists and celebrities were also guests. One other program we did lasted 25 years. It was called *Grandes Valores del Tango* (*The Great Talents of Tango*). And the greatest talents of tango passed through it. The tango ballet was ours.

Since 1960, we have both taught and appeared on many programs in Buenos Aires and throughout the world. We worked in the United States in 1967, before *Tango Argentino*. We traveled with our own shows through the Soviet Union, Japan, Mexico, in all the Latin American countries. Later, we were the choreographers for *Forever Tango*, which we did in 1990, and performed for the World Cup. It was miraculous.

Of all the productions we've been a part of, we have the most respect and gratitude for *Tango Argentino*, because it's the show that revolutionized tango throughout the world. After that show, the whole world became interested in tango. Because of that show, we have become internationally known for the thing we love—tango.

Both Gloria and I know all the different styles of tango very well. What style we dance depends on the purpose. When we introduce a show, we work to build a balanced show, and within this balance we have the possibilities of working with different aspects. And one falls in love with all those things. They are like children ("hijos") you give birth to. We pick a theme, and we work on it, and we develop it and make it deeper until it works. And then, we never touch it again. For example, we created choreography that we danced with Francisco Canaro in 1961, and we still dance it! It is like a painting; it is fixed and it can't be touched.

The proper style of tango is born from the dance. One can take tango to any height, even to the most modern place, by respecting the root of the dance. Tango is like a tree, when one cuts a tree at the root, what's above has no value. It will dry up. For what is above to have value, it has to be born from below. And the real tango is like that; it has to have the roots. Otherwise, it's another thing. It may be good, it may work, but it will not be tango.

When someone begins, he can be dazzled by things that are external, but the things of the tango are internal (points to his heart). A dancer arrives at the roots of tango when he falls in love. First, shall we say, he is like a tourist within the tango: He goes around and asks for one thing and winds up liking something else. But the passage of time makes the person capable of distinguishing that which is the root of the dance, which will be useful to him. And he is only going to be satisfied when he himself can assert himself. At that moment, the tango is inside of him. And he will then find tango only when he is able to put his own personality inside of it.

People talk about styles of tango, but there is only one tango. It accommodates itself to every place and every era. When the tango was growing, it took shape from location to location. For instance, when it first reached the outskirts of the city, it was danced one way. In the clubs, they danced it in a different way. In the city salons, it was forbidden to dance the way they danced in those other places. There you had to dance salon style. In my time, the salon style was an elegant, walked style, done on the floor, without figures. The feet were always on the floor. That's what I call salon style, and that's how it was defined in the competitions in the old days.

There was also the primitve canyengue style, which belongs to a much earlier time. Then came the tango cruzado, which was danced from 1935 to 1940. After that came the tango fantasia, which people don't understand very well. Tango fantasia came from the dance floor, not from the stage. The only thing that was different was that the man and the woman were allowed to do some figures separately, but they were tango figures, of course. This was born in the forties and fifties, in the practicas, among the men. The exhibitions were done by men. Later the woman was incorporated.

In the forties a style appeared with boleos and ganchos, footwork off the floor. It was something new, and it began a trend of style to attract attention. Later, in the fifties, people began to dance closer (club style) with their faces looking in the opposite direction. This was a more intimate dance, more for the couple, and some of the figures were reminiscent of the primitive tango. It had syncopations and dancers played with time and countertime. Again, that is more from the old, primitive tango and the orchestras played rhythmically. Among the first was Juan D'Arienzo. Juan D'Arienzo in 1935 was what *Tango Argentino* is for today. His orchestra got the whole country dancing.

Before 1935, the orchestras were heavy and slow. The tango that was danced in the salons was still somewhat forbidden. When the tango entered the mainstream society, not the high society but the middle class, it was forbidden to do "strange" figures. But, at the same time, in the outskirts of the town, they danced everything. The style of tango varied according to where it was danced.

In the twenties, when the tango went to Europe, they danced before the Pope. Canaro wrote a tango called "Ave Maria." I can only imagine how the woman who danced it was dressed...like a nun. Amazing. Meanwhile, in Buenos Aires, they were dancing another tango. The point is, there is only one tango, and the style can change according to the needs of the dancer or the place it's danced....Nobody is the owner of the tango. The most one can do for tango is to love it. When one believes that he is the owner of the tango, he is lost.

Over the years, I have admired many great tango dancers. Growing up in our neighborhood, there were many. Because if you couldn't dance, you weren't allowed to live there (laughter). Gloria's father was a phenomenal tango dancer. He even did exhibitions. Our friends did exhibitions. I was just a kid, but I liked tango so much that they let me in on their conversations. I wasn't allowed to talk; I just listened. Then, hanging around at two or three in the morning on a street corner, the conversation would suddenly turn into dance. They would start dancing and teaching. It was not like now. They did it quickly. They said, "Here, dig this," rapidly, and you had to grab it and take it just like that. This was a way of life, and it was imperative to learn to dance. For example, when a maestro came to teach me in a club, 200 people came to see how he would teach. It was a very big thing. There was a passion for tango. It was marvelous. And these were popular people with big names.

As Gloria would point out, the women learned to tango within the family, from their mothers, fathers, sisters, friends and brothers. It was a family affair. Then we would all go out together to dance, on Saturdays and Sundays.

The men learned in the clubs, among men. That's how we learned to lead. First we had to learn the part of the woman in order to know what the lead (las marcas) should feel like. Today, in a technique class I danced with all the women, and Gloria danced with the men, explaining the lead. This is rarely done anymore. These days, the woman help the men by doing things for them, and the men never really learn how to properly direct the woman with las marcas. They're in a rush.

In my day, I was in no rush (laughs). I was only 13 years old when I started, how could I be in a rush? Besides, I didn't learn with a business purpose in mind. I learned tango to have fun. I wanted to get ready to go out dancing with a woman. I wanted to have a good time. I had all the time in the world. Everyone would teach one another. It was a family thing where everyone would show you something. One day we'd go to one club, and the next day we'd go to another club in another neighborhood. We could see, watching somebody dance, whether he was from Valentin Alsina, Pompeya or Villa Urquiza. It was wonderful because every neighborhood had a different style. It was a great time for tango. [3]

Miguel Zotto

MIGUEL ZOTTO

A few words from Paul…
I met Miguel Zotto in 1986, when DanceSport took the first tango tour to Buenos Aires. This was at the very beginning of the new era for tango. On that tour, our friend Juan Carlos Copes helped set

3. Adapted from an article by Linda Valentino for ToTango.net.

up lessons for us with Maria Nieves and her sister Christina. Christina had a young assistant named Miguel Zotto. At the time, Miguel was one of the few dancers from the younger generation who was involved in tango. He was, in fact, the only young person I saw at the milongas, which were then frequented only by the older milongueros.

Some time later, when Rivarola and his partner left *Tango Argentino*, Miguel and his partner Milena took their place in the show. Before that, no one outside of Buenos Aires knew who Miguel was, but from there he went on to be one of the best dancers in the new wave of tango dancers and a groundbreaking choreographer as well.

Miguel and Milena are truly protégés of the older milongueros. Long before Pablo Veron gained fame as a tango dancer in Sally Potter's film *The Tango Lesson*, Miguel Zotto in classes, at milongas, and in shows such as *Tango Argentino*, *Tango x 2* and *Perfumes de Tango* became an inspiration for many young people to get involved with the dance.

MIGUEL ZOTTO'S LIFE IN TANGO...

Born in 1958 in Vicente López, Buenos Aires, Miguel Zotto came from a truly "tanguera" family. He grew up listening to tangos with his grandfather, who was a dancer, and his father, who was both a dancer and actor. From the time he was six years old, Miguel was dancing in the Buenos Aires milongas, and at the age of 17, he began studying tango with some of the greatest milongueros of the day. In 1985, Miguel shot to fame as the tango instructor and lead dancer in the show *Jazmines* by Ana María Steckelman, which was performed in both Argentina and Venezuela.

It was also in 1985 that Miguel met Milena Plebs, and they began their tango career as a couple. For four years, traveling throughout the United States, Canada, Venezuela, Europe and Japan, they performed in Segovia and Orezzoli's Broadway hit *Tango Argentino*. During those years, they continued to study with teachers such as Juan Carlos Copes, Rudolfo Dinsel, Petrolo, Virulazo and Elvira, Pepito Avellaneda, Hazel Grove, Finite, Petroleum, and they did an intensive study with the legendary teacher Antonio Todaro.

In 1988, Miguel and Milena created the company "Tango x 2," which they directed, choreographed and performed in as the principal dancers. With this company, which featured both legendary milongueros and young kids, they brought milonguero style tango to the stage. In 1989, they presented the company's premier show *Tango x 2*, which received excellent reviews in *The New York Times*, the *New York Post* and *Dance Magazine* where the critics declared *Tango x 2* "the best show of the season in New York." Four years later, they presented their second work, *Perfumes de Tango*, which not only included milongueros but actual scenes of milongas—something never done in a show before. Most recently they created *Una Noche de Tango*, which was hailed by the *Clarin* (an Argentine newspaper), as "the best dance show of the world." Since then, Miguel and Milena have continued dancing, creating and performing on TV programs, shows and festivals worldwide.

Miguel has also performed in the films *Tango, Bayle Nuestro* by Jorge Zanda, *Flop* by Eduardo Mingnona, *Oratoria Carlos Gardel* by Horacio Salgan and Horacio Ferrer and in the 1992 National Geographic Explorer documentary *Tango!* with Robert Duvall.

MIGUEL ON TANGO...

"Tango is not a fashion, but an addiction...a drug."

Milena and I were the first to take the traditional tango, tango of the dance halls and milongas, to the stage. That was quite an undertaking. From the time we started to dance, we realized that there were different principles involved in tango for the stage, but, nonetheless, we wanted to bring this traditional tango to the stage. Our desire was born when the show *Tango Argentino* had become a circus of pirouettes, and the only ones who were still dancing the slow and walked tango were Copes and Virulazo. When we studied with the milonguero Ramon "Fino" Rivera, he used to say that if we brought this dance to the stage, the Argentinean men and women would identify with us.

We did the show and carried on dancing simply. We returned to Buenos Aires and began studying with the great tango teachers, such as Antonio Todaro. I think we became an example for the young people because we kept going to the milongas while at the same time we were working in the show.

I got to know Antonio Todaro through the milongueros Virulazo and Jorge. Virulazo used to tell me "you must meet the Italian Antonio," but he would never tell me where to meet him, because at that time I was Virulazo's student. But later on, we did a program for television called *Grandes Valores del Tango*, and Antonio saw us and sent for us through another milonguero. We were the first professionals to study with Todaro. We realized that the way to move ahead in tango was with him and recommended Antonio to all the professionals and to all the young people in the milongas as well.

The genius of Antonio was that he was a machine for creating and combining the steps of tango. What he was teaching was authentic. He had the "whole thing" of the tango: the old school and the tango of the forties. The secret that he communicated to us and taught us was the *giro* and the *enrosque*. For us, that changed the subject of how to prepare and resolve a large part of the dance, since the professional dancer up to that time didn't do *giros* or *enrosques*. Another aspect of his genius was that he taught you to dance without saying a word. I think that in the history of tango, he was *the* teacher, in large because he was someone who *always* taught the dance; he didn't begin teaching just at the moment when tango became fashionable—as many do, so that now there are teachers emerging from everywhere.

Some say that tango is a fashion today, but I think one should say, rather, that tango is not a fashion, but an addiction…a drug. As such, the more you are exposed to it the more you become an addict. That's why they cannot kill it; it's more than a hundred years old and was always attacked, but they never succeeded in killing it.

It is vital to the survival of tango to keep a record of everything that is going on—to tape it. Imagine if Fred Astaire and Gene Kelly had not been captured on film as they were!

At one time, we began a project with Eduardo Arquimbau and

Copes to write down a methodology of tango, but we came to the conclusion that this is not possible. As soon as you begin to do this, you immediately lose the essence of tango. Tango is a social dance, a dance of the people. What would be the point of having lessons with teachers if we all taught the same? That's the charm of the tango: With each person, you find a different character and style. The same is true of orchestras. Musicians play the music, but if everyone played like Pugliese or Di Sarli, that wouldn't make any sense.

To me, Pugliese and Di Sarli are the best orchestras to dance to. Of course, this goes with my style—there are others who would say D'Arienzo or Tanturi are the best to dance to. There isn't one truth; it depends on the style that you want to be identified with.

Pugliese (the Pugliese of the forties, not of the present, which is much more pronounced) is more calm, more tuneful, and has phrases that allow you to dance the silences; and following the pauses is fundamental. The thing in tango is the rhythm, the timing one feels.

One has to dance with lots of different people—the men as well as the women. When Milena and I started going to the milongas, we mutually decided to dance with everybody. Of course, it was something that the milonguero of the old school, like Virulazo, didn't understand. He used to say to me, "How are you going to let Milena dance with that one?" And I'd reply, "Don't worry Viru, she's not going to be unfaithful to me; we're doing it so that we learn properly what the tango is about." The good thing is that nowadays this old attitude has gone.

The most important talent a milonguero must have is the ability to make the woman shine. It means nothing to execute a lot of steps with the woman just following you. The tango is like any action in real life. Tango is about the character in each one of us. Tango is the "ensemble" of life, reflecting all its idiosyncrasies. And without a woman you cannot dance tango; the woman fulfills as important a role as the man.

However excellent a dancer you are as a man—even if you are able to dance with every woman—when you dance with a woman who can't follow, you have more responsibility. You must dance perfectly, which means you can't relax, you can't think about your posture, and you can't rattle off a fine step; so what's the use of being able to do everything if they don't follow you?

You either feel tango or you don't. And the same goes for the character and the temperament of each person: If a guy is cold in life, he'll be cold in the dance. The tango is a reflection of what one is in life. I am passionate in what I do, and I feel it as much on the stage as in the milonga. Tango is about feeling and sensitivity; otherwise you are just doing gymnastics. You can do all the steps, but it has to have feeling and sensitivity to be authentic tango.

Tango is like writing a letter—it has a beginning, periods, commas, stops and an end. If you're doing figures and giros all the time, people don't see anything, and that is why there is the walk—the invention of all the people. In this dance of the people, which is what tango is, all the most famous couples have used the walk, and they use it constantly. The tango is on the ground. It's caressing the floor. It's the ball of the foot and the heel, the weight of the body right on the axis, and each person on his own axis. If you make pupils walk at the beginning, they get bored and want to learn steps, and then more steps—to show off at the dance hall. And that's understandable—it happened to me also when I started. So you need to have the luck of meeting a teacher who tells you, "No. Look: You must walk. First walk."

The woman must know how to wait for the man. Quite often you hear the milongueros saying to each other, "Look how that girl waits; it's fantastic how she waits." Waiting means to say that she's on her axis and the man can take her from it wherever he likes, like a feather. The woman needs to follow the man's torso and body with tiny adjustments. With regard to the man, the lead should be managed with the body, with the shoulders, with both hands and with the arm that is behind. The arm is fundamental because it's the support that keeps the woman from getting away from you; the woman dances within the arms of the man.

The young people try to do figures; they dance separated. This is because for 30 years dancing has been separated, not because of tango, but because of rock and roll and the discos. Because of that, the embrace has been lost. That's why what is most difficult for male students is to embrace, and for female students, to let herself be embraced in order to be led. The milonguero belongs to another generation, and he has assimilated this. In other words, for 40 years he's been embracing the woman in order to dance.

Without having met him, I consider Carlos Gardel my artistic father. Gardel broke with all the preconceptions of the singers and actors of his era. That cheerful element that he brought to the tango, that smile? With the expressions of his face, he is telling you the meaning of the tango lyrics. The first thing I listened to as a child was Gardel; and the smile I have is not, as many think, because I am imitating him. I have it because I have it assimilated into my life, and when I started to dance milonga, I said to myself, "If the milonga is a happy rhythm, why don't I smile when I dance it?" When I first met Milena, she was listening to Piazzolla; I got her to listen to Gardel. She understood how much I feel him, and today she feels about him as I do.

Piazzolla to me means the possibility of creating something more contemporary—more modern and stylized. At the milonga, one doesn't dance to Piazzolla either because he has a very syncopated rhythm or he hasn't got the essential pauses that allow you to resolve the step; or because he has those adagio phrases that are very slow for traditional tango. *Tocata en Re* or *La Tangata del Alma* are among the few tangos of Piazzolla that admit the traditional steps of the tango. Piazzolla's music is the real music of Buenos Aires, and it is ours. It has all the ingredients of tango, because this Italian was above all a tanguero. But to be able to create something and be different, you need to go out on a limb a bit, and he was a genius because he did it. He dared to step out of the mold. I don't dare to step out of the mold. There is an evolution in the tango that we dance, but the roots stay with the classic tango.

CARLOS GAVITO

A few words from Paul...

I met Carlos Gavito in the mid-nineties through one of my students who had studied with him at his salon in London, where he taught weekly tango classes. She often encouraged me to invite her former teacher to give workshops at my studio. She spoke so enthusiastically about him that, finally, I had to agree. Carlos's first classes were such a positive experience that we have invited him back ever since. To this day, he continues to hold his New York workshops and master classes exclusively at DanceSport when he visits New York, which over the years has become his home away from home.

Carlos Gavito

Aside from being a gifted teacher and performer, Carlos is also a fantastic choreographer and has been very generous in helping me and Eleny put together many different numbers. We still consider Carlos an important tango coach and a good friend, and we feel privileged that he shares his tango mastery with us and our students.

CARLOS GAVITO'S LIFE IN TANGO...

The poet-dancer Carlos Gavito is considered one of the last great dancers from the end of tango's Golden Age. Born in Avellaneda, a popular dance suburb of Buenos Aires, at 17 Gavito chose to make a career as a dancer and began studying ballet, flamenco, jazz and Argentinean folklore dance. At the age of 22, he devoted himself solely to Tango.

Over the years, Gavito has performed in the greatest tango shows of our time and with the most renowned orchestras. In 1964, with his first partner Mirta, whom he later married, he performed with Miguel

Caló's orchestra. Later with his second wife and tango partner Helen Campbell, he toured the world with other legendary orchestras, including the great Anibal Troilo. Nineteen hundred and eighty marked a turning point in Gavito's career. With the four shows they created, he and Helen performed at prestigious hotels and resorts throughout the world. In 1993, he returned to London, where he started his own tango salon ("Gavito's") and focused on a career of teaching not just show dancers but tango dancers of all levels.

A year later, producer and director Luis Bravo invited Gavito to join the cast of *Forever Tango*. The two numbers he created with his partner Marcela Duran immediately became a central and classic part of the show. After 15 months on Broadway, *Forever Tango* was nominated for the Tony Award for best choreography.

CARLOS GAVITO ON TANGO...

"Tango is a shared moment."

I never really learned tango—in the formal sense. Tango was part of the Argentine culture, and when I was a boy, it was in fashion. When I was seven years old, I used to go to the basketball court at the sports club in my town, Avellaneda, where three times a week they held tango "practicas." In those days, tango was practiced between men. The older men would use boys who were placed in a standing position, mimicking the women, and the men would practice their steps. They would say "hey boy, come, stand here, put your foot here, and now there," and they would try new steps and new ways. So at the beginning I was just a body, but I paid attention to the steps. When I was 15, it was then my turn to practice steps, and I did the same with a younger boy. In those days, there were no dance schools—and no television—so a kid like me would have soccer during the day and tango in the late afternoon.

I wasn't allowed to do any steps before I was 15 or to go to any milongas. What made me go back to the practice sessions each week was the music. I was always into the music. When I was 15, elsewhere everybody was listening and dancing to rock and roll, but all the clubs around my town were still playing tango. Tango was always there. From the beginning, I always liked tango. I found the music so beautiful that I always wanted to dance it—not as a profession, not as a performance, but in a social context.

By the way, I feel it is always important to make the distinction between social tango and the tango performed onstage: One has nothing to do with the other. Stage tango is done to sell tickets, while social tango is dancing you do for your own enjoyment. That's why I've never understood the "ganchos" (hooks) and kicks in social tango. I always make it clear to my students that I don't teach ganchos. I will only teach them if a student wants to become a professional and wants to learn a specific choreography from me; only then will I teach ganchos. But not for social tango. I feel strongly about that.

Although I started dancing at 15, I didn't decide to make tango a profession until much later, when I was around 23 or 24 years old. I was dancing jazz, and I was also taking ballet classes. I first became a jazz dancer, and then one day a friend of mine, Eduardo Arquimbau (from the well-known Gloria and Eduardo) came looking for me. He was putting together a television special and needed guys who danced tango, not just any kind of dancers, but dancers who understood both stage and social dancing. He knew I could dance tango, and so he came to talk to me. He told me about the possibility of doing this show, and I said "Okay, let's try; let's see what happens." We started to practice in a club, and it was fine. The show was called *Así Canta Buenos Aires* (*This Is How Buenos Aires Sings*). From that show, we went on and did another show, *Yo soy Porteño* (*I'm From Buenos Aires*). I wound up working with him for about three and a half years. Without really knowing it, I went back to my roots, to tango.

After that, Eduardo, Gloria and I started working in the milongas, where we performed four days a week as a trio. Later on, Eduardo formed a big company that I took care of when he was on tour in Japan and Central America. When he finally came back, I decided to go on my own to the Festival of Tango in Colombia with the orchestra of Aníbal Troilo.

Contrary to many tango dancers, I didn't have *dance* teachers; I had *tango* teachers. One was Julián Centeya, he was a poet—and a singer who wrote tango lyrics—and he was my best teacher. (If you listen to the tango "Café Domínguez," the one who is talking at the beginning is Julián.) He was my best teacher because he taught me tango from the inside. The other teacher who was important to me is Miguel Caló. I worked with him and his orchestra in Buenos Aires around 1963. He would say, "Listen to the music, now listen to the voice of Raúl Berón. Dance the voice, just the voice. Now dance the piano." He directed me like I was another musician in the orchestra. He made me understand how to listen to the music and what I should listen to. These were my two tango teachers.

There are no teachers like these two anymore. Today, when people dance tango you see every dancer rushing to do steps. There should never be a rush to do a step; one should enjoy it, make it last...dwell on it. I often say, I enjoy the step I'm doing so much, at the moment I am doing it, that I want to make it last. It's the same as when we were kids and we would get five pennies to get an ice cream; we would lick it slowly, trying to make the most of it, to make it last. So I don't understand the rush to finish one step just to go on to the next one. I think it's much more interesting to do one and stop—not really stop, but to take a pause and just do nothing for a while. Just enjoy the moment first and then go on to do something else. I think most people rush because they don't know how to do "nothing"; doing nothing is the most difficult. One problem is that even if your dance is not choreographed, you learn the basic step—the salida—then you think you have to do the whole step. But what happens if someone is in front of you, or next to you, and you cannot finish the step? In actuality, the step never ends. It's a three-minute step. It's the whole dance.

In social tango, you move with your partner and with the music. And that is also something that people should understand: The relationship between you and your partner is not personal. What is personal between the two of you is that you are both trying to caress the music with your feet.

Who is my ideal partner? My ideal tango partner...well, at the moment, it is definitely my partner in the show, Marcela Durán. We are a good duo. We understand each other without words. We don't need to talk, and we don't need to rehearse. Each of us tries to accomplish our own role: I lead, and she follows. Some girls get fed up with following, and they want to dance like a man because they say it's more entertaining. But I say you don't have enough time in your lifetime to learn how to follow well and to lead well also. So I would tell these girls to really learn how to follow.

My partner and I think very much alike. Even if she and I have a different idea, a different understanding or a different feeling of the music, we still think alike. What we share is the mood. She doesn't listen to my thoughts, I don't listen to her thoughts, but somehow we communicate the same mood to each other. Marcela and I don't have a personal relationship—we are friends and dance partners—but our souls communicate. We don't need to talk. So, right now I feel I am dancing with my ideal partner. But really, my ideal does not have a face. She's a dream of something I want in real life, but that ideal does not have a face. You know, when you dance tango, you should really put a little bit of your life into it. If you dance your life, you dance better.

A good tango dancer is one who listens to the music. That is the only criteria. We dance the music, not the steps. Anybody who aspires to dance well never thinks about the step he's going to do. What he cares about is that he follows the music. You see, we are painters. We paint the music with our feet. Musicians play an instrument and use their fingers, their hands. Dancers use their toes.

Teaching tango has been difficult at times, because tango was not always in fashion. To arrive at the point I'm at today took many years. Now I'm very much in demand, and I enjoy that because I've spent a long time dancing tango. I think I deserve it. I danced tango long before it became popular; I didn't become a dancer because it was fashionable. Some dancers started with folklore or flamenco, and then when tango became a commercial success, they started dancing tango. That was not my case. I danced tango when it was not in fashion, and even when it was politically dangerous. So, I deserve what I've earned. I've earned it through the years.

• • •

At the moment, I think teaching in the U.S. and teaching in Argentina is the same, because in Argentina it has also become very commercial. Teachers everywhere try to surprise and impress others. They sometimes teach steps they would not even do themselves. They say that if you teach simple things, students get bored. But a good teacher should never worry about that. He should teach social tango, not tango to impress others. I don't care if there are 10, 20 or 100 people in my classes. The way I dance is the way I teach, and I teach simplicity. Sometimes, a step can look very easy and simple, but when people try to recreate it, they can't, because simplicity is not always easy.

Its actually easier to dance fast than to dance slow. Sometimes the person who dances fast is actually trying to hide mistakes. The dancer who dances slowly does it because he's a hundred percent sure that what he's doing is perfect.

I don't think that understanding tango lyrics is so important. When I was a boy, I listened to Bill Haley. I didn't know any English, but I could tell whether the song was happy, sad or romantic. The lyrics in tango and the voice are very clear, and you can hear when there's romance, nostalgia or sadness. You can feel it, even though you don't understand the lyrics. Once again, the mood of the song, of the music, is important to listen to. For instance, I can never understand why a person who dances to Miguel Caló does ganchos when the tango is about love. A gancho is aggressive. Why would the woman agree to this aggression when the music is about love?

I don't really model my dancing after a person. My model would be the way a cat moves. When a cat moves, you see his paws and every single muscle. He moves slowly, but he's always ready to jump. You can't catch him. I like that when he moves slowly. There's a rhythm to his slow motion. It's something beautiful to admire, and I think all dancers should try to imitate it.

Because I've been dancing for so long, it's tough to say what my favorite tango is. There was a time when it was "Quejas de Bandoneón," another time it was "Chiqué," "La Ultima Cita" and also "Yunta de Oro." I'm very much in love with Pugliese's music, especially "Pata Ancha." One of my favorite tangos is "Café

Domínguez" because at the beginning you can hear the voice of my "godfather" Julián Centeya. I also love the tangos of Miguel Caló, each one of them. I love the voice of Raúl Berón, also Alberto Podestá. I love Pugliese and Ricardo Tanturi. But I'm not a big fan of Biagi or Canaro. These are not my kind of tango. Biagi is from the '60's, and I don't like the rhythm; it's too sharp on the beat. I prefer the music that goes away from the beat, that is softer, smoother, even looser. I don't like strong marks or accents on the music. I prefer tangos that are more like a dream, like flying.

It's difficult to say what my best tango moment has been. I swear to God that I enjoy every single tango I dance. That is why, when I go to a milonga, I don't dance the whole night. I dance a few selected tangos. What is important is that I always dance well. If I get tired, I go sit and watch, because I'd rather do that than dance badly. I dance to the inspiration of the music. I need inspiration. So first, I need the right music, and then I have to find the right partner. If I can't find the right partner, I won't dance. If I don't like the music, I won't dance. So, to describe to you my best tango moment is impossible, because for me every tango is a best moment.

I think those who say that you can't tango if you're not Argentine are mistaken. Tango was an immigrant music in my own country, so it does not have a nationality. Its only passport is feeling, and everybody has feelings. Passion is a plus. If you are a passionate person, you will dance better. There's a misperception that if a dancer knows a lot of steps, he's a good dancer. Knowing a lot of steps only means that a person has a good memory. I prefer the tango you dance while enjoying the moment, because then I will see that my partner is closing her eyes, and she is enjoying it, too.

Of course, I've met girls who thought they have to have their eyes closed to dance a good tango. That's a mistake, too. You close your eyes when you feel like it, when you're comfortable, and not because you have to or because it looks better. Trust is also important. When you dance with a partner, you are close, and the dance is very suggestive. But as I said before, it's not personal. Close is what the music inspires you to become. The embrace looks personal, but what we are actually embracing is the music.

If you go back to the beginning of tango, tango is defined as a feeling, a "sentimiento," which you dance to. So when you start the dance, you don't start with a step, you start with a feeling. That's why I think tango dancers are not like other dancers. Other dancers go through a combination of steps. Tango is improvised. It is improvised all the way. There are no combinations. In tango you can't be preoccupied with the steps. You need to express your emotions while listening to the music. You can spot a person who is actually thinking about the next step a mile away. On the other hand, the dancer who follows the music will move at the same time as his partner. They will move as one. The American language says it clearly: "It takes two to tango."

There is only one way that I want to be remembered as a dancer: that I was honest with my dancing. [4]

photo: Mike Nicolaides

Guillermina Quiroga and Roberto Reis

GUILLERMINA & ROBERTO

A few words from Paul...
I met Guillermina in 1991, when she came to New York with her first dance partner Osvaldo Zotto, whom she partnered in the original cast of *Tango x 2*. A year later, Guillermina returned to New York with her new partner and future husband, Roberto Reis. Since then, each has become a good friend, and when in New York, they often come to DanceSport both to perform and to conduct tango workshops.

Roberto and Guillermina are, in my opinion, two of the best tango dancers to have come out of the new generation of tango. Like their heroes, Copes and Nieves, they continue to push the limits of tango dynamics and powerful style. Inspired by composers like Piazzolla, they pave the way for tango's ongoing evolution as an artisti-

4. Adapted from an original interview in *ReporTango, The New York Tango Magazine,* January 2001.

cally expressive dance form. Since their first performances, they have continued to be an inspiration to audiences worldwide as well as fellow dancers, who often attempt to imitate their unique and innovative choreography.

Today Roberto and Guillermina continue to perform as featured dancers in our annual "TangoFest" held every year at Town Hall in midtown Manhattan. Over the years, they have generously shared their knowledge and inspiration with Eleny and me and have helped to create some of our best choreographies. They have also introduced us to many of their most prized teachers, who in turn became our teachers. Some of these tango legends include Nito and Elba, Raul Bravo and Puppy Castello.

GUILLERMINA and ROBERTO'S LIFE IN TANGO...

Since 1992, Guillermina and Roberto have performed together in numerous productions. Most notably, they were one of the central couples in the original cast of the Broadway hit *Forever Tango*, in which they choreographed the exciting final number.

After leaving *Forever Tango*, Roberto and Guillermina began touring with Julio Iglesias to promote his best-selling album *Tango*. During that tour, their performances thrilled audiences so much that Julio decided to make them a regular part of his show for more than three years.

Among Guillermina and Roberto's most significant appearances are the performances they rendered in Gloria and Eduardo's production of *Tango Tango* and *Corazon de Tango*, their choreography in Sony Productions' *Tango Magic* at Carnegie Hall, and their famous rendition of "Tanguera," "Couprasita" and other new works such as "Zoom" at New York's "TangoFest."

With each performance, Roberto and Guillermina reaffirm the quality of their artistry and make clear that they are in a class of their own. While each currently dances with various other partners, on special occasions they still perform together. Most recently they appeared in *Assassination Tango*, a film currently being produced and directed in Buenos Aires by tango fanatic Robert Duvall.

GUILLERMINA ON TANGO...

"Many dance, very few move and reach the heart of people."

I started dancing when I started walking, I believe. I studied ballet from age six until 22, and when I was 23, I began studying tango. Only at 23...I was old! Once I began studying tango, I never stopped.

I had seen tango on TV, sometimes in Vergara Leuman's *Botica de Tango* or in *Grandes Valores del Tango*. Every so often, I would watch the shows, but at that time, I was in another world, ballet...and tango was very popular and did not really attract me. Then one day I saw Copes and Nieves dance, and I was amazed. I thought it was incredible...and I said I want to learn to dance *that*. But I thought it was so difficult, and I didn't feel capable of dancing even one of those steps. For a while, I researched places where they taught, but I would never go. But finally, I said to myself "Okay, let's go, I have nothing to lose, and if I can't do it, I'll never go back" (laughs).

The first day I went to La Casa del Tango (The House of Tango) in La Plata, and Fabian Salas (who still teaches) was there. There wasn't really a formal instructor, just a person who would guide beginners. We met and he said: "Okay, now I'll teach you the basic step." And I couldn't do it to save my life (laughs). It was an absolute failure. The next Wednesday I decided to give myself one more chance. I vowed, "If I can't do it, I'll *never, ever* go back." Then I went and I let myself go, and I did everything. Suddenly I could do the basic, the ochos (forward and backward), the molinetes. I do not know where it came from, but I was suddenly able to do every-thing. I danced waltz, milonga, tango, everything. And I would do boleos; I would do plenty of boleos. I was ecstatic, so I went home and said to my mother: "I found what I want to do with my life!" And my mother said: "Oh, yes?" and I told her: "Yes, this is my life." And it was like that....

For several months, I went to La Casa del Tango. A few months later, I took classes in Canning with Miguel Balmaceda, who has now passed away. He was an excellent teacher. Miguel and his partner Nelly became my first real instructors. I studied with them for about one year. Later I met Puppy [Castello], and I spent a lot of time with him, too. After that, I studied with Pocho Pizarro; later they introduced me to Todaro, Pepito Avellaneda, Raúl Bravo, and, of course, Petroleo, from whom I learned a lot. So, I studied a bit with everybody.

I think the dancer I liked the most at that time was Copes. However, I never learned with a teacher like that—a show dancer. I always learned with milongueros—the teachers from the milongas. When I started going to the milongas, there weren't many young people there. I would go and stay in a corner until, finally, the older people, the old milongueros, would dance with me. I learned a lot in the milongas, dancing with everybody.

Tango por Dos was the show I really started in. I stayed with it for two and a half years. At that time, I danced with Osvaldo Zotto —he was my first partner. We began together—we had been introduced at a practica. Before we started in *Tango por Dos*, Osvaldo and I won the first annual "Hugo del Carril" contest '89, and the award was a season at the Teatro de las Provincias, along with some incredible stars. One of them was Virulazo. I was just starting and to be dancing next to him…this was incredible.

I have been lucky to perform with some of the best dancers in the world. When I became partners with Roberto, we danced at the opening of the '94 World Cup with Mayoral and Elsa Maria, Rivarola and Maria, Copes and Nieves, Nelida and Nelson, and Los Dinzels. And in *Forever Tango* with so many couples. Later, Roberto and I danced with Julio Iglesias. Our work with Julio was something very different; another type of show.

The *Tango Magic* performance at Carnegie Hall was very important for us—especially for Roberto, because it was his dream to dance in Carnegie Hall.

I was also part of the remake of *Tango Argentino*, and I liked the show a lot. There I partnered with Pablo Veron. For me, it was also marvelous to share in this last work Copes and Maria Nieves did together. They are people I admire a lot, and to be next to them. It is very special. Especially, Maria Nieves who, as a female dancer, is the best; there is no other.

Dancing on a stage and dancing in a milonga are very different. To dance onstage, for me, is an absolute pleasure. However, I also like to improvise something relaxed, without thinking, without any-body looking at me. This is why I still go to the milongas—because at the milonga I am just another person. I can make mistakes. I can improvise. And I love dancing with each person at a milonga because each dances differently. Each man, for instance, gives a dif-ferent embrace. There are men who give you space, but who at the same time hold you—that is perfect. When they give you space, you can experiment and add things. Whether onstage or at a milonga, it is ideal when both partners contribute what they feel to the music. The wealth of a tango couple resides in that they both contribute to the choreographic creation, the improvisation, the emotion that each feels, which is materialized in steps.

When I feel the music inspires something, I do it. When my partner allows me to, when it is the proper moment, when there is a pause and the music asks for something...but I never do some-thing that interrupts the lead.

The future of tango? I think it will be fantastic, because I see new people working to do new things. I always tell students: Don't do what is always done...don't do the same. Don't copy...don't mimic. The best will always be what occurs to them based on the knowledge they have. And I see that there are young people, new people, aiming for that.

When I started dancing at the end of '89, Petróleo, who was an innovator and an extremely creative guy, taught me how to do boleos. He taught me a lot of things. (All the molinetes, all the things that are still being done today—he invented them before the forties.) One day he said to me: "Enough, girl. This tango is over; don't dance it anymore. With the music of tango, you must force yourself not to repeat things. Find new things." "Like what?" I said. "I don't know," he said, "you have to find them." And yet we are still repeating the molinetes and ganchos.

Roberto, who was my partner for so many years, is among the people looking for new things. He is a very creative person, and he invented a lot of new things in the dance that perhaps you see now—I know they came from him. And just like him, there are other people who dare to use all their creativity, and that will bring a different form of expression.

I really don't worry about how the traditional milongueros will react to the new expressions in tango. I don't worry because, first of all, I learned with them and I continue dancing with them and, second, because Petróleo, who was the milonguero of the century, implored me to create something new with the other young tango dancers.

To women who want to improve in tango, I would advise, first of all, stop thinking about individuality. One of the big questions I hear from my students is, "How do I let myself go?" And I always tell them the same: Relax and enjoy. You have to relax and not think so much; let the man guide you. In the few moments that the man gives you the space to improvise, you can create something new. You must insist and you must practice. And you must never try to be like somebody else. I know students sometimes look at somebody and say: "Ah, I want to dance like her." Never try to be like somebody else.

You must, certainly, follow the rules of tango, follow the techniques you learned and follow the man's lead, but try to move like yourself. The form of movement should be absolutely personal, with its own dynamics, with its own expression. It's also important for a woman learning tango to learn to perceive the man—to be able to follow him in every step, in each pause, in each breath. Let yourself be led, and let yourself be filled with the music to be able to interpret it.

An emotional connection is also important in tango. You need to have your emotions stirred to dance. If the music does not move me inside, I can't dance. You don't necessarily need an emotional connection with your partner, but an emotional connection must exist with the music in the tango dance. If this is missing, it is better to devote yourself to something else.

When I hear "tango," I think of something that is my own. I think "Oh! It's mine." I know it sounds very possessive, but I know there are many people who work in tango as much as I do, who when they hear a tango in the street they say: "Oh no! Not tango again!" The first thing I think is "Oh! How nice!" It is something I do, that I share, something that makes me very happy.

ROBERTO ON TANGO...

"Tango belongs to the world..."

When I began dancing, I began as a folklore dancer. I was eight years old. When I was 13, I became a professional dancer with the group "Ballet Brandsen." I was there until I was 17. Afterwards, I went to the ballet of Chúcaro, where I stayed for two years. And I also worked a lot with small companies until 1987.

In 1988, tango became fashionable because of *Tango Argentino*. At that time I was working in San Telmo dancing folklore, and the tourist shows had no professional tango dancers to dance onstage. That's when they began putting me onstage. Let's say they pushed me there—I wasn't that interested at first. The first thing I did with tango was a show with Copes called *Tango Tango*, and after that I began working in the San Telmo shows.

There are certainly differences between folklore and tango— there were issues with the poise of the chest and leaning backwards. At that moment, however, there weren't many tango teachers—and the few who danced tango didn't want to teach "kids like us." So when I was beginning, all we did was invent new things or recreate some things we had seen. Only after that did some instructors begin appearing. Obviously, the first one I began imitating was Copes, with whom I was working. I also spent a year as an assistant to Copes, so I learned in his classes. After that, I studied with Todaro, Raúl Bravo...many of the great tango dancers.

The first time I went to a milonga was in 1987 or 1988—and the old people kicked me out with a broom. The truth is, they treated us very badly. They didn't even let me watch. The older men didn't like the younger men watching because then the women would look at us—since we were young—and the old men would get jealous. I was only able to go back in 1989 or 1990, when other young people started going. With so many of us, they had no alternative but to put up with us. When I was working onstage, I also started to enjoy going to the milongas.

I began learning tango in a way that is opposite to how most learn. I mean, I began as a professional in a show, and it was only after that I went to the milongas. The old men would tell me: "You, kid, are only good for the stage…." They would treat us so badly, pushing us, elbowing us, etc., and many quit. Because of that, there are actually few people left [in tango] who used to go dancing at the milongas in those days. It was a good filter; only a few of us, the really obstinate ones, kept going.

From the very beginning, I had to create my own steps. The first I invented were with my first partner. Some of those steps are part of the public domain now; everybody uses them. After dancing with my first partner, I stopped dancing for a year. When I joined with my second partner and returned to the milongas, I realized that one style was predominant, which was the style of Miguel Zotto. I did not identify with that style at all, so that's when I noticed that I was doing different things. And I guess in some way I always knew what I wanted to do. Many students also made me realize that I work with a special technique, which is nothing more than working with natural movement. I can't define what my style is. It's a style that just comes out of me and which is always renewing itself in some way.

Music is something very particular with me, because the truth is, I used to hate tango, and I hated the music. I had grown up believing that tango music was a thing for old people. My dad would play it every Sunday morning, and it would really bug me. When I finally got over that, when I began dancing, the first tango I identified with was Troilo. And after that, I started to identify with Pugliese and Piazzolla. It's what I feel the most. More than the music, it seems to me that one of the biggest attractions in tango is this form of bodily communication.

I have done a bit of everything in tango. *Tango Tango* in 1988, *Michelangelo* in 1989, *Casablanca* in 1990. I went to Japan several times. I was in the opening of Soccer World Cup in the United States in 1994 with *Forever Tango*, and in 1996, I did choreography work with Eleonora Cassano (a renowned figure of Argentine ballet), with the Russian ice-skaters Pasha Grituk and Evgeni Plator, with Julio Iglesias, and with *Tango Magic* at Carnegie Hall.

I was an actor for a time. I worked in a play on Corrientes,

Buenos Aires' Broadway. For a while, I was debating whether I should stop dancing and just act. But I realized that I still have something to say with dance. I still don't know what it is, but there is something else I'm missing. I feel that from the beginning, I started moving the public with the choreography or with some clear-cut technique. Now I'm busier trying to move the public from my own emotions. And I feel that slowly I'm achieving that. Every time I do a performance or I come out onstage, I'm beginning to enjoy the dance, and I am not burdened with that tension or weight of responsibility as I was before. I feel that at this stage I don't have to prove anything, and instead I enjoy what I am doing.

The first time I came to New York was in December of 1992. I remember it was night, and it was snowing. I had come to work, to give classes and to dance. The tango scene in New York has changed a lot since then. At that time, it was a struggle, since there hadn't been a good tango show there in a while. Now, there are milongas every day; there are some places that get really crowded. There's the magazine, *ReporTango,* which is some sort of vertex in all this. Because if the magazine exists, it fills a need for a great number of people.

Tango in Buenos Aires has an infrastructure that is very commercial. There are some very good teachers, but there are also many, many bad ones. Nevertheless, cultural things are still done and people still tango for the mere pleasure of doing it. But there are many who teach and just turn students out as if on an assembly line. They push them out, and out, and out, and it doesn't matter how good they really are when they leave. So now when you go to the milongas, because it's full of beginners, you get kicked a lot. The old milonga codes are somewhat lost. But I think there is a friendlier climate, too. The milongas are not as artificial as they were before. For those who like tango, it is still a place to go, and breathe tango 24 hours a day. However, there are places that may be better. I went to Amsterdam, and I found dancers that wow! They are simply not in Argentina. Perhaps there are really good dancers outside of Buenos Aires because, on one hand, for the foreigner, tango is the discovery of something marvelous, that perhaps we don't give so much importance to in Buenos Aires. Outside of Argentina, dancers obsess and invest a lot in tango. On the other hand, for commercial reasons, the good teachers are always working abroad. So, a Dutch person has more opportunities to learn with the top instructors than somebody from Buenos Aires does.

Many people confuse the elementary concepts of tango. Even in the United States, I found many people who say "this is tango, this is not tango." When tango began, this kind of judgment did not exist. One day somebody who wanted to do *ganchos* appeared and did ganchos, even though ganchos didn't exist the week before, and the same thing with the *arrastradas* [sweeps]. It was a bit like that. Today people judge that tango as what already exists, and they close their minds to what is new. The fault is somewhat with the old people for whom "everything in the past is better" and for whom everything new, everything that young people do, doesn't exist. Because of this, people don't dare to do new things, and this happens a lot with the professional dancers also. There are many professionals who are still concerned about what an old milonguero would say. I always find the old milongueros respectable, but I don't think there is a rule that must be followed. We have to dare…and there are a few people today who do dare.

The role of the woman in tango is fundamental. Tango without a woman doesn't exist. The sensuality and everything that characterizes tango wouldn't exist without the woman. If anything defines my dancing, it is that it needs a woman. There are some people for whom the woman is simply a means to do steps. But for myself, I find it very inspiring to make the woman dance.

I think the future direction of tango is very uncertain. Clearly, tango has been established in the rest of the world, and I think it is something that will last forever—with ups and downs. Though there are new faces, more beginners, etc., there are no new tango shows, which is what keeps tango alive in the world. Nonetheless, I think tango is established now. Tango belongs to the world. It'll exist forever. [5]

5. Adapted from an original interview in *ReporTango, The New York Tango Magazine,* May 2001.

NITO & ELBA

photo: Piero Introncaso

Nito and Elba

A few words from Paul…

Internationally acclaimed as tango masters, no other couple expresses the elegance and style of tango like Nito and Elba. Nito emerged as a dancer in the twilight of tango's heyday, winning awards in 15 dance contests between 1955 and 1965, and then went on to perform as the principal dancer with Osvaldo Pugliese's orchestra.

I finally met Nito and Elba a few years ago in New York, when they were passing through on a world tour and contacted me about teaching out of my studio. Their reputation as consummate teachers preceded them, so I was honored to have them at DanceSport. Since then they have become regular visiting coaches, holding special workshops and master classes for my staff and students.

Partners both in life and in tango, Nito and Elba began their tango partnership in 1975. Since then they have performed, choreographed and taught throughout the world. I think it is safe to say that anyone who knows show dancing knows their work. While they teach dancers of all levels, their specialty is advanced choreography, built with clean lines and balanced phrases. What makes Nito stand out is his style of tango, which is founded on unique attention to foot and leg positions.

Together with Raul Bravo, Nito created a unique system of how to teach dance. This was called the Todero-Bravo System, and it has become the foundation for most teaching today.

A CONVERSATION WITH NITO and ELBA…

"Tango is not a fashion, it is a way of life…"

Nito: I grew up in Avellaneda, Buenos Aires. In 1970, I moved to a town called General Oblin, and that's where I met Elba, in 1973. Elba didn't know how to dance then, but it was very important to me that she learn, so I taught her.

Elba: I remember the first time Nito and I went out dancing. I was embarrassed at how little I danced, so I told him, "No, I can't dance...I'm shy." He got a bit upset and said, "Okay, let's go." But I didn't want to leave because we had just arrived. Then he told me something that I always remembered. He said: "If you want to make me happy, learn tango and dance with me." So from then on, I worked hard at learning how to dance.

Nito: We got married in Junin in 1976, and soon after we started dancing with a very important orchestra from Junin; it had 13 musicians and three singers. We traveled every weekend to the different Argentine provinces to perform. We lived in Junin until '84, when we moved to Mar del Plata.

In 1990, the San Francisco Tango Association invited us to the States to teach. After San Francisco, our tour kept being expanded to the rest of the States. And now that's our life: dance. More than dancing, though, our thing is teaching. When in Argentina, we live in Mar Del Plata during the week, but teach in Buenos Aires on the weekends—on Fridays in "Torquato Tazo" and on Sundays and Mondays in "Gricel."

We have taught in New York many times over the years. Since meeting Paul Pellicoro, we have made DanceSport our teaching base in New York, where we conduct classes and workshops. When outside of Argentina, being with the friends we have made in New York is like being with our other family.

Nito: Our specific style of tango comes from our focus on trying to position our feet correctly. We are very strict about that. That's what we are known for. I am already 66 years old, and each time I dance it's a little bit more difficult to do certain things, but that's our specialty.

Elba: What also makes Nito such a special dancer is that he always has the right weight in the step. When you follow him you cannot make mistakes; he always gives the right lead.

Nito: Elba also has the right weight for me. (And she adds a lot of beauty to the couple...a lot of beauty.) We are an even couple. We believe we must dance together; if we do a step for one, we must make it for both.

Tango is very much about the woman. I think that the mere fact that the woman stands in front of the man is what makes the tango. Two men could dance marvelously well, and it wouldn't be worth a thing. That is why the woman is the most important part of the man: You can do nothing without her.

Elba: I think that the women in New York are generally better dancers than the men. You can tell that they practice a lot, and that they persist in trying to position their feet well. They interpret well, and they work based on that.

When I teach, I like the steps, as in the fifth closing step, to be very smooth, very sensual.

Nito: In general, our classes start with half an hour of exercises that are tango steps by themselves. This helps to achieve balance and a good walking style. If the student does the exercises well, she will dance well, and it will accelerate her dancing.

After the exercises, we make students dance a tango so that we can see what level they are at. That is how I decide what I will do in the class. I don't divide by levels. Since we all learn differently, within the same class we give different assignments to different people.

I think the biggest difficulty male students have is learning to lead the woman. Sometimes men have blocks, and they may think they have given the lead, but they haven't. Often they are distracted by the rhythm, or by watching other couples, or by thinking of the next steps. The women, however, seem to have the most difficulty with the molinetes, the turns. So often I see a woman move her foot backward by not placing it correctly, and when she does this, she moves the man from his center. In our classes we work on these things.

I think one of the most important things for a student to remember is that each step has a beginning, a middle (or development) and an end. And each end starts the next beginning. Often we see someone dance where the end is not reached, and the middle is just mixed up. That continuous movement without an end makes a visual impact, but it lacks balance, and dance must be balanced. If you dance above, you must also dance below, to the floor.

Sometimes we Argentines criticize foreigners for the amount of ganchos and sacadas they do, but we must remember that most foreigners began dancing tango because of shows they attended, and they're only trying to imitate what they saw. Now, because many more milongas are taking hold in the States, people must begin dancing a more social tango—and this takes time.

For me, tango is a way of life. I think you have to listen to a lot of tango music in order to dance well. You can't be listening to another music all day long and at night go dance tango. Also, one must dance what they hear and what each particular piece of music provokes in them. I cannot, for instance, dance to D'Arienzo with the same steps I use when I dance to Pugliese. Of course, understand this is also a process that takes time. Every time I go in a plane and I see the pilot's controls, with all those clocks and buttons I wonder: "How long did it take for the pilot to learn the purpose of every one of those things?" And I think it takes a man the same amount of time to get tango into his head and to understand it so that he can let it out in a fluid way. It takes time for many people to advance to the point where they don't think too much about what they are doing. I always say: "The musician thinks from the heart to the hands. But dancers must think from the brain to the heart, to the feet." This must be done in milliseconds so that we can continue with the choreography that we have in our minds, because what we do is improvise.

We had the fortune here in New York to have Luis Bravo invite us to dance in *Forever Tango*. It gave us tremendous pride to be invited, even if it was only for one performance. It was recognition that I will always remember and that I will always be grateful for.

Elba: For us, it was emotional, very emotional.

Nito: We are salon dancers, not stage dancers, and that is also what we teach. Because of that, it was very different to dance in *Forever Tango*, a show that is so heavily choreographed.

Although we think tango has triumphed, I think we are going to see more changes. Tango is not a fashion; it is a way of life, and few that start with tango leave it. Tango is a creature that gets inside of you, and then it does not allow you to let even one weekend go by without dancing.

Puppy with Graziela Gonzales

PUPPY CASTELLO

A few words from Paul....
Puppy Castello is a real milonguero. He is also one of the most established tango dancers and teachers today. Puppy is known primarily for having taught many of today's best female tango dancers, including Guillermina Quiroga, Graciela Gonzales and Vanina Bilous.

I met Puppy through Guillermina, who had praised him as one of her best teachers and recommended that I invite him to teach a workshop at my studio. When I first saw Puppy dance, what stood out was his very smooth and sensitive dance style—a style characteristic of 1940's tango. It is a very strong and steady style, which gives the appearance of great simplicity while at the same time being full of rich subtleties. Today this style is imitated by many of the best tango dancers in the world.

When in New York, he holds his workshops exclusively at DanceSport. We enjoy his visits not only because Puppy is one of the best teachers in tango, but also because he's got a lot of personality. If you go dancing in Buenos Aires, chances are you'll run into him, as he is still one of the main figures in the Buenos Aires milonga scene.

PUPPY ON TANGO...

"The most difficult thing to learn in tango is how to walk...."

How did I get into tango? Well, when I was a child—which I was once—if you turned on 10 radio stations, you would hear 10 tangos. Tango was like one of the products today that gets a lot of promotion—it was everywhere. I always wanted to dance tango, since I was a little child, and to sing it, because it was what was listened to. If you listen to rock all your life, I think you'll like rock. I listened to tango.

I didn't really come from a tango family. My father danced, and my sister, but...none of the Castello wives has ever danced tango. I don't know why. My dad danced, but my mother didn't dance. My son dances, but his wife doesn't. And nobody imposed tango on them.

Today, you hear that tango was danced among men. It isn't true. Well, it was true in the practicas, but not in the milongas. In the practicas at that time, mothers didn't let their girls go alone. It is not that they guarded them, it was about respect. When you went to a practice, there were usually three women and 30 guys...this is why men practiced with men. It was a necessity.

At 15, I was, of course, underage. But I never had trouble getting into the dance halls—but there were other problems. Back then, there were clubs we called "el liso" [literally meaning "the plane surface"]. We called them this because they did not let you dance across, meaning with steps and breaks. You had to dance simply in these places. Basically, they just walked. At that time, the "social" clubs didn't let you do things like ganchos and boleos; it was not considered proper. But tango, unfortunately, is competitive, and if a guy next to you does one thing, you want to do two, and if I do two, the guy next to me wants to do three, and it was a disaster. They must have kicked me out of 20 clubs. They would kick all of us out.

My favorite places to dance were the Social from Beccar, the Unión from Boulogne, Círculo from Vicente López. At the Unión, I won my first contest when I was 20 years old. I didn't have an established partner then. I've really never had a fixed partner because then it is not a tango anymore—it's choreography. I think that becomes monotonous. Imagine, for example, the professionals. The other day we were talking about this with Miguel Zotto. And he was saying: "Puppy is a case; he dances with anybody….Instead, I practice a choreography for six months and I dance it for three years." Well, I think you have to get bored dancing the same thing for three years.

I think that choreography can be very good and is needed for the stage. But, I don't see myself onstage very often. (Perhaps I don't because I'm a social dancer, and I'm not trained for the stage—I would end up giving my back to the public.) I understand the artists who dance onstage, but I am not an artist. With social dancing, you feel another flavor of tango, because the girl has to pay attention to what you are going to do. It's not a set step. And you have to pay attention to what you are going to indicate to her. With choreography, you know you have to do two steps here and two steps there…it's a different way to dance.

I think I have always been a teacher. In the past, you did not have "tango teachers." If you wanted to learn, you'd go to the practica, and there would be [Juan Carlos] Copes. We would practice with Copes, and we'd try to get whatever we could out of him. (Copes was my idol!) It was like that when I was learning. There wasn't a specific teacher who would let you know what to do. That is, you'd see 20 dancers who each had a different style. This is not the case now, because now dancers stay with one teacher, and students become Xerox copies of that teacher. He who likes Puppy, dances like Puppy; he who likes Naveira, dances like Naveira; he who likes Chicho, dances like Chicho.

When I was learning, of course, I had people I modeled myself after. Copes was one of them. There were so many different styles of tango to learn from. Each neighborhood had its own dancing style. Copes, for instance, was from Chacarita. Eduardo [Arquimbau] was from Pompeya, and you could tell. Just by watching these dancers, you could say: "He is from Avellaneda, this one is from Pompeya, that one is from Chacarita." I was mostly from Chacarita, although I lived in San Isidro, because Chacarita was closest to where I lived.

I started teaching professionally—on a whim. I started because of a teacher whom I used to help. Back then, I had a good job, and I didn't care to teach for money. I danced because I liked it; that was the only reason. Then one day, this teacher did a wrong thing to me; and I told him I was going to start teaching by myself, and that is how I became a teacher.

The best publicity for a teacher is really "word of mouth." For example, Graciela González, Vanina [Bilous], Guillermina [Quiroga] studied with me, and that did a lot. Imagine! Today they are the great dancers in tango. And because I taught them, 20 more came, and the men came also. It was the best publicity I could have.

I have taught in many places around the world, and teaching abroad is always different than teaching in Buenos Aires. I don't know if it is because of the economic level, the advances in New York or that the people there are more educated, but I note that in New York they are more serious about learning. Perhaps they have less feeling, but technically they get tango quicker than the Argentines. Germany is where they are the most serious about learning. You show a step, and two minutes later they are doing it. Perhaps they are doing it well, or just so-so, but they are doing it. But in Argentina, you show a step and it takes them 10 months to learn it.

I like teaching abroad, because there is more money (laughs), but I also like to teach in Argentina. I like to teach as long as people really want to learn. Because the most difficult thing to learn in tango is how to walk it, you really have to want to learn. If students are not committed and you have a guy walking for six months, he'll want to smack you. I had one student who now has a show in France that is very successful. His name is Federico Moreno Rodríguez. He has a contemporary show called *A Fuego Lento*. I had him walking for six months, and now he has triumphed in Paris. He wanted to learn.

I don't particularly like the way tango is evolving. I just don't identify with it. The thing with the new tango, which perhaps is the tango of the future, is that partners dance very far apart; they move all around and, on the crowded dance floor, they bother the other dancers. I don't criticize this new tango, because when I began dancing my style of tango, my Dad would laugh, because he had another style that for him was the real tango.

Couples today all do choreographies. But among the current male dancers that move me are [Gustavo] Naveira, Osvaldito Zotto, to name only two. Among the women, Vanina and Guillermina. I also like Graciela a lot. And from the very latest, Geraldine.

When it comes to the music, I like all the orchestras from the forties. Tanturi, Láurenz, Di Sarli, Pugliese, D'Arienzo. And among the singers, Floreal Ruíz, Alberto Morán, Angel Vargas, and one that was with Gobbi—who for me was a phenomenon—Alfredo Del Río, Edmundo Rivero.

My favorite tangos are "El Cencerro," "Gallo Ciego" and "N.N.," but "El Cencerro" is a marvel of a tango. I've danced it for 20 years.

What do I want people to associate with my name? Look, what matters is that they talk about you, whether the say good things or bad things, as long as they speak, and they remember that I exist! (Laughs). I would like them to remember me as a good person, which I think I am and as a great dancer, although I don't feel that way—but I would like people to remember me that way. [6]

Raúl Bravo

JORGE RAÚL BRAVO

A few words from Paul...
I first met Raul Bravo when Eleny and I were in Argentina visiting Roberto and Guillermina. What makes Raul distinctive as a dancer is his very strong, nearly explosive, style and the dynamic of this style made an immediate impression on me; one can say that Raul is a real Porteño (a native of Buenos Aires). He is also one of the few really strong show dancers performing today.

6. Adapted from an original interview in *ReporTango, The New York Tango Magazine*, August 2001.

RAUL BRAVO'S LIFE IN TANGO...

Raul Bravo was born in Gálvez (Sta. Fe) Argentina in 1934. In 1950, he began learning the basics of tango, waltz and milonga, with the Gianelli teaching brothers in Buenos Aires. By 1952, Raul began performing in the clubs, salons and bars of the Cap. Fed. He stood out as a dancer, performing in numerous shows at well-known theaters and bars throughout the city. In the early days of his career, he danced with the greatest orchestras, such as Raul Calo, Juan D'Arienzo, Pugliese, Jose Colangelo and Mariano Mores, to name only a few. From 1962 on, accompanied by great tango singers, he performed in shows throughout Buenos Aires and Latin America, the United States, Europe, Asia and South America. He also made appearances on many international television shows in Israel, Italy, Mexico and Argentina.

In 1969, Raul began his career as a tango teacher with the famous Antonio Todaro, with whom he taught for 17 years. Together, they invented the most highly regarded system of teaching tango, now known as the "Todaro-Bravo method." With this system, Todaro and Bravo taught most of the great tango dancers of our time, and their system continues to be used by most professional dancers today.

PABLO VERON

A few words from Paul...
One afternoon, Eleny and I were at the studio working on the choreography of "Gallo Ciego" with Carlos Gavito, when in walked a man who could only be described as an artistic-beatnik type. He had curly long hair in a pony tail, sunglasses and a beard. He stumbled into the studio to inquire about Salsa lessons. The next thing we knew Carlos screamed out, "Oh, my God, it's Pablo." The two laughed and greeted each other with a big hug and kiss, like long-lost friends.

Pablo Veron

Eleny and I stood there wondering who is this odd character that Carlos is paying such respect to? He, of course, was Pablo Veron.

Carlos introduced Pablo as both a friend and a great tango dancer from Argentina. We learned later that he was also one of the new generation of tango stars who had joined the original *Tango Argentino* in 1989 in Paris. He continued touring with the show until it ended 1991.

Today, Pablo is perhaps one of the best-known tango dancers in the world. While the theater-going public may have learned about him through *Tango Argentino*, he was brought to international attention (along with Gustavo Neiver and Fabian Salas) with the lead role he played in Sally Potter's film *The Tango Lesson*. Today, he is still an avid tango dancer and instructor. On his frequent visits to New York, Pablo holds his tango workshops at DanceSport and frequents the many milongas around town as well, where, on occasion, he can be seen dancing with *The Tango Lesson*'s director, writer and star, Sally Potter.

PABLO VERON ON TANGO...

"There is no one tango; there are an infinite number of tangos."

I was eight years old when I began ballet. But I had wanted to dance from the time I was five. One day, my family noticed my desire to dance was very serious and though I wanted to do tap; they enrolled me in ballet because it was clear that ballet technique gives the basics to a dancer. Still, I insisted that I wanted to do tap. After three years of studying ballet they then sent me to study tap with a new instructor where I lived, in La Plata.

Tango came later. I continued dancing, going to the San Martin Contemporary Dance School. I took modern jazz classes. When I was 15 years old, I came to New York to study for a few months. Early on, I had a small company where we danced on a cruise ship, the Eugenio Costa. Then on my 18th birthday, my friends said, "Come on, we want to take you to a place." And they took me to a milonga in Once (a barrio of Buenos Aires), not far from where I lived.

It was a very dark place. I remember there were red and blue lights, and in the middle of that darkness suddenly appeared a guy dressed in white. He was extremely elegant, very mysterious. He danced with one girl, left her, danced with another one. At that time, I only danced choreography. The idea of improvising was new to me. But then I saw that guy dancing with another woman, and doing another thing, within the same style…but somewhat different. I kept watching him. He had a gangster ["malevo"] face, like an assassin dressed in white. I loved it. A bit later a friend told me: You have to go see a milonguero. She took me to "Canning," and there I was with Miguel [Balmaceda] and Nelly; I remember it was in January of 1988. I saw him dance, and I was in awe…by the moves…by the elegance…and this whole thing of the improvised milonguero dance. His milonguero style was very evolved. It was more evolved than the basic milonguero dancing you see now. Today, people say milonguero dancing is very limited, but the milongueros who live in the north of Buenos Aires, places like Villa Urquiza, danced in a more avant-garde way. Well, that's what got me interested, and I started investigating. (I never found out who the man in white was.)

After studying with Miguel Balmaceda, I went on to study with Todaro, and after that I studied with Pepito. I also learned by watching many dancers from Villa Urquiza. I always went there to dance, because it had the most interesting dance style. And I watched *a lot*. I would spend entire nights watching these guys and trying to understand their movements. I guess I used the milongas as a school. I was a bit self-taught. I learned by deduction. To dance tango, you really have to teach yourself. There is so much to learn. It's not that there weren't plenty of schools. But nobody can tell you exactly what to do. Everyone reformulates things personally, according to what they see, what they try, what suits them.

When I first started improvising with tango I realized I had to put everything else aside. Tango was like going back to my roots. Before then, I became very Americanized. Musicals always fascinated me, both in the theater and in movies. Tango, however, was something different. It was returning to the dance of my neighborhood, something that was more universal. I loved that. So I started from scratch. I realized I had to learn to walk, and to communicate everything to the woman. In the past, when I had done other dances and danced other rhythms with a woman, I loved it. But when dancing tango, I realized I could channel that feeling *with* the woman. Tango forces you to be with the woman the whole time, unlike other dances where you can separate and then come back together again and again.

What I like most about tango is the freedom and the intimacy. In some ways, you have that with tap, but with tango you dance what you feel within the unit of the couple. Tango is all about the communication between a man and a woman. I can't define what it is I like the most about tango. I believe that choreographically it's very rich, that there is a lot to investigate. It is perhaps the most difficult dance because it has the most freedom. However, to obtain this freedom you first have to understand your partner. I like tango, too, because it is from my homeland. It is in my blood.

What makes tango different from the other dances I have done is that, in a sense, tango is finding one's roots—if you are Argentine. It is my country's culture made into dance. Tango is the result of multiple influences from several cultures; that's the history of tango, of how it got created. And at the same time, tango is also a call to individuality. There is no one tango; there are an infinite number of tangos. To dance this dance is to stake a claim in the search for something personal in tango. Tango can be very nice, very choreographed, very show-like, but it can also be something very simple, and both things have a very clear place. It is not like other dances, where it is just about the exhibition, the show.

Both show and social tango are very evolved and I find both fulfilling. I am very interested in creating choreography, but I am also drawn to improvisation, which is the other thing that fascinates me about tango.

The first work I did in Paris was with *Tango Argentino* in 1989. I had only been dancing tango for a year when I auditioned for the show. They selected me at the audition and a year and a half later they said: "Okay, you're in." The other dancers hated me. There were guys who had been dancing all their lives who wanted to be part of *Tango Argentino*, because it was the only show that was touring, but I got it and I danced with Carolina Lotti. Paris fascinated me....I was fascinated by the city and by a woman, and, well, I've been living there ever since.

I go to Argentina each year to visit. I miss it when I am abroad too long. But Buenos Aires is not my present world. At present, I choose to be connected to my roots through tango but at the same time connected with the rest of the world.

Doing *The Tango Lesson* was a great experience. It made me evolve as an artist, as a dancer, as a person. It was very positive. Since I was both the choreographer and the lead, it was a big thing. It was also a lot of responsibility. I always liked acting; I had studied theater. I always liked the movies and dancing in the movies. So *The Tango Lesson* was like a dream come true. It changed my perspective on the place of dancing in the movies.

The movie was Sally Potter's artistic vision. We had an understanding between us in the way we danced, and that understanding was used in the movie; it was then put into dialogue and incorporated into a story. The movie speaks essentially about real things. She was an English director who wanted to dance, and I was a dancer who was in Paris and wanted to act. That was the base from which we started. The driving force of the movie, however, was Sally's desire to dance. That was the constant impulse. What is interesting is how Sally gives dancing such an important, almost metaphysical, place. To her, dancing has a healing function, and dancing regenerates you. I also feel that way, as do many other people.

Sometimes people ask how much of the movie was fiction and how much reality. Movies are fiction. A documentary is a documentary, and this was a movie, not a documentary. It used reality as a springboard and then fictionalized it. Like the character I play in the movie, sometimes I feel uprooted. At the same time, in another sense, I feel deeply rooted. For me, tango is a way to get back to where I came from. I don't know where that feeling comes from, but I like it. And I express myself in tango, and I evolve in it and believe in it. It is creative.

What interests me about tango is where it came from and its popular appeal. I don't want to feed the cliché image of tango; I want to open tango to popular trends in other kinds of dance. Although tango is danced sometimes by people who dance ballet, tango is essentially a dance of the people and I want to preserve that aspect of it. I think it's also fantastic when people from other disciplines get involved with tango. We shouldn't try to keep the dances apart. All popular music tends to fuse, to unite, but tango has remained isolated. It is played like classical music, like Mozart. There is some sort of canonization of tango that I find very negative for its evolution. The dance itself is very modern. The music is very rich, but there is somewhat of a retrograde attitude—a fear of tango being opened to outside influences. When you shut something off, it decays inside and dies; we have to let it evolve.

It's true that for a long time nobody danced, or just the old-time milongueros were dancing. Finally, now there is a new generation dancing tango in Argentina and around the world. In tango, there have been some of us who have advanced the dance, who have proposed new things. But it is not the same in the musical environment. As a result, the dance is limited because the music is not evolving with the needs of the dancers. There has to be a musical evolution. Dancers are still dancing to a music that was recorded 50 or more years ago. It's not a bad thing, I like it, but today there is no musical equivalent in terms of musical productivity that is rich and lively. There has to be a guy like Piazzolla who says: "I formulate the music from myself." I open up to the reality of the world, and I go to other places, without conservative notions, without cowardice regarding others' judgments.

There's an attitude of "El tango no me lo toquen" ["Do not touch my tango"]. We have made a myth of the past. That is why tango has been left the way it was and has not changed. All the great creators, who left their mark on tango in its early stages were innovators. Today, we should take their example and be creative in a popular way, both in the musical and the dance, so that each can be fully integrated. We could explore other unsuspected connections that would give tango another sound and a new dimension. This is what tango is missing now.

It is not that I want to do something so progressive. I dance. I dance tango and other dances; and I approach other venues, and I see how there the exchange exists between the musical genres, and yet how tango continues to be an arena where things do not change....I am only stating an observation of the phenomenon. Variety is necessary. The past, the present, the future....

When it comes to teaching, I find it interesting because when you teach you are constantly adapting to the needs of the people. It is also a discovery; the instructor evolves. And it gives me pleasure when I help people understand the knots of tango, because there are no real schools for tango. (Nobody taught me one technique in tango, but I try to teach what I know in the clearest way possible. It gives me a lot of pleasure to see people learn and to pass on the culture of my country. You can say it's like being a cultural ambassador. I don't feel that it's a heavy responsibility. It's natural. It's a path.

I've researched a lot in tango. I feel I have been trying to rescue or preserve something. I have often gone to the old milongueros and asked them to explain something to me. It's like doing archeological work in the history of tango. When I started, there were still many good dancers, old-time milongueros, but now many have died. Unfortunately, few archives—like film or video or photographs—of early popular tango remain. When people come to me with their stories and their knowledge of tango, I try to act as a record keeper, an archivist. When I am in Buenos Aires, the milongas feed my knowledge. And even if I don't want to, I go anyway. It pulls me....I go to the old and new places. I love "Sin Rumbo," I also go to "La Viruta," where younger people go.

People often ask me whom I admire in dance. I've always admired the creative work of Fred Astaire in the movies. He is one of my models in tango. And I've always liked the elegance and mastery of Juan Carlos Copes. He is the most authentic dancer on the stage. He manages to give a tango show that maintains a real connection to the source of tango.

As for having a favorite tango, it changes. Right now it is "Emancipacion" by Pugliese. As for a favorite orchestra, it depends. Each orchestra has its strong points, and each has a unique instrumental mark. Some are unique because of the singer they have or the way they incorporate the voice and some because of the space they create. Others because of some emotion they generate, so that if you listen intently, you don't even feel like moving, but just listening.

A good tango dancer is someone who has rhythm and who has a good musical ear. He also has to respect the woman; to know what to do at the right time with the right partner. He adapts himself to the woman. He makes her feel that she is the best dancer. He dances for *her*. If he can execute complicated figures gracefully, he's good. But as long as he can dance in harmony with his partner, then he's an excellent dancer.

A good partner is one who not only follows me but who also listens to me and who dances. There's got to be such a connection between us that it does not look like she's following me. She also has to take pleasure in following. She has to be able to lose herself in the music and lose herself in me. [7]

photo: Adriana Groisman

Tete and Silvia

TETE & SILVIA

A few words from Paul...
Tete and Silvia are widely known in the tango world as experts in the close embrace. When I went to Buenos Aires with our annual tango tour, I arranged for them to teach our group and share their expertise in this club or milonguero style, which has become so predominate in milongas worldwide.

TETE'S LIFE IN TANGO...

Tete was born in Buenos Aires in 1936. At the age of 11, his mother taught him how to tango, and by the time he was 14, he was

7. Adapted from an original interview in *ReporTango, The New York Tango Magazine,* April 2001.

already dancing at the neighborhood dance halls. In the sixties, Tete gained fame and won many contests as a rock and roll dancer. Today, he lives for tango and can be found—every night of the week —at one of the various Buenos Aires milongas.

In 1995, Tete met contemporary dance choreographer and icon Pina Bausch in Plaza Dorrego and began working with her on *Wuppertal.* That year, he also made his first dance tour of Europe, both teaching and performing, and has been doing so every since.

Silvia Riani (born in Buenos Aires in 1961), first met Tete as his student in 1994. Two years later she became his partner and joined him on his second European tour. Since then, they have toured the continent three times and the United States twice.

SILVIA ON TANGO...

I was blessed with the chance to learn tango from a man who dances it with his body and his soul, who always gives priority to the spirit of the music, and who preserved the sensibility and freedom of movement. Because of the man who taught me, teaching to me means sharing this treasure, while remaining aware that these concepts are valid for other styles and practices as well.

I'd like to assume that this art, which arises from movement, will be the first and last faith in the world; and I like to dream that for the first time in the world, men and women will achieve this result together. Here I'm quoting Gordon Craig, whom I used to read some 20 years ago, when I hadn't even dreamt of dancing professionally. But even then, I felt something ignite inside me—the search for something new and beautiful.

TETE ON TANGO...

From the heart of a milonguero...

Let's speak the truth. Let's not disguise tango, because it'll get ruined in the end. Not wanting to give offense, I love tango, so let us please not disguise it.

Tango can be danced in a thousand different ways, but let's step on the ground first, because that is where the energy comes from. Therefore, this is where we ought to dance to the music.

Let's not forget pleasure and love for tango. Kids these days tend to dance in the air. You can do many nice things, but please do them on the floor. Great masters did all those nice things, but mostly on the dance floor.

The music, the beat of tango, is very beautiful. It's a shame to ignore it. Either on or off a stage, a dancer must live the music. Please, wake up and realize what you must do with the music; otherwise, the moment will come when Europeans will return and try to sell tango to us. I speak from the heart. I'm just another guy who dances.

I've taught workshops to teachers abroad. I never thought they could surpass our dancers. I wouldn't like this to ever happen. There are people here that can dance ferociously well. So let's stand up within our axis and avoid looking down to the floor.

Let's not dance for an audience but for ourselves. Even onstage one has to dance for oneself; it shows better. Not because I'm showing others—do I forget who I am or what music I'm dancing to?

There are two in tango. No dancer can dance without a lady. And a lady can make her partner stand out when she really understands him. Even if tango becomes a job, you mustn't practice it without the music. You cannot teach a step for its own sake.

My first loyalty remains with tango: Without the music, there's no dance, no tango. No teacher, no student. A true teacher can only transmit the teaching music has left him.

The Music of Tango

Pablo Aslan

A few words from Paul…

Pablo Aslan was one of the first tango musicians I met back in my early days when we all performed at Nell's nightclub in 1988. At the time there were (fortunately) a few local tango musicians who had relocated from Argentina to the New York City area. Because of the different culture and language, it was difficult to work together. Born in Argentina, Pablo, who is fluent in both English and Spanish, was able to be a liaison between me and the musicians.

Since that first gig at Nell's, I have brought Pablo on board for many other tango projects. In addition to organizing and playing with tango bands for my milongas at DanceSport, he also helped me put together orchestras for our tango nights at Il Campanello's on 31st Street. On more than one occasion, he has participated in and helped me to organize the orchestra for "TangoFest," our annual concert at Manhattan's Town Hall.

PABLO ASLAN ON THE MUSIC OF TANGO...

By most accounts, it has been said that the music of tango emerged out of a mixture of different music styles and dance influences that were in vogue at the turn of the century. In and around Buenos Aires and Montevideo, the music of the polka, mazurka, habanera and milonga were the sounds bringing people together. In this exciting time, social dancing was very much in vogue. As a result, many new and original moves were being created on the dance floor. This innovative style of dancing was contagious to the musicians who were inspired to be innovative in their playing as well.

By the first decades of the 20th century, tango music became a distinct genre. The first recordings, made around 1911, demonstrate a simple style, guided by the rhythm of the guitar. The dance, on the other hand, was complex and virtuosic.

The popularity of the tango, and, more importantly, the acceptance of the dance in polite society, attracted many musicians and bandleaders. Tango music gained in sophistication as conservatory-trained musicians formed orchestras that filled an increasing demand. Apart from the downtown cabarets and the aristocratic dances, tango was present in cafes and theaters throughout Buenos Aires. In silent movie houses, where some of the great musicians of the time found steady employment, audiences sometimes enjoyed the sounds of these small orchestras more than the movies themselves.

Unlike the isolation of today's recording studio, years ago there was an interactive live experience between the musicians and the common people, particularly in the dance hall. Musicians inspired dancers, and the dancers inspired musicians. This natural play off of one another was typical.

As it continued to evolve, tango music became a listener's art. Starting with the 1920 recordings of the Tipica Select, and continuing with the seminal Julio De Caro sextet recordings of the mid-1920s, a new style known as the Guardia Nueva (New Guard) propelled the music to a protagonistic role.

The new music was complex, virtuosic, just like the dance that inspired it. It took two decades for the music to express in sound what the early dance pioneers had invented with their bodies.

The Guardia Nueva sound was supported by the rhythm of the piano, although the violins would sometimes leave their melodic function and scratch away snappy accompaniments. The bandoneons, by now tamed and conquered by the early virtuosos, took on a prominent role in the orchestra. The roles of all the instruments became more defined, and the arrangements better organized than in the older style. Yet some orchestras continued to favor the simple sound of the old guard. It was the beginning of a division among tango lovers: the innovators against the traditionalists.

With the growing popularity of the tango song, a new way of experiencing tango had taken root. Singers generally accompanied guitar players, but in the late twenties, some orchestras began incorporating singers as well, though in a limited role. Tango music became obligatory in staged productions, and many new songs were given their first performance in the theater. Recordings, radio and soon films brought the singers into contact with their audiences. It was mostly due to the song form that the tango survived the 1930s Depression and the Hollywood invasion.

But the tango had many years of life ahead: In the mid-1930s tango dancing became a highly popular phenomenon in Buenos Aires. The music that went along with this popular dance was a simplified rhythmic style more similar to the conservative old guard than to the sextets of the 1920s.

Fast and steady, propelled by the piano and bass, these enlarged orchestras played for huge crowds. The simplified style was a necessary change from the days of the cafe and theater. Musically, the focus was on rhythm, and every section of the orchestra engaged in this function in one way or another.

Singers, who were now a regular feature in the orchestra, adapted their style to the steady dancing beat. So, while the tango song remained popular, it was subordinated to the rhythmic structure of the dance style.

In the early 1940s, dozens of orchestras found work thoughout Buenos Aires. The city was a mecca for talented musicians from all over Argentina. Regular radio broadcasts, dances, cafes, tours and recordings kept a large pool of musicians in constant activity. The leading orchestras refined their style, searching for a distinctive sound. Dancers had their favorites among these orchestras and their featured singers. For the most part, the more simplified, old guard orchestras had a large following among amateur dancers. And once again, in cafes and cabarets, many orchestras developed a following of listeners more interested in the music and the song than in dancing. Some orchestras were able to bridge the two worlds, producing music that stimulated ears and feet alike.

As the dance boom subsided, toward the early 1950s, the tango once again survived as a song form. This was truly the era of the singer. Many compositions that had been recorded during the dance days were now redone with rhythmic liberties that allowed the melodic and lyrical content to come to the foreground. Free to pause, to slow down, tango arrangements became elaborate poems in themselves. As the dancing public shifted their interest to other music, tango became a marginalized cult of things past. By 1960, with very notable exceptions, the popular art form of Buenos Aires had lost its lifeblood. What remained was a recreation of the repertoire, which for the most part had been written before 1950. Some recordings of the time, though, are among the best ever made: The concert style of 1960's tango brought life to many pieces that had not been suitably interpreted in the dance era style. Once again, it seemed that tango music had acquired a dramatic choreography and turned it into sound and poetry.

The revolutionary style of Astor Piazzolla, resisted and maligned by traditionalists, in effect extended the life of the tango. A fierce opponent of the dance style, Piazzolla treated rhythm differently and extended the form of his compositions by introducing slow sections. His pieces were meant to be listened to, and those who dared dance to it, did so with a modern choreography only marginally related to salon style tango. This new tango had may followers among musicians, but its popular appeal was reduced to a devout following of music lovers. Yet, by incorporating influences from jazz and classical music, Piazzolla created an audience for tango outside Argentina.

The revival of tango dancing in the last decade has created a paradoxical situation in music. Dancers prefer the simple style of the 1940's, and recordings from that era have replaced live music in most dance salons.

Musicians today resist going back to a style they considered old-fashioned and have not been able to come up with a suitable, contemporary replacement. While concert tango still continues to attract audiences, and the style pioneered by Astor Piazzolla has been adopted by many musicians worldwide, the absence of live music in today's dance events is conspicuous. Part of the problem is attributable to the wide gap between the last generation of traditional tango musicians and the bands now starting to appear. This gap in which tango bands did not perform, let alone create, is making the transition back to musical performance harder to negotiate.

Since a great part of the skill in performing tango music was passed on via the oral tradition, musicians today lack the necessary knowledge to perform adequately—let alone innovate—with dance style tango music. This knowledge from the past, however, is buried in the recordings of the forties, the same recordings that are keeping musicians away from the dancing public. In order for tango to renew its life it must go feet first—the music, once again, must follow the dance.

Tango: The Best Recordings

Paul Pellicoro

Now that you're on your way to becoming a tanguero, it's important to dance tango with the right music. What follows is an introduction to some of the best. The first eight selections on this list are what Keith Elshaw, of totango.net, calls the Big Eight tango orchestras. The leaders of these orchestras are legends, and while most are now deceased, their music will forever live on as the heart and soul of the tango dancer's tangos.

After a brief statement about each orchestra is a list of their most popular dance style tangos. These selections were made by renowned tango DJ, Carlos Quiroga. These are tangos that you'll hear played at most milongas you attend, and were they not played they would be truly missed. Many of the numbers are instrumentals with a solid beat. This beat is important, since it will help you develop both an ear for the music and also a solid walk in the dance. Each of these tangos has a uniquely identifiable sound that enjoys a nearly universal acceptance in milongas. It is important to know that while various orchestras may play their own version of a well-known tango, some are quite renowned for their particular interpretations, and that's why I am recommending these specific versions; they're the best.

The importance of the relationship between music and movement cannot be overemphasized. One of the best ways of becoming an accomplished tango dancer is to be familiar with the music that is played at the practicas or milongas. The greater your familiarity, the more you will intuitively dance inside the mood of the music and begin to develop a sense of what figures are most in sync with particular sounds. For instance, a steady even beat may inspire a walk, whereas syncopated sound will more likely inspire a corrida—a little run. I always find that when you can sing along with the sounds of the music in your head, your body will do the same. How you interpret the music, that is, how you are inspired to dance, is truly the essence of self- expression in tango and it is mastering this that will take you from being an amateur to a virtuoso tango dancer.

For the beginner, I recommend starting with Di Sarli, D'Arienzo and Canaro because they play mostly instrumentals with a consistent, solid beat and rhythm. There are also some vocal tangos in this mix, and while you need not know Spanish to sing along, you may be inspired to learn. Many tango enthusiasts find themselves learning to speak Spanish the more they get involved with this dance. But whether you know the language of the songs or not, if you just follow your heart, and really listen to the emotion of music, the rest will fall into place.

While you can go to a record store and look for these various songs and CDs, some of them are rather hard to track down outside of Argentina. If you can't locate your music choice in traditional shops, an easy way to get them is to order from our website, *www.dancesport.com*, where you can also find various videos and other tango paraphernalia.

THE BIG 8 TANGO ORCHESTRAS

Carlos Di Sarli (January 7, 1903-January 12, 1960)

Di Sarli's originality is breathtaking; his beat is so sexy, and by all accounts, he was a tyrant to work for. A perfectionist, Di Sarli's exquisite rhythmic sound grew out of an early period when he didn't always use bandoneons. Instead, he scored the strings to mimic their sound. When he did use bandoneons, he stuck with his unique string voicings. His melodic signature came from how he constructed his chord resolutions.

Di Sarli was a wizard on the keyboard, and his arrangements were magical. Many teachers around the world use Di Sarli's music for teaching because it is an excellent choice for beginners who often have trouble hearing "the beat" of tango.

Early Di Sarli's arrangements were fast; he slowed everything down in the '50s. The best sound of Di Sarli is found on his Phillips recordings from 1952-1958, and they are very pleasing to hear today.

Carlos Di Sarli Discography:
Instrumental:

A LA GRAN MUÑECA
BAR EXPOSICIÓN
CHAMPAIGNE TANGO
DIDÍ
EL CABURÉ
EL RECODO
LA CACHILA
MI REFUGIO
RACING CLUB
SHUSHETA

with Alberto Podestá (Singer):

QUE SOLO ESTOY
VA A CANTAR UN RUISEÑOR
VAMOS

JUAN D'ARIENZO (December 14, 1900-January 14, 1976)
When he arrived in the late 1930s, Juan D'Arienzo infused new life and energy into tango. His orchestra brought throngs out to dance. As a result, every other orchestra had to change its style to be more like what he made fashionable in terms of energy and fun. D'Arienzo was the engine that drove the Golden Age by virtue of his orchestra filling the dance halls. His beat, his sound, his musicians were nothing short of amazing. Not all his work with vocalists is totally satisfying for use at a social dance. D'Arienzo happily expressed a hard-core Lunfardo

attitude that is the Porteño way. His glorious milongas are sexy and irresistible. His recording of the milonga "La puñalada" was the first million-seller Tango record (1950). Two of his great pianists—who provided a large portion of his fantastic sound—went on to form their own notable bands: Rodolfo Biagi and Fulvio Salamanca.

Juan D'Arienzo Discography:
Instrumental

---

9 DE JULIO
ATANICHE
DON JUAN
EL CENCERRO
EL CHUPETE
EL IRRESISTIBLE
EL TAMANGO
ESTE ES EL REY
PAPAS CALIENTES
QUE NOCHE

with Héctor Mauré (Singer):

HUMILLACIÓN
MIRAME EN LA CARA

Tango brujo with Alberto Echagüe (Singer):

LA BRUJA
PENSALO BIEN
QUE IMPORTA

FRANCISCO "PIRINCHO" CANARO (November 26, 1888-November 14, 1964)
Born near the end of 1888, this maestro brought humor, sophistication, rhythm, showmanship, worldliness and business savvy to the great tango party. He conquered Paris in the '20s; at his last big show in the '50s, he introduced Juan Carlos Copes and María Nieves to the top of the world. He composed many tango standards.

Canaro's music is like a glue you use to stick all the parts together, because it recalls the old tango feel while capturing the sound of the Golden Age. It ranges from sophisticated large orchestras with clarinets and trumpets to pared-down quintets (Quinteto Pirincho). Much of his recorded work is instrumental, although he utilized vocalists as well. Canaro had a prolific period composing between 1908-1920. Some classics of his from that time include: "La tablada," "El pollito," "Milonga con variación," "Nobleza de arrabal" and "Mano Brava."

Across his catalogue you find quaint old-style tango and canyengue, mellow and sedate tango and recordings with a drive only D'Arienzo also achieved. His valses, such as "Corazón de oro" and "Vibraciones del alma" are intoxicating; as are his slow (as "Milonga de mis amores") and fast milongas such as "Milonga brava," "La milonga de Buenos Aires" and "Reliquias Porteñas."

Starting in 1928 he was the first person to work in the area of "Tango Fantasía," elevating tango to a theatrical level it had never aspired to before. From this period came "Halcón Negro" among others. He had the biggest orchestral sound, traveled the most (he was the ambassador for tango in Europe and North America), and had the most rich and eclectic arrangements (muted trumpet, clarinet, organ). Canaro was the very first president of SADAIC, the Argentine Composers and Authors Society.

Francisco Canaro Discography:
Instrumental

EL TIGRE

FELICIA

LA MALEVA

LA TABLADA

LORENZO

PAMPA

RE-FA-SI

RETINTÍN

SÁBADO INGLÉS

SENTIMIENTO GAUCHO

with Quinteto Pirincho (Instrumental)

EL GARRÓN

LA REZONGONA

LA SONÁMBULA

ANÍBAL "PICHUCO" TROILO (July 11, 1914-May 18, 1975)
Troilo took tango to new heights of sophistication. He showed how big the sound could be; he showed how sweet it could be. His bandoneon could make you feel so many emotions. Interestingly, his entry into the professional world came when he played in the Pugliese/Vardaro group as a young man. Troilo had a unique style, too—sweet is one word that comes to mind. Sweet, even when exhibiting power. His work with vocalists, especially Roberto Goyeneche, gave tango a refined splendor. He helped take tango in a startling new direction by letting young Astor Piazzolla arrange for him. The powerful "Para lucirce" in 1946 gave people the feeling that the revolution was coming. At the other end of the spectrum, his duos with Roberto Grela (the guitarist) are also beautiful in their revelation of what tango music really is.

Many original masters of his music were burned in a 1950 warehouse fire. Fortunately, Troilo rerecorded many of his standards again in the '60s, and they sound great.

For a particular period, Troilo went in a direction where the music is more suitable for listening rather than social dancing. "Quejas de bandoneón" is his signature piece. He always claimed that he would die playing it. On May 18, 1975, after finishing it in a Copes Show, he walked offstage and collapsed, never to recover.

Aníbal Troilo Discography

Instrumental

CACHIRULO

COMME IL FAUT

CTV

EL ELEGANTE (CHIQUÉ)

GUAPEANDO

MILONGUEANDO EN EL '40

OJOS NEGROS
PATÉTICO
QUEJAS DE BANDONEÓN
TINTA VERDE

with Francisco Fiorentino (Singer)

A BAILAR
GIME EL VIENTO
SENCILLO Y COMPADRE

RICARDO TANTURI (January 27, 1905-January 24, 1973)
What he produced added strength and breadth to the overall tango sound. It is really interesting to compare the same-song recordings he made with his two different vocalists, Alberto Castillo and then Enrique Campos (from August 1943).

Tanturi knew how to get dancers to places other people hadn't accessed through his combination of sharp sound and crisp beat. There is no better example of what wondrous results come from a special union of sound, arrangements and vocalists. His recordings are absolutely essential to have in any collection.

Ricardo Tanturi Discography
with Enrique Campos (Singer)

LA URUGUAYITA LUCÍA
MUCHACHOS COMIENZA LA RONDA
OIGO TU VOZ
SOMBRERITO
UNA EMOCIÓN

with Alberto Castillo (Singer):

ASÍ SE BAILA EL TANGO
BARAJANDO RECUERDOS
ESE SOS VOS
ME LLAMAN EL ZORRO
POCAS PALABRAS

ANGEL D'AGOSTINO (May 25, 1900-January 16, 1991)
ANGEL VARGAS (October 22, 1904-July 7, 1959)
Whether tango, vals or milonga, D'Agostino and Vargas made sweet music for 15 years that will sound great forever. More than any other combination, they are linked as one in their legacy. It was known that D'Agostino didn't lead his own orchestra very successfully, but when Angel Vargas was singing with Angel D'Agostino ("Hotel Victoria" is a classic, as are the milongas "Compadreando," "El porteñito" and "Señores, yo soy del centro"), his voice is tango personified. Pianist/composer D'Agostino actually formed his first group—with D'Arienzo—at age 11. His way of posing intimations inside the beat is one of his appealing qualities. His playing style was economical in comparison to other more flashy pianists. He displayed his brilliance with an overall orchestral effect while leaving lots of room for the singer. His sense of dynamics was bold and satisfying. His intro to "Hotel Victoria" is a call to tango.

Angel D'Agostino Discography
with Angel Vargas (Singer)

BAILARÍN DE CONTRASEÑA
CARICIAS
EL YACARÉ
HOTEL VICTORIA
MANO BLANCA
NO CREAS
PALAIS DE GLACE
PERO YO SE
TRES ESQUINAS
UN TROPEZÓN

MIGUEL CALÓ (October 28, 1907-May 24, 1972)
Miguel Caló's selection of musicians, songs and arrangements became the quintessential sound of 'the 1940's and of today's tango. Caló's best recordings are what you find when you look up chemistry. He had the ring, the bounce, the push, but he also had the delicate touch that is refined tango. Credit the players for this, of course,

along with the arrangements and the recording producer. Listen to any one of his songs once, and you think you've heard it a hundred times before, because he nailed it. And he chose fabulous songs: "Tristezas de la Calle Corrientes," "Jamás retornarás," "Al compás del corazón," "Que te importa que te llore," "Lejos de Buenos Aires," "El vals soñador," "Cuatro compases" and "Un crimen."

Caló's recordings with Raúl Berón singing are classic. His recordings with Alberto Podestá are just as pleasing to the ear and feature better technical quality.

Miguel Caló Discography
Instrumental

ELEGANTE PAPIRUSA
SALUDOS
SANS SOUCI
TIERRA QUERIDA

with Raúl Berón (Singer):

JAMÁS RETORNARÁS
LA ABANDONÉ Y NO SABÍA
LEJOS DE BUENOS AIRES

with Alberto Podestá (Singer):

DOS FRACASOS
PERCAL
YO SOY EL TANGO

OSVALDO PUGLIESE (December 2, 1905-July 25, 1995)
Pugliese is the great innovator. So radical, but never over-the-edge: always tango.

Pugliese influenced a change in the sound and feel of tango in each of five decades following his first hit "Recuerdo" (1921), written when he was barely a teenager. His "La yumba" in 1943 was like a revelation from on high. You can hear his influence in almost every arranger's work since the start of the twenties.

Formed in 1939, it wasn't until 1943 that his own orchestra's recordings were first released as 78s, and then only with four or eight songs per year.

Pugliese was effectively blacklisted because of his Communist Party card and was actually jailed for a few months for such iniquities as paying his sidemen the same amount as he was paid. Those were the times—during his absence—when his orchestra would perform without him but they would always lay a red rose over the piano to indicate his absence.

Pugliese's lush and compelling recordings from the '50s and '60s represent the ultimate in passion and expressiveness. It's a controversial issue, but some consider his '60's material somewhat chaotic, while others consider it to be the ultimate in felicitous expression. It has been said that Pugliese lost control of his musicians during this period by giving them too much freedom.

If you could only buy one Pugliese CD, "From Argentina to the World" would be the one. This is his best '50's collection.

Some notable songs are "Chiqué," "Nochero Soy," "Pata Ancha," "Gallo Ciego" and "Emancipación." There are many others.

Pugliese made great music right up to the end of his long and wonderful creative life.

Osvaldo Pugliese Discography
Instrumental

CHIQUÉ
EL ANDARIEGO
EMANCIPACIÓN
GALLO CIEGO
LA MARIPOSA
LA YUMBA
MALA JUNTA
NOCHERO SOY
PATA ANCHA
SEGUIME SI PODÉS

THE BEST OF THE REST—TANGO ORCHESTRAS

Alfredo De Angelis When you want valses ("Pobre flor," "Soñar y nada más" and the beautiful "Flores del alma"), you can't go wrong with De Angelis. He was practically born to play them. Many vocal tracks are duets with the vocalists shining in classic settings. The musicians are superb, in the *Tango Argentino* tradition and the feel is exciting; the result is that his music makes you want to dance all night.

Horacio Salgán crafted a big sound like Troilo and also worked closely with Goyeneche. When he took off in a jazzy direction, he created unique new tangos that were still in the context of dance tangos. He introduced a concept used in northern hemisphere music: starting the song over again at the end. Like Troilo and mid-Pugliese, he's a bridge from the Golden Age to what would come. His music is featured in Saura's recent film *Tango* and is available on the movie's soundtrack.

Roberto Firpo is absolutely unique in his approach. With a small orchestra, Firpo explores rhythm in exciting ways.

Pedro Láurenz composed classics and made strong recordings for a very long time.

Julio De Caro is hugely important and influential. You have to know his music to really know about the history of tango. The feel of his music is different when dancing than any other orchestra. "El monito," "Mala junta," "Boedo," "El arranque," "Tierra querida" and "Mala Pinta." He was one of the five most important composers of tango music.

Lucio Demare had a recognizable "sound" and made good dance music (many tracks are with the singer Raúl Berón).

Rodolfo Biagi has in his body of work many wonderful and exciting tangos.

Francisco Lomuto is known for great classic music. His music should be included at the milongas. His most important songs are milongas such as "Parque Patricios" and "No hay tierra como la mía."

Los Tubatango recreates the original milonga/tango/vals feel. Great fun.

Enrique Rodriguez sounds like a cross between Lomuto and Demare. He would have been more well-known, based on his music and sound, but he was shunned in many tango circles from the '50s through '70s for his right-wing views. Today, however, he is quite popular in Buenos Aires' milongas. His recordings of his compositions "Son cosas del bandoneón," "Llorar por una mujer" and a few others are classics in their own right. Roberto Flores and Armando Moreno were his singers.

Donato Racciatti has recorded some excellent instrumental milongas and vals.

Florindo Sassone has released good quality recordings. In the beginning, he went for a Di Sarli sound, then broadened.

Alfredo Gobbi has recorded some great tracks, but good quality is hard to find.

Domingo Federico is the composer of "Saludos," "Al compás del corazón," "Percal" and many others. He came from the Caló orchestra.

Francini-Pontier composed and recorded a handful of nuggets, including the modern classic, "A los amigos." (He also came from the Caló orchestra.)

Osvaldo Fresedo recorded extensively from the mid-'20s. Many of his records became very well known. One distinct element of his sound was the use of vibes, which added a nice touch.

Elvino Vardaro was a violinist who was a part of so much great music. He co-ran a group with Pugliese that had Troilo and Gobbi in it; he played with so many others.

Orquesta Típica Víctor was made up of an exceptional group of musicians that released records between 1925-31. Here is the best example of typical tango, without the star power of a major leader attached.

Astor Piazzolla left Troilo and started his own tango orchestra in the late 40s. He made dance music for about three years before going on to create "Nuevo Tango," with which he entered the realm of jazz. Although many dancers have choreographed numbers to his music, Piazzolla's later compositions would not be typically categorized as music for dancing social tango.

What To Wear

Paul Pellicoro

Long skirt, short skirt? Tight pants? Shorts? High heels? No heels? When you begin to dance tango, it's natural to wonder if there is a dress code. The truth is, you'll see people dressed in anything from faded blue jeans to stylish gowns.

While the style of your clothing may change from night to night, the most important thing to consider in tango are your shoes. Many dance studios, including mine, sell a variety of dance shoes for men and women. These shoes have special split suede soles that offer you a secure feeling on the floor without being too slippery or too sticky. These days, with tango's popularity, you can find a wide variety of fashionable styles.

In the beginning, basically any shoe can be a dance shoe if it's light and flexible while still being comfortable and giving the foot the support it needs. In fact, I don't encourage my students to buy dance shoes until they've had a few lessons. By then, they will have figured out what kind of shoe they like. Until that point, you can probably get by with something that you've already got in your closet.

For men, a simple classic dress shoe with a thin leather sole will do fine. Basically, you want to avoid a large boxy shoe with thick, sticky soles. Ladies should avoid "extra" high heels in the beginning, especially if they aren't accustomed to wearing high heels very often.

The simple facts are that if the shoe is comfortable, has a leather sole and doesn't fall off your foot, it's acceptable.

As for the color of the shoes? For men and women black is usually most popular, but color is of no importance. The heel of a man's tango shoe is generally angled, the leather soft, and the soles are nearly always leather. On women's shoes, which come in a variety of styles and all sizes of heels, the soles are often felt, which, like leather, are best for ease of movement on a wood floor. Most importantly, the shoe should fit comfortably and have straps or closures so that it doesn't come off the foot.

When it comes to clothing, I have seen some men and women dress up in the traditional nightclub look and others dress pretty grungy, in jeans and even sneakers. Black is the most popular color seen on tango dance floors, but don't let that hold back your inner colorful self. If colors are what you like, go for it.

Personally, I like to dress with the respect I have for tango and I suggest men wear slacks and a clean shirt—a tie is optional. A good quality sweater works, too. Jackets are not often worn these days, but personally I like to wear a light, fashionable, suit jacket if it's not too hot and the air conditioning is working. Basically, you can wear what you like.

Ladies always have more options. Many find pants are both attractive and give freedom of movement, particularly if the legs are not too wide. But then again, dresses and skirts are popular, too. If you imagine skirts with slits, you're not imagining. A skirt may indeed have a slit to give the dancer the ability to free her legs. If a skirt is too long, it may interfere with the dance.

After you've tried a variety of styles, you'll soon figure out what looks nice and works best for you. Most important to keep in mind when deciding what to wear is that you want to be comfortable, look appealing to your partner and be able to move freely. But don't be afraid to find your own style. Have fun!

And ah, one last thing…out of respect for your partner, I would pass up the garlic for dinner, hold off on heavy perfume and don't forget to bathe! You're going to be dancing pretty close and won't want to offend.

Tango Terms

These are some of the Spanish terms that will continually come up in tango classes and the tango world at large.

- In Buenos Aires "ll" or "y" is pronounced "zh," almost an English "j";
- a "qu" sounds like the "c" in cat;
- a "z" is pronounced like "c";
- and a Spanish "j" is a hard, throaty "h" sound.

ABRAZO (*ah-brah-so*) The embrace; a hug; or dance position, dance hold.

ADORNO (*ah-dor-no*) Adornment; embellishment that is done with the feet and legs.

AMAGUE (*ah-mah-gay*) From amagar—to make a threatening motion, or a feint: To fake a step and retreat. An amague is used as an embellishment. It is either led or done on one's own. It may be used before taking a step. An example of an amague may be a beat before taking a step. The foot may do a sharp in/out motion before taking a step.

ARRASTRE (*ah-rah-stray*) From arrastrar—to drag. See *barrida*.

BARRIDA *(bar-ree-da)* A sweep; a sweeping motion. One dancer slides or sweeps their partner's free foot along the floor and places it in a new position without losing foot contact. *Barridas* are done from either the outside or the inside of the foot of the receiving party. The technique is different for the inside and outside. *Barridas* are also called llevadas and arrastrars.

BASICO *(bah-see-koh)* A basic pattern of steps used while dancing tango. There are several basic patterns the most common of which is the eight-count basic or *salida*.

BOLEO *(boh-lay-oh)* From bolear—to throw; to swing a free leg. This is usually done by checking the lady's body rotation in mid-turn. The boleo, a whip-like action of the free leg, is done while swiveling on one foot. A boleo may be executed either high or low depending on the power and intention in the lead. These can also be done forward or back.

CADENCIA *(kah-den-see-ya)* A check and replacement of weight, usually led by the man. Useful for avoiding collisions and making direction changes in small spaces. This may also refer to a subtle shifting of weight from foot to foot, done in place and in time with the music. Cadencias are often done by the man as a means of commencing the dance just after the embrace, to communicate to the woman the rhythm he intends to dance with and to ensure that she will begin with him on the correct foot.

CAMINAR *(kah-mee-nar)* To walk.

CAMINADA *(kah-mee-nah-dah)* A series of walking steps.

CORRIDA *(cor-ree-dah)* From correr: to run. A sequence of running steps. A series of syncopated walks.

CORTE *(kor-tay)* From cortar—to cut. In tango, *corte* means cutting the music either by syncopating or by holding a step for several beats. May also refer to a variety of dramatic poses.

CRUZADA *(croo-sah-dah)* From cruzar—to cross; the cross. A *cruzada* occurs any time one foot is crossed in front of or in back of the other. The position of the woman's foot at the fifth beat in the eight-count basic. May also be called *trabada*.

DIBUJO *(dee-boo-ho)* Drawing; sketch. A dibujo is done by drawing circles or other small designs or movements on the floor with one's toe. Also *firulete, lapiz* and *rulo*.

ENROSQUE *(en-ross-kay)* From enroscar—to coil or twist; a corkscrew. While the lady dances a *molinete,* the man pivots on his supporting foot, hooking or coiling his working leg behind or around in front of his supporting leg.

FIRULETE *(fee-roo-leh-tay)* An adornment; a decoration; an embellishment. To draw or doodle with your feet on the floor. Complicated or syncopated movements of the feet and legs which dancers use to demonstrate their skill and to interpret the music. Similar to *dibujo*.

GANCHO *(gahn-cho)* The hook. When one dancer swings a leg backwards to engage or hook a partner's leg. Ganchos are usually performed on the stage. They may be executed from different positions to the inside or outside of either leg and by either partner.

GIRO *(hee-row)* Turn. A turning step or figure.

LAPIZ *(la-peez)* Like a pencil on a compass. To turn on one foot and draw a circle around the body with the free foot. See *dibujo, firulete and rulo*.

LLEVADA *(yay-vah-dah)* From llevar—to transport; to carry; to take. Occurs when the man uses the upper thigh or foot to "carry" the lady's leg to the next step.

MARCAR *(mar-kar)* From marque—to plot a course; guide. To lead. The man leads or guides the woman's movements and steps throughout the dance. He must communicate this to her through use of his body, hands and arms so that she can feel his lead and follow effectively; his foot pattern does not necessarily create the mark.

MOLINETE (*moh-lee-neh-tay*) Windmill—wheel. A figure in which a partner (usually the woman) dances a grapevine action in a circle around the other, stepping side-back-side-forward in a continuous manner. The man usually directs the woman around his body while he is positioned in the center of the turn.

MORDIDA (*mor-dee-dah*) From morder—to bite; the little bite. One partner's foot is sandwiched or trapped between the other partner's two feet. Sometimes called *sandwich* or *sanguchito*.

OCHO (*oh-cho*) Eight; a figure eight. A continuous crossing and pivoting action that may be done forward or backward. The man usually leads the woman to do forward or back walks that swivel and change direction on the spot, The name comes from the figure-eight pattern created on the floor. The *ocho is* considered to be one of the oldest steps in *tango,* along with *caminada,* the walking steps.

PARADA (*pah-rah-dah*) From parar—to stop; to wait. Though his lead, the man stops the lady from continuing her movement. Commonly led from a back ocho, the man stops the woman midway through the ocho with her feet apart and one foot extended forward on the floor. The man often follows the parada with a sandwich. See *mordida.*

RULO (*roo-low*) See *firulete, lapiz, dibujo.*

SACADA (*sah-kah-dah*) A kind of displacement in which the man steps between the woman's legs in such a way that the contact appears to send her leg to its next position.

SALIDA (*sah-lee-dah*) From salir—to exit; to go out. Commonly known as the basic figure in tango. It serves as an entrance or exit to many other figures and movements.

SANDWICH (*sand-wich*) When a dancer holds one of his partner's feet between both of his own.

SENTADA (*sen-tah-dah*) From sentar—to sit. A sitting action. A figure in which the man leads the woman to create the illusion of sitting on his thigh or knee.

SYNCOPA (*sin-ko-pa*) Syncopate; double time. A musical term adopted by dancers to describe cutting the beat, or stepping on the half-beat to dance faster, as in the *corrida*.

TRABADA (*tra-bah-da*) To block or to cross.

TRASPIA (*tras-pee-ah*) To stumble, to slip up. A style or way of dancing milonga with syncopations or triple steps. See *syncopa*. Three steps usually done in a 1-2-3 or a quick-quick-slow timing. (Three steps done to two beats of music.)

PARTS OF THE BODY
Cabeza = Head
Brazos = Arms
Pierna = Leg
Pie = Foot
Torso = Torso

Where To Find Tango

As of publication time, all of the listings in this directory were accurate. However, because things do change and clubs open and close all the time, we encourage phoning ahead and checking to make sure that the information is still correct.

—Editors

ARGENTINA

BUENOS AIRES

Note: This list of milongas in Buenos Aires was kindly compiled by Pichi of Buenos Aires, who offers the "Do-it-yourself Tango Tour to Buenos Aires" as your personal guide. E-mail: jantango@feedback.net.ar

Subway information kindly supplied by Alberto Gesualdi. If subway info isn't shown, it means that there is not a subway nearby. Subways are now open until 11 PM, so are useful for evening milongas, too.

MILONGAS
SUNDAY

AKARENSE—Villa Urquiza
Donado 1355 8 PM-2 AM
Tel: 4543-1109

CARIBEAN
Ave. Rivadavia 2217
Afternoon at 3:30 pm
Evening at 9 PM-3 AM
Tel: 4812-4067 / 4958-4825

CIRCULO ARMADA—Caballito
Av. Jose M. Moreno 355 8 PM
to 1 AM Tel: 4903- 6531
Subway: A line, Acoyte station

CLUB GRICEL—San Cristobal
La Rioja 1180 8 PM-2:30 AM
Tel: 4957-7157
Subway: E line, Urquiza station

CLUB SOCIAL RIVADAVIA—Flores
Av. Rivadavia 6465 9 PM-4 AM
Tel: 4632-8064

CONFITERIA IDEAL—downtown
Suipacha 384, p. 1° 3 PM-9 PM
Tel: 4326-0521

Subway: D line—9 de julio station/
B line—Carlos Pellegrini station /
C line—Diagonal Norte station
EL BESO—Congreso
Riobamba 416 9 PM Tel: 4953-2794
Subway: El Beso station
EL MOROCCO—Congreso
Corrientes 2048 8 PM-1:30 AM
Tel: 4954-6911/4931-5381
Subway: B line—Callao station
EL SALAMANCA
Ave. Independencia 2542. 10 PM-
Tel: 4942-7498 / 0551
GLORIETA BARRANCAS—Belgrano
11 de Septiembre y Echeverria. 4 PM
*Dancing in a Gazebo in Belgrano
Park—not really a milonga.
Subway: D line—Juramento station
(5 blocks)
GRICEL NORTE
Juramento 2379 (corner of Ave. Cabildo)
10:30 PM-5 AM
Tel: 4785-6470
**LO DE CELIA TANGO CLUB—
Constitution**
Corner of Humberto Primo 1783 and
Entre Rios 8 PM-midnight
Tel: 4371-1030 / 15-4184-4244
Subway: E line—Entré Rios station
(1 block)
PLAZA DORREGO—San Telmo
Humberto 1° y Pje. A. Aieta
6 PM-10 PM
SALON CANNING—Old Palermo
Av. R. Scalabrini Ortiz 1331
7 PM-3 AM Tel: 4832-6753
SALON RODRIGUEZ—Caballito
Gral. Manuel A. Rodríguez 1191
6 PM-11:30 PM
Tel: 4581-5189
TORQUATO TASSO—San Telmo
Defensa 1575 10 PM Tel: 4582-9057
VIEJO CORREO—Caballito
Av. Diaz Vélez 4820 10 PM-4 AM
Tel: 4958-0364

MONDAY
CARIBEAN
Ave. Rivadavia 2217
Afternoon at 3:30 PM
Evening at 9 PM-3 AM
Tel: 4812-4067 / 4958-4825
CONFITERIA IDEAL—downtown
Suipacha 384 1° piso 3 PM to 11 PM Tel:
4326-0521
Subway: D line—9 de julio station
B line—Carlos Pellegrini station
C line—Diagonal Norte station
LAS MIREYAS (Caribean)—Congreso
Rivadavia 2217 4 PM -11 pm
Tel: 4773-6029 / 4902-8766 Laura and
La Tana
Subway: A line—Pasco or Alberti stations
PARAKULTURAL—Old Palermo
Av. Scalabrini Ortiz 1331 11 PM-
4 AM Tel: 4932-8829 Oma
VIEJO CORREO—Caballito
Av. Díaz Vélez 4820 10 PM-4 AM
Tel: 4958-0364
TUESDAY
CARIBEAN
Ave. Rivadavia 2217
Afternoon at 3:30 PM
Evening at 9 PM-3 AM
Tel: 4812-4067 / 4958-4825
CONFITERIA IDEAL—downtown
Suipacha 384, p. 1° 3:30 PM-10 PM Tel:
4326-0521
Subway: D line—9 de julio station
B line—Carlos Pellegrini station
C line—Diagonal Norte station
EL ARRANQUE—Congreso
Bartolome Mitre 1759 3 PM-10 PM Tel:
4371-6767
Subway: A line—Congreso station
LA TERRAZA—Vicente Lopez
Av. San Martin y Segurola 9 PM
Tel: 4796-2959 / 4702-2324
LA TRASTIENDA—San Telmo
Balcarce 460 10:30 PM
Tel: 4342-7650

Subway: A line—plaza de Mayo station (5 blocks)

PARAKULTURAL (La Catedral)— Almagro
Sarmiento 4006 11 PM Tel: 4932-8829
Omar
Subway: B line—Medrano station

PORTEÑO Y BAILARIN—Salon de Baile
Riobamba 345. 10 PM-3 AM
Tel: 4372-6080 José Garofalo
Subway: B line—Callao station

UN MONTON DE TANGO—Congreso
Riobamba 416 6 PM-midnight
Tel: 4953-2749
Subway: B line—Callao station

VIEJO CORREO—Caballito
Av. Diaz Vélez 4820 10 PM-3 AM
Tel: 4958-0364

TANGO CHAT

Not a milonga but an informal meeting to discuss all things tango amongst English speakers. Subjects range from different styles of tango, teachers, codes and customs of the milongas, where to go to dance and lots of other things. It all happens every Tuesday between 5 PM-7 PM at:
Academia Café, Callao 368
nr. Corrientes

WEDNESDAY

CONFITERIA IDEAL—downtown
Suipacha 384 1° p 4 PM-10 PM
Tel: 4326-0521
Subway: D line—9 de julio station
B line—Carlos Pellegrini station
C line—Diagonal Norte station

EL BESO—Congreso
Riobamba 416 10:30 PM
Tel: 4953-2794
Subway: B line—Callao station

MARACAIBO—Salon de Baile—down-town
Maipú 365 10 PM to 2 AM
Tel: 4326-2534
Subway: B line—Florida station

LA NACIONAL
Adolfo Alsina 1465 10 PM-4 AM
Tel: 4307-0146—Pablo Banchero

SALON CANNING—Old Palermo
Av. Scalabrini Ortiz 1331.
3 PM-11 PM Tel: 4832-6753

SALON RODRIGUEZ—Caballito
Gral. Manuel A. Rodriguez 1191 6 PM
Tel: 4581-5189

SIN RUMBO—Villa Urquiza
José P, Tamborini 6157 9 PM-3 AM
Tel: 4574-0972

VIEJO CORREO—Caballito
Av. Diaz Vélez 4820 10 PM -3 AM
Tel: 4958-0364

THURSDAY

EL ARRANQUE—Congreso
Bartolome Mitre 1759 3 PM-10 PM
Tel: 4371-6767
Subway: A line—Congreso station

CONFITERIA IDEAL—downtown
Suipacha 384, p. 1° 3 PM to 9 PM
Tel: 4326-0521
Subway: D line—9 de julio station
B line—Carlos Pellegrini station
C line—Diagonal Norte station

DANDI—San Telmo
Piedras 936 (between Estados Unidos and Carlos Calvo)
9 PM-4 AM Tel: 4307-7623 / 4361-3537
Gloria Garcia
Subway: C and E lines—Independencia station (3 blocks)

DR. JEKYLL—Belgrano R
Monroe 2315 10 PM-1 AM
Tel: 4543-0018
Subway: D line—Congreso de Tucuman station

NIÑO BIEN—Constitution
Humberto 1° 1462 11 PM-4 AM
Tel: 15-4147-8687 Luis Calvo
Subway: E line—San José station

VIEJO CORREO—Caballito
Av. Diaz Vélez 4820 10 PM-3 AM
Tel: 4958-0364

FRIDAY

CARIBEAN
Ave. Rivadavia 2217
Afternoon at 3:30 PM
Evening at 9 PM-3 AM
Tel: 4812-4067 / 4958-4825

CIRCULO ARMADA—Caballito
Av. Jose M. Moreno 355
10 PM to 3 AM Tel: 4903-6531
Subway: A line—Acoyte station

CLUB GRICEL—San Cristobal
La Rioja 1180 10:30 PM to 5 AM
Tel: 4957-7157
Subway: E line—Gral Urquiza station

CLUB SOCIAL RIVADAVIA—Flores
Av. Rivadavia 6465 9 PM-4 AM
Tel: 4632-8064

CONFITERIA IDEAL—downtown
Suipacha 384, 1° p. 1 PM to 8 PM
Tel: 4326-0521
Subway: D line—9 de julio Station
B line—Carlos Pellegrini station
C line—Diagonal Norte station

LA ESTRELLA—Old Palermo
Armenia 1366 (ex Acevedo)
11 PM-6 AM Tel: 4774-6357

LO DE CELIA TANGO CLUB—Constitution
Corner of Humberto Primo and Entre
Rios 11 PM-4 AM
Tel: 4371-1030
Subway: E line—Entré Rios station

LAS MIREYAS (Caribean)—Congreso
Rivadavia 2217 4 PM-11 PM
Tel: 4773-6029 / 4902-8766 Laura and
La Tana
Subway: A line—Congreso station (4
blocks)

PARAKULTURAL Old Palermo
Scalabrini Ortiz 1331 11 PM-
Tel: 4932-8829 Omar

SIN RUMBO—Villa Urquiza
José R Tamborini 6157
10 PM to 4 AM Tel: 4574-0972

TORQUATO TASSO—San Telmo
Defensa 1575 11 PM-5 AM
Tel: 4582-9057

VIEJO CORREO—Caballito
Av. Diaz Vélez 4820 10 PM to 4 AM
Tel: 4958-0364

SATURDAY

CIRCULO ARMADA—Caballito
Av. Jose M. Moreno 355
10 PM to 3 AM Tel: 4903-6531
Subway: A line—Acoyte station

CLUB GRICEL—San Cristobal
La Rioja 1180 10:30 PM to 5 AM
Tel: 4957-7157
Subway: E line—Gral Urquiza station

CLUB SOCIAL RIVADAVIA—Flores
Av. Rivadavia 6465 9 PM to 4 AM
Tel: 4632-8064

CONFITERIA IDEAL—downtown
Suipacha 384, 1° p. 1 PM to 8 PM
Tel: 4326-0521
Subway: D line—9 de julio station
B line—Carlos Pellegrini station
C line—Diagonal Norte station
EL ARRANQUE—Congreso
Bartolome Mitre 1759 3 PM-9 PM
Tel: 4371-6767
Subway: A line—Congreso station

EL TROVADOR—Vicente Lopez
Av. Del Libertador 1031 10 PM-4 AM
Tel: 4542-5902

LA CALASITA/CLUB I.M.O.S.—Nunez
Cdoro Rivadavia 1350 11 PM-4 AM
Tel: 4744-5187 / 4799-7069

LA TERRAZA—Vicente Lopez
Av. San Martin y Segurola 10 PM-
Tel: 4796-2959/4702-2324

LA VIRUTA—Old Palermo
Armenia 1366 11:30 PM 4 AM
Tel: 4774-6357

LO DE CELIA TANGO CLUB—Constitution
Corner of Humberto Primo 1783 and
Entre Rios 11 PM-4 AM

Tel: 4371-1030 / 15-4184-4244
Subway: E line—Entré Rios station
MARACAIBO—Downtown
Maipu 365. 10 PM-5 AM
Tel: 4326-2534
Subway: B line—Florida station
SALON RODRIGUEZ—Caballito
Gral Manuel A. Rodriguez 1191
10 PM Tel: 4581-5189
SIN RUMBO—Villa Urquiza
J.P. Tamborini 6157 10 PM-4 AM
Tel: 4574-0972
SUNDERLAND—Villa Urquiza
Lugones 3161
Tel: 4541-9776
TORQUATO TASSO—San Telmo
Defensa 1575. 11 PM
Tel: 4582-9057
VIEJO CORREO—Caballito
Av. Diaz Vélez 4820 10 PM-5 AM
Tel: 4958-0364
GRICEL NORTE
Juramento 2379 (corner of Ave. Cabildo)
10:30 PM-5 AM
Tel: 47-85-64-70

*The following milongas are out of the center
of the city. Pichi points out that unless you
go with someone you can dance with, be
prepared to just sit and watch all night.*

GRAN BUENOS AIRES
**BOMBEROS VOLUNTARIOS DE
LANÚS**
Gral. Rodriguez 1039, Lanús.
Saturdays 10 PM-4 AM
**CENTRO GALLEGO DE VALENTIN
ALSINA**
Armenia 740, V. Alsina.
Saturdays 10 PM
Tel: 4208-1005
CÍRCULO FRIULANO
Av. Mitre 2154, Avellaneda.
Fridays and Sundays 9 PM
Tel: 4204-3384

CLUB A. PLATENSE
Zufriategui 2021, Vte. Lopez
Tuesday, Friday, Saturday 10 PM-
4 AM
EL BOLICHE
Peyrera Lucena 270, L. de Zamora.
Wednesdays and Sunday 10 PM-2:30 AM
Tel: 4392-0190 / 4299-1416
TÍA LOLA
H. Yrigoyen 5248, Lanús.
Monday 9 PM-2 AM, Tuesday 10 PM-mid-
night, Thursday 10:30 PM-4 am
Tel: 4225-1426
PUEBLO UNIDO
Lavalle 23, Avellaneda. Tuesday,
Thursday, Sunday 6 PM-midnight
RACING CLUB
Av. Mitre 934, Avellaneda.
Saturdays 10 PM Tel: 4222-3393

MAR DEL PLATA
CHIQUÉ
Hipólito Irigoyen 2067, Centro Casilla y
León. Saturdays 10:30 PM
Tel: 4496-0294 / 156-827407 (m)
LA MILONGA DE MAR DEL PLATA
Details from Mariana Gonzalo and
Claudio Fortes, who also give classes,
seminars and shows.
Tel: 223-4803-993 / 223-4952-412
e-mail: nanitango@copetel.com.ar

MENDOZA
**ACADEMIA DE TANGO ARRA-
BALERA**
Chile 1754. Classes on Tuesdays,
Thursdays and Fridays 8 -10 PM
Tel: 0261-420-4224 Veronica Gai

PRIVATE/CLASSES
Roberto Herrera 15-5347-4242
Ricardo and Nicole 4361-5725*
Gustavo Naveira and Giselle Anne
4374-6550 (and Fax)*
Los Dinzels 4777-0405

Puppy Castello 4864-2076
Carlos Rivarola & Alicia 4584-1995
Osvaldo Zotto 4932-8519
Facundo and Kely 4805-6388
Carlos Alejo and
  Jacqueline Bourgin 4244-9454
Carlos and Inés Borquez 4861-7713
Maria Pantuso 4383-6878*
Teresita Brandon 4306-0978*
Graciela Gonzales 4931-9950
Mingo Pugliese 4805-1652
Pocho Pizarro 4205-8464
Monica Romero and Omar Ocampo
  Tel/Fax 02322-430890*
Milena Plebs Tel/Fax: 4804-5595
  e-mail: milenaplebs@interar.co.ar

*The following are teachers of the style which
has, rightly or wrongly, become known as
"milonguero" style.*
Raul Cabral (group classes) 4385-3911
Luis Canan 4963-3252*
Cacho Dante (group class with
  Alica Pons) 4922-2085
Lidia Ferrari and José Luis Lussini
  4776-0897*
Marisa Galindo 4543-0018*
Laura Grinbank 4812-4067*
Vilma Martinez 4545-9344
Susana Miller and Ana Maria Schapira
  4981-6869*
Nestor Ray and Patricia Garcia
  4901-9332*
Ariel Romero 4856-2091 / 4383-2137
Pedro Sanchez 4923-2774
Ruben Terbalca 4554-1374*
Tito Villa and Maria Telma 4863-0185
* Speak English

TANGO SHOWS
CAFÉ-CONCERT—selected
BAR SUR
Estados Unidos 299 Tel: 4362 6086
CAFE HOMERO
J.A. Cabrera 4946 Tel: 4736-1979
CAFÉ TORTONI

Av. De Mayo 829 Tel: 4342-4328
Most Days
CLUB DE VINO
Cabrera 4737 Tel: 4833-0048
Fri.-Sat. 9:30 PM
EL VIEJO ALMACEN
Independencia and Balcarce
Tel: 4307 7388 / 6689
ESQUINA CARLOS GARDEL
Pasaje Carlos Gardel 3200
Tel: 4867-6363
EL GATO NEGRO
Av. Corrientes 1669 Tel: 4371-6942
MICHELANGELO
Balcarce 433
Tel: 4331-9662 / 15-4960-1945
RESTAURANTS WITH SHOW—
selected
CAMINITO TANGO SHOW
Del Valle Iberlucea 1151
Tel/Fax: 4301-1530 / 20
DANDI
Piedras 936 Tel: 4307-7623 / 4361-3537
SEÑOR TANGO
Vieytes 1653 Tel: 4303 0231
MICHELANGELO
Balcarce 433 Tel: 4328 2646
LA VENTANA
Balcarce 425
THEATRES—selected
THEATRO GENERAL SAN MARTIN
Av. Corrientes 1530 Tel: 446 8611
TEATRO AVENIDA
Av. De Mayo 1222- Tuesday and Friday
9 PM, Saturday 10 PM, Sunday 8 PM Tel:
4381 0662
LA TRASTIENDA
Balcarce 460 Tel: 4342 7650
MUSEO MITRE
San Martín 336. Tel: 4394-8240
PIGALLE RECOLETA
Roberto M. Ortiz 1835 Tel: 4806-8051
ROOMS TO RENT IN B.A.
ZENKA
Sanchez de Bustamante 233, 5° p. "A"
Tel: 4864 7033

MARIA VILLALOBOS

Flats or rooms to let—long or short stays. Write to: Cochabamba 472, San Telmo, 1150.

Tel: +54 11 4307 7715

e-mail: acp_sh@sminter.com.ar

MARIA TERESA LÓPEZ

Rosario 178, 1424. Tel/Fax: 4902 5059

e-mail: mariatango@topmail.com.ar

MARTA DIAZ

Montiel 4657, CP Tel/Fax: 687 4184

LINA ACUÑA

Estados Unidos 780, 1101 C.P.

Tel/Fax: 54- 11-4361-6817

e-mail: lina@internet.siscotel.com

CASA DE GERARD

alojatango@aol.com

MARIEL ARANDIA

Defensa 1111, 3° "H"

Tel/Fax: 4361 6715

LA CASITA

Cochabamba 286. Tel: 4307 5073

SOL ARAMENDI

Balcarce 776, San Telmo. Tel: 4343 3951

e-mail: Marisol@siscor.bibanl.edu.ar

NORA LEDA DISTILO

Independencia 2277 2°, Tel: 4941-6670

e-mail: noraleda@topmail.com.ar / noraleda@hotmail.com

Single $150 pw/double $200 pw.

Web: www.casatango.com.ar

VICTORIA AREJOLA

Matheu 143 PB "6"   Tel: 4951-0828

Single $150 pw/double $200 pw.

NELLY VIDAL

Muniz 376, PB "4". Tel: 4983-4414 / 15-4-034-8889

VOLKER

Tel: ++54 11 4854-7421

GRAN HOTEL HISPANO

Av. De Mayo 861 Tel: 4345-2020

Fax: 4342-4431 e-mail: h.hispano@sminter.com.ar

ARMANDO ORZUZA

Avenida Santa Fe 3900.

Tel/Fax: ++1 818-487-8516

e-mail: datango@aol.com

DIEGO DI FALCO and CAROLINA ZOKALSKI

Located in congreso, half-block from Callao

Tel: ++1 -818-694-1414

e-mail: ElBulinApts@aol.com

JORGE LUIS

Calle Brazil, 24 de Noviembre in Parque Patricios 7°.

e-mail: jlgb2-@pacbell.net

Tel: +1 626-794-8713

RODOLFO WINDHAUSEN

Cabello 3355, near Paunero in the middle of Palermo Chico.

Phone, cable TV, bathroom and single room suitable for two people.

Convenient for downtown and milongas in Palermo and el Centro. $350 pw.

Contact in BA (English spoken) 4822-6965. Contact in New York (212) 599-6545.

e-mail: windha@mindspring.com

JUAN MEDRANO-PIZARRO

"Lo de Ana". Tango bed and breakfast in newly renovated turn-of-the-century house in San Telmo. Near El Tasso, Nino Bien. Private Rooms. San Telmo. 2 bed-room apartment. Recently renovated.

Tel: 603 643 9264

e-mail: Medrano@Dartmouth.edu

JENNI BARBIERI

One room to let in a beautiful 9th floor flat in central location (Plaza Congreso). Quiet with conservatory balcony viewing Corrientes, Obelisco and North. English spoken. Tel: 4371 0435

e-mail: barbi@altargentina.com

ANDREW POTTER

Many flats available - Tel: 11-4300-8042

EL SOL DE SAN TELMO

French Italian house, newly restored in 19th century. Central to the most impor-tant milongas. 14 well-equipped, spa-

cious rooms, shared or private. Dance studio, internet, cleaning services available. Chacabuco 1181, 1p.
e-mail: elsolst@yahoo.com.
www.elsoldesantelmo.com
Tel: 0054-11-4300-4394
SUSANA WHEATLEY
Studio apartment in fashionable Recoleta. All mod. cons.
Tel: ++5411-4803-4728

USEFUL WEBSITES FOR B.A.

www.expatvillage.com
Information for foreign visitors—good page on safety in the streets.
www.loscolectivos.com.ar
Bus route information.
www.microbus.com.ar
Microbus to the provinces information.
www.buquebus
Information for boats to Colonia and Montevideo, Uruguay.

For additional information on Tango in Buenos Aires, contact: Tito Palumbo
B.A. TANGO
Moreno 2562, piso 1 3° "H"
1094 Buenos Aires
Tel/Fax: 0054 11 4863 5298
e-mail: abatango@yahoo.com

AUSTRALIA—0061
BRISBANE
LA MILONGUITA DE MILTON
20/20 Park Road, Milton (behind the Eiffel Tower, upstairs)
Saturdays 8 PM-midnight
ROSITA RIVAS
Classes and Milongas.
Tel/Fax: 61 7 33512858
MARIA ELIANA BOSAANS
96 Osborne Rd., Mitchleton.
Tel: (61) 7 3355 3032
e-mail: mbosaans@one.net.au
TANGO CAFE
Sunday nights at 6:30 PM. Contact:
Michael Higginson
e-mail: dancing@riorhythmics.com.au

CANBERRA
TANGO SOCIAL CLUB OF CANBER-RA
Tel: 0414-871-801
e-mail: tango.canberra@bigfoot.com

HOBART
TANGO
All Bar One Gastrodome, 24 Salamanca Square.
Tel: 3 62247557

MELBOURNE
PLAYPEN
Once a fortnight Contact: David Backler
e-mail: tangobar@netspace.net.au
VIVA TANGO—TANGO BAR
"The Stage", 231 Smith St. Fitzroy.
Last Sunday of the month live tango band and floorshow.
Also: Practica on Mondays 8 PM-late at VIVA CLUB, First Floor 3a Johnston St., Collingwood.
Tel: 613 9415 8166/Fax: 8266
Contact: Ruben Espinoza
Tel: Melbourne 98882205

PERTH
TANGO TALK
Piazza Piano Bar, 677 Beaufort St. Mt. Lawley Wednesdays 7 PM
Also: Dance Factory, 28 Delhi St., West Perth.Thursdays 8-10 PM
For info: Tel/Fax: 8 9386 1264
e-mail: tango@space.net.au
THE TANGO SALON
296 Churchill Avenue, Subiaco.
Tel: 08 9382 3235
Fax: 08 9381 4873
e-mail: juan@starwon.com.au

SYDNEY
ARGENTINO TANGO SCHOOL
11, Bay Street, Rockdale.
Tuesday 6-9 PM
also: 47, Norton Street, Leichardt.

Thursday 7-9 PM
Contact: Luis (2) 580 7367 CARINA (2)
305121-
MR. RIVAROLA Tel: 96 666 4080
MR. ROBERTO ROUCO
tango@glebe.net.au
EL SATURNO MILONGA
Glebe Town Hall, 160 St. John's Rd.
Glebe. 1st and 3rd Fridays of month
8 PM Tel: 9692-9248 / 9351-6105

AUSTRIA—0043
VIENNA

MONDAYS
COLOR TANGO
"Titanic", 6 Theobaldg. 11 8-9 PM free
class/ Milonga 9 PM-2AM
Tel: (1)968-33-41 Laura Suarez
e-mail: colortango@chello.at
TOLEDO TANGO CLUB
LIMA, Florianigasse 16, A-1080
9 PM-1 AM Hernan Toledo
Tel: 1 4031815 / 1 403 8961
CLUB TANGO ARGENTINO VIENA
Club International Universitaire,
Schottengasse 1, Mezzanin. A-1010.
8:30-midnight Tel: (664) 13-198-13
(Christian and Andrea)
e-mail:tangoargentino@netway.at
www.tango-argentino.at/viena
WEDNESDAYS
LA MILONGA
"U.S.W.", 8 Laudongasse 10 9 PM-
Tel: (1)403-36-72 Mark and Jane
PRACTICA
"LIMA", Florianigasse 16. 9.15 PM-
Tel: (1)403-18-15 Hernan Toledo
THURSDAYS
TOLEDO TANGO CLUB
LIMA, Florianigasse 16, A-1080
9 PM-1 AM Hernan Toledo
Tel: 1 4031815
"ALMA DE TANGO"

"Café Nautic", 4 Schleifmühlgasse 2.
Free class 8 PM Salon 9 PM-
Tel: (664)260-7727 Jutta.
e-mail: jutta.bloechle@gmx.net
FRIDAYS
CLUB TANGO ALMAGRO (Practica)
"Studio 0.1", 4, Rienösslgasse 4a, A-1040
9 PM- Tel: (676)4212-313
e-mail: tango@almagro.at
http://tango.almagro.at/
SATURDAYS
GoTanGO
"Museumsquartier," 7 Museumsplatz 1.
9 PM-
Tel: (1) 405-47-68
e-mail: gotango@vienna.at
SUNDAYS
PRACTICA
"Studio 0.1", Rienößlgasse 4a. 7-10pm
Tel: (663)920-08-11 Traude and Luciano

BELGIUM—0032

ANTWERPEN
TANGOSCHOOL ANTWERPEN
Wolstraat 1 Practica on Wednesday
evenings.
Tel: 03-232-6720
TANGOFABRIEK EL SUR
Hertsdeinstraat 29B, 2018 Every second
Sunday 4 PM-8 PM

BRUGGE
TANGO SALON
Taverne and Zwart Huls, Kuipersstraat
23, 8000.Every second Friday of the
month. 9 PM-2 AM
Tel: Gert/Frank 50 382686

BRUSSELS
ILUSION
Place Communale 18, 1080 Molenbeek-
St-Jean.
Every fourth Sunday 4:30 PM-9 PM
Second Saturday 8:30 PM-3 AM

AMAUTA
La Tentation, rue de Laeken 28, 1000.
(From January)
Tel: 2 733 2702
SALON
35, Rue De L'Argonne, 1060 (St.Giles) 10
PM-1 AM Every Friday. Tel: 0477-68-26-
97
SALON PIANOFABRIEK
Pianofabriek, 35 rue du Fort, 1060.
3-8 PM every first Sunday of the month
(first Sunday with Trio Gomina—live
music) Not in Summer Tel: 2 538 09 01
AL COMPAS DEL CORAZON
La Roseraie, Chaussée d'Alsemberg
1299, 1180 Brussels. Every fourth
Saturday of month. Class: 8:30-10 PM
Salon 10 PM-3 AM Classes every Tuesday
7:30-11 PM
Tel/Fax: 2 345 6891
e-mail: marisa.vanandel@rosas.be
www.rosas.be/alcompas.html
EL DORADO
9 Kerkstraat, 1851 Humbeek. Every 3rd
Sunday 4PM-9pm
Tel: 02-270:3060

TEACHERS
Nathalie Prudon and Pedro Andrade
  2 7365302
Christiane Tamine and Miguel Gabis
  2 687 9253
Fedor Villafane
  2 733 2702
Marisa van Andel and Oliver Koch
  2 345 6891
Patricia Lafourcade
  0473 641130
Gisele Graf Marino and Sergio Molina
  2 270 3707

GENT
Vzw POLARITEIT
Verkortingsstraat 55, 9040 Practica on
Fridays
Tel: Polariteit 09 238 2630

HASSELT
**SALONITA DE TANGO DE PRIMA-
VERA—MEDIA LUZ**
Kunstencentrum België, Burgemeester
Bollenstraat 54-56, B-3500 Wednesdays
8 PM-midnight
Tel: (0) 89-380168 (Jo and Brecht)
e-mail: media.luz@planetinternet.be
Web: home.planetinternet.be/~switten1

BRAZIL—0055

BELO HORIZONTE
BAR ACADEMIA DANÇARTE
Av. Getúlio Vargas 820.
Mondays 10 PM Tel: 262-0066
KINA-NÚCLEO DE DANÇA
Av. Do Contorno 8471 First Thursday of
the month 8 PM
Tel: 291-0451

RIO DE JANEIRO
TANGOMANGO
Café Cultural, R. São Clemente, 409
Botafogo. First Friday of the month
10 PM-2 AM Tel: 2536-1620(21) Marcia F.
"LUGAR COMUM" (PRACTICA)
Rua Alvaro Ramos 408, Botafogo.
Every Monday 9:30 PM-midnight
Tel: 541 4344
TRANSNOCHANDO
Gafieira Estudantina, Praça Tirandentes
79—Centro Wednesdays 9:30 PM-
2 AM Tel: 232 1149
Tel: 294 5041
C.D.JAIME ARÔXA
Rua Sâo Clemente 155-2° andar-fundos
(Botafogo) every second
Saturdays 10 PM-2 AM Tel: 539 8779
BELLA TANGO
Rua Fernando Magalhães 396 Jardim
Botânico
Saturdays monthly 10 PM-2 AM
Tel: 9982 3212
PLANETA TANGO
Av. Mem de Sá 66-68 (Lapa) Sundays
8 PM-midnight Tel: 220 6020

ESTANGOSTOSO
Beco da Bohemia, Rua General. Góis
Monteiro 34 (Botafogo)
Every Thursday 9 PM-1 AM
Every third Sunday 7 PM-midnight
Tel: 542-6296

CAFE XANGÓ
Rua da Passagem, 172-2° andar Friday
9:30 PM-1 AM
Tel: 541-5184

TANGO NAS MARRECAS
Rua das Marrecas, 9 Centro Every two
weeks Saturdays
9 PM-2 AM Tel: 220-6500

TANGO CAFE
Atlantico Palace Hotel, Rua Raul
Pompeia 94—Copacabana.
Every Thursday 9:30 PM-midnight
Tel: 295 2276 / 556 7765

QUE-SÉ-YO?
Far Up (Cobal do Humaita)—Rua
Humaitá, 448-2° piso, Cobal. Every
fourth Sunday 9 PM-midnight
Tel: 9219 1827

SÃO PAULO
VELHO PIETRO
Rua 13 de Maio, 192, Mondays and
Thursdays 9 PM-2 AM
Tel: 3885-4547

**CANTINA E PIZZARIA CARLO
MAGNO**
Rua Dr. Veiga Filho, 237, Tuesdays
11 PM Tel: 825-6293

BAILE TÍPICO TANGO UNO
Av. Vereador JoséDiniz 491
(SantoAmaro)
Milonga on Thursdays 10 PM-2 AM and
Saturdays at midnight
Tel: 521 3946

PIZZARIA PAPA GENOVESE
Rua Cayowaa, 44. Thursdays 10 PM-
2 AM and Sunday at 9 PM
Tel: 263-9197

CLUB DEL TANGO
Alameda Sarutaiá, 222 Saturday 9:30 PM
Tel: 3884-7105

CAFÉ PIU PIU
Rua Treze de Maio 134 (Bexiga)
Last Sunday of the month 10 PM-2 AM
Tel: 258 8066 Cesar.

CANADA—001

MONTREAL
LA TANGUERIA
5390 Boulevard Saint-Laurent
Tel: (514) 495 8645
Fridays andSaturdays 10 PM-3 AM

TANGO LIBRE
1650 Marie-Anne est
Tel: (514) 527 5197 Friday, Saturday
and Sunday 9:30 PM-3 AM

STUDIO TANGO MONTREAL
1447 De Bleury. Wednesdays 8:30 PM-1
AM Tel: 514-844-2786

ACADEMY DE TANGO ARGENTIN
4445 Boul. Saint-Laurent. Thursday,
Sundays 8 PM-1 AM
Tel: 514-840-9246

AL SUR
370, Jean-talon Est (274-9003). Sundays
2-6 PM

QUEBEC
LES SALONS d'EDGAR
263 rue St. Vallier Est, Sunday 8 PM-
1 AM Tel: (418) 523 7811

AVENUE TANGO (Nancy Lavoie)
280 St. Joseph Est, 1er étage.
Saturday 9 PM-1 AM
Tel: 418 524 8264

SALTSPRING ISLAND
POR EL AMOR DEL TANGO
The Lion's Hall, Bonnet Avenue. Lots of
classes and a milonga once a month
Contact: Margie Korrison, 115 Bayview
Rd. Tel: 250-537-2707
e-mail: margietango@yahoo.com
www.geocities.com/porelamordeltango

TORONTO

EL RANCHO
430 College Street. Every Sunday. Class 8-9 PM
Milonga 9 PM-midnight
Tel: 416 921 2752

STRICTLY TANGO
College United Church Banqueting Room, 502 College St. (entrance on Bathurst St). Second Friday of month 9 PM-midnight Tel: 416 422 1067

MILONGA SAN TELMO
La Classique Night Club, 1069 St. Clair West (St. Clair east of Dufferin) Sundays 8 PM Tel: 416-240-0808

CLUB VIVA TANGO
Paradiso, 412 Richmond St. East, 3rd Floor. Wednesdays and Fridays at 9 PM
Tel: 416-968-2782

VANCOUVER

TANGO PRACTICA (Claude Esposito)
Polish Community Centre, 4015 Fraser St. and 24th Ave.
Tuesdays 8:30-10:30 PM
Tel: 604 987 3937

STRICTLY TANGO
Forufera Centre, Mezzanine, 505 Hamilton Place. Last Saturday of month 9 PM-midnight Tel: 604-633-2623
strictlytango@canada.com

BAILÁ TANGO
For address see www. bailatango.com
First and third Fridays of month 8 PM-midnight Tel: 604 874 8707
e-mail: dancetango@hotmail.com
Also at: The Polish Hall, 4015 Fraser (at East 24th Ave E)
Practica Tuesdays 8:30-10:30 PM Classes on Sunday evenings
with Semiral and Elaine Carson.

TANGOVANCOUVER—Practica
Yasel Danceport Studio, 4603 Main Street—2nd floor (at 30th Ave). Sundays

8:30-11pm. Also occasional Saturdays
Tel: 304-924-9557 e-mail: susana@tangovancouver.com

VICTORIA

TANGO MILONGA
459 Chester St. (off Fairfield, one block east of Cook Street) Second an fourth Friday. 9:15 PM-midnight Also: Practica every Sunday 8-10 PM
Info: The Victoria Tango Association Tel: 250-384-1879 (Pamela) or 250-477-6360 (Hilda)

CHILE—0056

SANTIAGO

AGUSTIN MAGALDI
Nataniel 1220 Tel: 5566761 Sunday, Friday, Saturday 7 PM

ARGENTINO LEDESMA
Portugal 1288 Tel: 5561786 Sunday and Thursday

BUENOS AIRES
Recoleta 1267. 9.00 PM-
Fridays, Saturdays Tel: 7779226

ENRIQUE S. DISCEPOLO
San Francisco 668 Fridays, Saturdays Salon: 10 PM

EL CACHAFAZ TANGO BAR
Guardia Vieja 188, Providencia.
Wednesday, Friday, Saturday
Tel: (2) 233 4949

For additional information in Chile contact the magazine: EstampaTanguera Compañia 1291.-3° Piso, 717359 Santiago.

CHINA—0086

BEIJING

BEIJING TANGO CLUB
3/f Capital Club (inside the health centre), Chaoyang District. Tuesdays 8:30-10:30 pm. Tel: 10 6505 9614 (Sandrine Chenivesse)
e-mail: Beijingtango@iname.com

COLOMBIA—00577

MEDILLIN

LA MAGIA TU BAILA
Tel: 574 266 9422 Fernando Gonzales

CUBA—0053

HAVANA

ACADEMIA DEL TANGO DE CUBA.
Justiz, 21 Bajos, La Habana Vieja
ASOCIACIÓN CUBANA AMIGOS DE TANGO
Casa Del Tango, Neptuno No.305, Entre Aguila y Galiano, Havana 2.

CZECH REPUBLIC—0042

PRAGUE

DIVADLO V DLOUHÉ
Dlouhá tr. 39 Tel: 02 248 26807

DENMARK—0045

AALBORG

TANGO
"1000 Fryd", Kattesundet 10, 9000.
Sundays 7-10 PM

AARHUS

TANGO AT GØGLERSKOLEN (Practica)
Klosterport 4D, 8000 Aarhus C. Fridays 7-9 PM and Sundays 6-10 PM
Tel: 86120790

COPENHAGEN

"EL BAILONGO"
Vesterbro Kulturhus, Lyrskovgade 4,3.
Tuesdays 8-11:30 PM Tel: 3332-9088 or 2650-1023
LA PRACTICA
"Tingluti", Valhalsgade 4. Fridays 8:30-11:30 PM Buses 10 and 39
Tel: 3314-1489

COPENHAGEN TANGO SOCIETY
Meeting Room at the Nyboder Skole, Oster Voldgade 15, close to Osterport Station. Sundays 2-5 PM
EL SALON
Park Café, Osterbrogade Sundays 8 PM-midnight Tel: 3314-1489

ODENSE

TANGOCAFE
Skibhus 17:48, Buchwaldesgade 48.
Second Fridays of month 7.:30 PM-12:30 AM

DOMINICAN REPUBLIC—0011

JUAN DOLIO

TANGO GRILL
Av. Boulevard frente al Hotel Playa Real.
Tel: 809 526 1578
Armando and Analia Nazarre

FINLAND—00358

HELSINKI

AMIGOS DEL TANGO
Balanssi-studiot, Kaapelitehdas, entrance D.
Wednesdays 8-10 PM Tel: 9 498994
HELSINKI INTERNATIONAL FOLK DANCE CLUB
Olympic Stadium, entrance D. Sundays 2-4 PM (September-April)
TANGO DEL JUBILADOS
Malmin Virkistyskeskus, Latokartanontie 9. Wednesdays 1:30-3:30 PM

FRANCE—0033

ALES

TANGO EN LIBERTÉ
Place de la Paix, Wednesdays (Open-air , Summer only) 7-10 PM

ARRAS

DANCE CLUB ARRAGEOIS
Maison des Societiés, 16, rue Aristide
Briand, 62000
Tel: 2107 30 31

BORDEAUX

CRUZ DEL SUR
rue du Port, 33800 Tel: 56 31 47 13
**ECOLE DE DANSE "ESPACE
FORME"**
Espace Dulau, 33470 Gujan Mestras.
Tel: 56 66 00 25

CLERMONT-FERRAND

TANGO VOLCANIQUE
Le 1513, 3 rue des Chaussetiers, F-
63000.
(Centre of town by Cathedral) Thursdays
from 8 PM
Tel: 04 73 28 1263
e-mail: I.Langlois@univ-bpclermont.fr

GRENOBLE

TANGO-TANGO (Practica)
95 Galerie de L'Arlequin.
Thursdays 8-9 p.m
Tel: 76 42 82 45

IBOS (TARBES)

ASSOCIATION TANGUEANDO
5, rue du Sovy, 65420 Tel: 62 90 03 05

LILLE

TANGO? TANGO!
3 rue Watteau, 59800
Tel: 01033 20 30 94 59 /
20 50 54 01
MJC-MAISON POUR TOUS
23, rue Alsace Lorraine. 59350 St.
André-lez-Lille
Tel: 20 51 66 67
LA BOUCHERIE
rue Massena à Lille. Every third Sunday
of the month

LYON

TANGO DE SOIE
Nomade's Land, 35 rue Imbert Colomés
Mondays 8 PM Tel: 78 39 24 93
LA BARATHYM
1 Rue Dumont Durville, 69001.
Mondays and Thursdays 8:30 PM-
TANGO OPEN AIR
Guinguette "Les Pieds dans l'Eau,"
Chemin de la plage, Rochetaillée sur
Saône. Sundays 6 PM-
Tel: 04 7227 8572

MARSEILLE

LE BOMPARD (Practica)
7, rue Marius Thomas, 13007
Thursdays 8:30 PM-10 PM
Tel: 04 42 44 89 11
EL TANGO (Practica)
13, Quai de Rive Neuve, brasserie Beau
Rivage. Mondays 8:30 PM-11 PM Also last
Friday of month at Café de Paris, rue de
la République Tel: 04 91 84 32 40
LA MORDIDA DU PORT (Practica)
Studio Yette Résal, 30, cours d'Estienne
d'Orves. Wednesdays 9 PM
Tel: 04-91-33-1223 (Elisabeth)
LE WEBBAR
114 rue de la République 13002. First
Monday of month 7 PM
Metro: Joliette Tel: 06-0392-4592
Nadine
LA MORDIDA DU PORT
La Brasserie des Danaïdes, place
Stalingrad, 13001. Third Friday of
month 7-10 PM
CARRÉMENT TANGO
Rue Venture. Practica First and third
Sunday of month 5 PM-9 PM
Tel: 04-96-12-0878 Valérie Lafore
LA NOCTURNA
Marseille Dance Centre, 8 rue Lieutenant
Meschi 13005. Practica last Friday of
month 10 PM-2 AM
Tel: 04-91-49-0478

MONTPELLIER

TANGO PRACTICA

La Faluche. 2nd Friday of month

7 PM-1 AM

Tel: 04 67 60 54 80

TANGO BAL

La Faluche. Third Sunday of month

8 PM-2 AM

Tel: 04 67 47 10 12

NICE

BAR DES OISEAUX

8 rue de L'Abbaye. Every last Saturday of the month.

EL GATO TANGUERO

Espace Magnan, 31 rue Louis de Coppet. Practica Wednesdays 9:30 PM-midnight

NÎMES

MILONGA DEL ANGEL

54 route de Beaucaire, 3000.

Saturdays 9 PM-

Tel: 06-60-86-97-26 Felix

ORLÉANS

ACADEMIA DEL TANGO ARGENTI-NA

106 rue de la Barriere Saint Marc, 45000.

Tel: 2 38 86 37 90

PARIS

SUNDAY

BAL TANGO ARGENTIN

BALAJO, 9 rue de Lappe, 75011.

Metro: Bastille

9 PM-1:30 PM

Tel: 01 47 00 07 87 / 01 39 78 50 68

BALLCABARET SAUVAGE

Cabaret Sauvage, Parc de la Villette au bord du canal, 75019. First Sunday of month 8 PM-1 AM

Tel: 01-40-03-75-15

Metro: Porte de la Villette

LE TEMPS DU TANGO (practica)

La Sourdiére, 23 rue de la Sourdiére, 75001 4:30-8 PM Metro: Pyramides.

Tel: (0)146-55-22-20

IACP

32 Rue du Capitaine Marchal. Last Sunday of month. 5 PM-8 PM Metro: Porte de Bagnolet. Tel: 01425-13654

TUESDAY

ACCORDS TANGO

11 Rue St. Luc, 75018. 9 PM-midnight Metro: Barbés-Rochechouart.

Tel: 0145-883155

MJC POINT DE JOUR

MJC point de Jour, 1 rue du General Malleterre, 75016 9:30 PM-midnight Metro: Porte de St Cloud

Tel: 01 45 25 14 19

WEDNESDAY

PRACTICE PETER GOSS

Studio Peter Goss, 7 rue des Petites Ecuries, 75010

10:30 PM-midnight Metro: Chateau d'Eau Tel: 01-44-83-9346

OXYGÉNE

Espace Oxygéne, 168 rue Saint Maur, 75011 10 PM-1:30 AM Metro: Place Clichy ou La Fourche

Tel: 01 48 05-0060

LE BISTRO LATIN

20, rue du Temple, 75004 9:30 PM-1 AM Metro: Hotel de Ville

Tel: 42 77 21 11

THURSDAY

MJC

1 Place Parmentier, 92200, Neuilly sur Seine 9-11:15 PM Metro: Porte Maillot

Tel: 01462-40383

PRACTICE PETER GOSS

Studio Peter Goss, 7 rue des Petites Ecuries, 75010 10 PM-1 AM

Tel: 01-46-06-1575 Metro: Chateau d'Eau

LE BISTRO LATIN

20, rue du Temple, 75004

10:30 PM-1 AM

Metro: Hotel de Ville
Tel: 42 77 21 11
PRACTICE PARIS 8
Université Paris 8 St. denis, 2 rue de la
Liberté, 93210 St. Denis. 7-10 PM Metro
Université
Tel: 01-53-28-0743
FRIDAY
LE BISTRO LATIN
20, rue du Temple, 75004 9 PM-2 AM
with live music Metro: Hotel de Ville
Tel: 42 77 21 11
MJC ST. MÉDART
3 rue du Gril, 75005 12:30-2:30 PM
Metro: Censier-Daubenton
Tel: 0142-804797
TANGO LIBERTÉ
Studio Liberté, 195bis rue de Paris,
Charenton-le Pont.
9:30 PM-2 am. Metro: Liberté.
Tel: 01 47-07-8728
SATURDAY
LE BISTRO LATIN
20, Rue du Temple, 75004 9 PM-
2 AM Metro: Hotel de Ville
Tel: 42 77 21 11
ESPACE OXYGENE
168 rue Saint Maur, 75011. Metro:
Goncourt. Second Sat. of month 10 PM
Tel: 01 49 29 06 77
TANGO MAISON VERTE
Maison Verte, 127 rue Marcadet, 75018
5-8 PM
Metro: Lamark-Caulaincourt.
Tel: 01-4364-1032 / 01-4818-7801
LE TEMPS DU TANGO
Salle d'Erlimont, 25 bis Avenue de la
République, Montrouge.
9 PM-1 AM metro: Porte d'Orleans.
Tel: 01 46 55-22-20
QUAIS DE SEINE (Outside by the
Seine—not when raining)
Quai St. Bernard, 75005. 9 PM
-midnight in the Summer
Metro:Gare d'Austerlitz / Jussieu
Tel: 01 43-74-4942

BALL RÉPUBLIQUE
Ecole de Danse de Paris, 17 rue du
Faubourg du Temple, 75010 8:30 PM-
12:30 AM Tel: 01-42-40-2283
Metro: République
*For additional information on Tango in
Paris contact: Marc Pianko
Le Temps du Tango
73, av. Henri Ravera, 92220 Bagneux
Tel: 46 55 22 20 Fax: 46 55 48 61
e-mail: tango@club-internet.fr
http://www.club-internet.fr/perso/tango*

PAU
ROCKING CLUB PALOIS
1, rue Taa, 64230 Lescar, with Maryse
Filc and Thierry Leray.
Tel: 59 02 80 71 / 59 80 07 08
VIGNES PASCAL
18, rue de la Republique, 64400 Bidos
Tel: 59 39 2919

PERNES LES FONTAINES
TANGO PROVENCE
Centre Culturel des Augustins, Place
Giraud, 84210. Wednesdays Class 7:30-
8:45 then practica until 10:30 PM
Tel: +33 0682 653964 / 06 12135094
Florent Mazzitelli or Josiane Monard

REIMS
FOYER RURAL " L'EVEIL DE SARRY"
6 rue de L'Eglise, 51520 Sarry
Tel: 26 64 10 11
CHAMPAGNE DANSE
Centre de Loisirs, route de Sogny les
Moulins, 51520 Sarry.
Tel: 26 67 53 16 and 26 64 33 88

RENNES
ASSOCIATION BRAISE TANGO
MJC La Paillette, rue du Pré de Bris,
35000 Practica Fridays 8:30 PM-
midnight or later.
Tel: 0299443022 or 0299315710

ST. HERBLAIN (NANTES)
LES ALLUMÉS DU TANGO
5, Bd. du Val de Chezine, 448

TOULOUSE

ASSOCIATION TANGUENDO
31 rue Escoussiéres-Arnaud Bernard, 31000.
Tel: 61 22 01 33 Fax: 61 23 45 37
STUDIO ELYSABETH BECLIER
6, bis impasse Marestan, 31100
Tel: 61 41 23 77
CORINNE FATTALINI
16 bis rue des Potiers Tel: 61 20 28 98
CHRISTINE MONTICELLI
av. Françoise Verdier, 31820 Pibrac.
MILONGA DE LAS MOROCHAS
Bar Le Petit Diable, 99 Allées Charles de Fitte. Wednesdays 9 PM
Tel: 05 61 42 86 95
PRACTICA
La Salle Jean Rancy, 10 rue Rancy.
8-10 PM Thursday

UZES

ASSOCIATION TANGUEANDO
BP 32, 30702 Uzes Cedex.
Tel: 66 03 02 40
CATHERINE DE ROCHAS and HENRI VIDIELLA
Centre Social de St. Quentin, 30700
Tel: 66 22 75 99 and 66 85 75 97

VAULNAVEYES LE HAUT

ASSOCIATION TANGO TANGO
chemin des Guichards, 38140.
Tel: 76 89 05 82 (Simone Vladich)
*For further information on Salons, etc.
in Southern France, contact:
Les Trottoirs de Marseille
18, Rue de Lodi, 13006
Tel: 91 48 09 29*

GERMANY—0049

AACHEN

TANGO NIGHT
Café Roncalli, Theatrestr. 17 Fridays twice a month at 11:30 PM
Tel: (0)241 4011 266

Also at: Bleiberger Fabrik, Bleiberger Str. 2 Saturdays twice a month.
Tel as above.

AUGSBURG

BLAUER SALON
Krankenhaus, Pulvergasschen 6a.
Saturdays 9 PM-1 AM
Tel: 0821-156841

BAMBERG

TANGO Y MAS
Obere Sandstr. 5 Saturdays at 9 PM
Tel: 0951-56288

BERLIN
MONDAY

CHECKPOINT
Leipziger Str. 55, Berlin-mitte. 9 PM Tel: 2082995
8:30 PM-12:30 AM Tel: 6922100
THEATRE TANGO
Windspiel Theatre, Berliner Str. 46
9 PM Tel: 8736583
SODA TANGO CLUB
Neue Kulturbrauerei, Knaackstr/Prenzlauer Berg
8:30 PM Tel: 030-391-19-98
TUESDAY
KALKSCHEUNE
Johannisstr. 2. 9 PM
Tel: 030-28-39-0065
EL BARRIO
Potsdamer Str.84, berlin-Tiergarten.
10 PM-
SEHPARÉE
House in Kölnnischen Park 6-7 (Turmeingang), 10179. 9 PM
Tel: 50378608 Fax: 50378609
WEDNESDAY
ROTER SALON
Volksbühne, Rosa-Luxemburg-Platz, direct on tube,
Berlin-centre From 9:30 PM-3 AM
Tel: (030) 28-59-8538

HOPPETOSSE (Gastronomieschiff)
Eichenstr. 4 9 PM
CLÄRCHEN'S BALLHAUS
Auguststr. 24/25, Berlin-Mitte 9 PM Tel:
78913243
THURSDAY
GRÜNER SALON
Rosa-Luxemburg-Platz. 9 PM
Tel: 030-391-1998
TRIALARIT
Gervinusstrasse 12, 10629. 9 PM
Tel: 323-7468
FRIDAY
HAUS DER SINNE
Saarbrücker Str. 36-38, 10405 Berlin-
mitte. 9 PM
Tel: 44049155
BEPOP
Mehringdamm 33 9:30 PM
Tel: 030- 69-41-101
LA MILONGA DE BERLIN
Ballhaus Walzerlinksgestrickt,
Tempelhofer Berg 7d, Kreuzberg (U7)
9:30 PM Tel: 030-323-4502
HEXENKESSEL-THEATRE
Monbijoupark, Monbijoustrasse 3,
Berlin-Mitte 11:30 PM
TANZART
Hasenheide 54, Berlin-Kreuzberg.
10-11.55 PM Tel: 6936109
SCHOKO-CAFÉ
Mariannenstrasse 6 / HH, 10997. Every
third Friday of month 9 PM
Tel: 615-1561
SATURDAY
TANGO
Balhaus Rixdorf, Kottbusserdam 76
9:30 PM Tel: 030-440-17406
BAILONGO
Böckhstr. 21, Kreuzberg. 8-10:30 PM Tel:
030-787-05640
SUNDAY
BAILONGO
Böckhstr. 21, Kreuzberg. 3-6 PM
Tel: 030-787-05640

TANGOVIVO
Mehringdamm 33 7-9:30 PM
Tel: 030 691-9328
B-FLAT
Rosenthaler Str. 13. 10 PM
Tel: 030 7870-4191
CAFÉ LAMPENFIEBER
Hallesches Ufer 32, Berlin-Kreuzberg.
3-6 PM Tel: 61507013
ESTUDIO SUDAMERICA
Brunnenstr. 181, Berlin-mitte. 7-10 PM
Tel: 2823952
TRIALARIT
Gervinusstrasse 12, 10629. 7 PM
Tel: 323-7468

BIELEFELD
TANGOTREFF
Freizeitzentrum Stieghorst, Glatzer Str.
21. Tuesdays once a month. 8 PM
Tel: 0571-387-0630
Also at: Café Tropical, Weberei Str. 5.
Sundays once a month.
Tel: 0521-3051371

BOCHUM
TANGOABEND
La Boca, Nehringskamp 1. Thursdays
and first Friday and third Saturday of
month 9 PM Tel: 0234 949-0933
TANGO RIFF
Bermudahalle, Konrad-Adenauer-Platz 3,
44787. Mondays 6 PM
Tel: 0234-9490933

BONN
CAFÉ PAUKE
Endenicher Str. 43 Thursday
8 PM-midnight
Tel: 02 28- 634290
TANGOTREFF
Theatre in Ballsaal, Frongasse 9. Second
Sunday of month 8 PM
Tel: 02-28-79-7901
LA VIDA
Plittersdorfer Str. 48, Bonn Bad-

Godesberg. First Saturday of month.
9 PM-2 AM Tel: 0228-9140877

BRAUNSCHWEIG

MILONGA BRUNSVIGA
KarlStr. 35 Mondays 8 PM-midnight Tel:
0531-334094
GALERIEHOF
Madamenweg. Sundays 5 PM-8 PM Tel:
0531-343440
SALON
Piccolo Theatre, Kasernenstr. 20. Fridays
twice a month 9 PM-1 AM
Tel: 053-53-3938

BREMEN

LAGERHAUS
Schildstrasse 12-19 10 PM-midnight
Mondays
TANGUERO
Sielwall 44, 2800 Tuesdays 9:30 PM Tel:
0421-702691
LA MILONGA
Staderstrasse 35. Tuesdays 9 PM,
Sundays 8 PM
Tel: 421 44 22 84 (Michael Domke)
LA CITA
Grundstr. 10. Thursdays 9:30 PM-1:30
AM Tel: 0421-7020691
TANGOABEND
Bürgerhaus Hemelingen, Godehardstr 4.
Fridays twice a month at 9 PM
Tel: 0421-498-4679

BREMERHAVEN

LAUBENPIEPER
Van Heukelum Str. 26 Wednesday
8 PM Tel: 04743-7426

CHEMNITZ

VOXXX
Horst-Menzel-Str. 24. Wednesday 9 PM
Tel: 0371-3541-300
ATOMINO
Schloss Str. 7. (Entrance in Theunerstr.in
Hinterhof) Sundays twice a month.
7-11 PM Tel: 0179-21-38202

DACHAU

TANGO NIGHT
Konrad Adenauer Str. 1
Wednesday 8 PM

DARMSTADT

MEDIA LUNA TANGOCAFÉ
Tanzwerkstatt Markplatz 13. Every first
and third Sunday in month. 7-10 PM Tel:
061-51-97-77-73
TANGOTREFF
Café das Blatt, Wilh-Leuschner-Str. 30.
Fst Saturday of month 9 PM
Tel: 061-51-997711

DIEPHOLZ

TANGONIGHT
Hotel Carstendiek, St. Hülfe. 1st and
3rd Thursdays of month. Tel: 044-42-
5471

DETMOLD

TANGONIGHT
Tanzschule Wiggie'z, Bielefelder Str.5
One Saturday a month. 8:30 PM
Tel: 052-31-302830

DORTMUND

TNT
Heyden-Rynsch-str.2 (Dorstfeld)
Wednesdays 9 PM and Sundays 8 PM Tel:
023-24-31811 / 023-05-15857
TODO TANGO
Lütgendortmunder Str. 40. Second
Saturday of month 10 PM
Tel: 0231-69-2588
BAILAR
Schüruferstr. 119. Second Friday of
month. 10:30 PM
Tel: 0231-445795
THEATER IM DEPOT
Immermannstr. 39. (Hafen), Every last
Friday 10 PM
Tel: 0231-826023

DRESDEN

GARE DE LA LUNE
Pillnitzer Landstrasse 148, Dresden-Wachwitz.
Saturday 9 PM-1:30 AM
Tel: 0351 2678554

ANDORINHA TANGO NIGHT
Park Hotel Weißer Hirsch. Tuesdays once a month 9 PM

DUISBURG

STUDIO TANGO
Mercatorstr. 4, 1.Etage. Every first Saturday of month 9 PM
Tel: 02159-2332

DÜSSELDORF

MOVE and DANCE TANGO
Move and Dance Tanzzentrum Wersten, Leichlingerstr. 3-5. Every second and fourth Sunday 7:30 PM
Tel: 0211-761454

TANGO DE BUENOS AIRES
Tanzhaus nrw Erkrather Str. 30. Second and fourth Tuesdays 9:30 PM
Tel: 0211- 721412

ERFURT

ESQUINA DEL TANGO
Saal des Johannes Lang Haus, Karl-Marx-Platz/ entrance Puschkinstr.
Fridays 9 PM Tel: 0361-212-50004

ERLANGEN

TANGOFEST
Erba-Villa, Äußere Brucker Str. 49. Every third Saturday of month. 9 PM-1 AM Tel: 9131 16986

TANGOBAR
UNICUM, Carl Tiersch Str. 9. Sundays twice a month 8 PM Tel: 09131-16986

SABADOS DE MILONGA
TTC Münchener Str. 55. Saturdays once a month 9 PM-1 AM
Tel: 09131-205600

ESSEN

TANGONIGHT
Zeche Carl Wilhelm-Nieswandt-Allee 100. Saturday once a month 9 PM
Tel: 02324-31811

FALLHOVEN

TANGOFALL
Tchorznickistr. 39. Saturdays 10 PM-3 AM Tel: 2334-8172

FLENSBURG

VOLKSBAD FLENSBURG
Schiffbrücke 67. Mondays 9 PM
e-mail: simeondimitrov@hotmail.com

FRANKFURT

CASABLANCA
Behind Casa di Cultura Italiana, Adalbertstr. 36 (Bockenheim). 9 PM-1 AM Second Saturday of the month.
Tel: 069-7077548
e-mail: kontakt@cyber-tango.com

TERRANOVA
Mörfelder Landstr. 64, 2. Stock (Sachshausen) 9:15 PM-12:30 AM Wednesdays. Info: academia@fabiana.de

TANGO TREFF
Die Brotfabrik, Bachmannstr. 2-4 (Hausen), Frankfurt AM Main. Mondays 9 PM-1 AM Subway U6+U7 Industiehof.

TANGO CAFÉ
Am Industriehof 7-9, Frankfurt Hausen, Saturday 4:30-7:30 PM
Tel: 069-78800426

TANGO BAR
Tanzschule Weber, Bolongarostr. 113 65929 (Höchst). Fridays 10 PM-3 AM
Tel: 069/ 302976

TANGO CAFÉ
Romanfabrik, Hanuer Landstr. 186. Sundays 7:30-midnight.
Info: Academia de Tango 069-811234

FREIBURG

TANGO CLUB CORAZON
Wallstrasse 14. Sundays 9 PM-midnight

TANGO IN DER FABRIK
Habsburgerstraße 9, 79104. Thursdays 9
PM-1 AM, Saturdays 10 PM until late.
Tel/Fax: 07-61-70-00-80
e-mail: rafaelbusch@gmx.de
ESTATION DEL TANGO
Wiehre Bahnhof, Gerwigplatz. Fridays
10:30 PM

FRIEDLAND
TANGONIGHT
Sportpavillon, Vor dem Waldtor 3. First
Saturday of month 9 PM
Tel: 03960-120231

FULDA
LALILALU
Severiberg 1. First and third Fridays of
month. 9 PM
Tel: 06 61-22334
CAFÉ FLAMME
Friedrichstr. 9 (near Dom) Second and
fourth Fridays of month 9 PM
Tel: 06 61-22334

GIESSEN
TANGO BAR
Café Zum Rodtberg, Reichenberger Str.
9. Second and fourth Wednesday of
month 9 PM Tel: 06 406-907254

GÖTTINGEN
TANGONIGHT
KAZ Spiegelsaal, Hospitalstr. 6 (Junges
Theater)
Tuesday 10.15 PM Tel: 05 51-3793-299
TANGONIGHT
MUSA , Brotfabrik, Hagenweg 2a.
Sundays 6 PM
Tel: 05 51-35865

GREIFSWALD
TANGONIGHT
Café Caspar, FischStr. 11 Tuesdays 8:30
PM
Tel: 038-34-843374

TANGONIGHT
Jacobiturm, Raum der
Studentengemeinde, Domstr. Sundays
8:30 PM Tel: 038-34-843374

HAMBURG
TANGO CAFE BALADIN
Stresemannstr. 374 Friday and Sunday
once a month 7 PM
Tel: 040-898908
ENTRE AMIGOS
Kulturhaus Eppendorf, Martinistr. 40.
Saturday once a month 9 PM
Tel: 040-4225039
**TANGOFATAL (Lesbians, Gays and
Friends)**
Stresemannstr. 374 Once a month
9 PM Tel: 040-898908
LA YUMBA
"Tangofrauen," Kastanienalle 9, Hamburg
20359 St. Pauli. Once a month 11 PM
Tel: (0)40 721 2119 / 317 32 24

HANNOVER
TANGO MILIEU
Leinaustr./Ecke Berdingstr (Linden)
Tel: 0511 44 02 02 Sunday 9 PM,
Wednesday 9 PM, Friday 10 PM
TANGO MIO
Plathnerstr. 5b. Tuesday and Thursday
9:30 PM-midnight, Saturday 8 PM-
Tel: 0511-2833200
DESAYUNO EN TANGO
Plathnerstr. 5b. Second Sunday of
month. 11 AM-3 PM
Tel: 0511-2833200

HEIDELBERG
THE GOLDEN ROSE
Hegenichstr. 10. Thursdays 9 PM-
1 AM Tel: 06221-385025
CONDETANGO
Hauptstr. 190 (outside Apothecary)
Fridays and Sundays 10 PM
Tel: 06221-602070

JENA

TANGONIGHT
Ricarda-Huch-Haus, Löbdergraben 7.
Wednesdays 9 PM
Tel: 03641-605530

KAARST/WILLICH

TANGONIGHT
Zollhaus, Hardt 29. Fridays 10 PM
Tel: 02159-2332

KAISERSLAUTERN

BAILEMOS TANGO
Cotton Club, Kulturzentrum Kamgarn,
Schönstr. 10. Sundays 8 PM
Tel: 0631-67497

KARLSRUHE

SIEMPRE TANGO
Walhalla (Restaurant El Greco),
Augartenstr. 27.
Tuesdays 9 PM Tel: 0721-9375393
MILONGUEANDO EL SABADO
Callas Ziegler, Baumeisterstr. 18.
Saturdays 9 PM
Tel: 0721-9375393

KASSEL

TANGO TS SEYLER
Salztorstr 14. Mondays 9:30 PM
Tel: 06406- 907254
TANGO ZERO
Sanderhäuser str. 77. (Raiffeisengelände)
Every Wednesday from 9 PM
Every Sunday from 8 PM-11 PM
TANGO OFFENES WOHNZIMMER
Goethestr. 34 Thursdays 5-8 PM
Tel: 0561-32455
TANGO DOCK 4
Lower Karlstr. 4 Thursdays 9 PM-midnight Tel: 0561-713618
TANGO CAFÉ / TANGO SALON(Tango Suerte)
Gleis 1 / Hauptbhf. Sundays 5-8pm /
9PM-midnight
Tel: 0561-5280065

KEMPTEN

TANGONIGHT
Haus International, Beethovenstr. 2.
Mondays 9 PM Tel: 08370-1758

KIEL

TANGONIGHT
Estudio Latinoamerica, Sophienblatt 88-90. Sundays 7-10:30 PM
Tel: 0431-676705
TANGO IN DER PUMPE
Haßtraße. Every Wednesday 8 PM-midnight

KIRCHEIM

TANGONIGHT
Villa Dettinger Str. 95. Fridays once a
month Tel: 07021-82642

KÖLN

EL CASTILLO IN THE BASEMENT
Herwarthstrasse 22 (under the church)
Wednesdays 9:30 PM
Tel: 0221 9610153
DON TANGO CLUB
Krefelder Strasse 18. 50670 Friday 9 PM-1 AM, Sundays 6-10 PM
Tel: 0221 732 7669
TANGO KULTOR 5
Helmholtzstr. 8-32 Sundays 9 PM
Tel: 0221 9545025

KONSTANZ

GEBHARDSHALLE
St.-Gebhard-Str. 6. Wednesdays at 9 PM
Fridays at 9 PM Tel: 7531-34730
e-mail: arthur@tangolibre.de
www.tangolibre.de

KREFELD

TANGO NIGHT
Café Kulisse, Virchowstr. 130. Mondays
8:30 PM-1 AM

LANDSBERG

TANGONIGHT
Foyer of Stadttheatre. Thursdays 10 PM
Tel: 08191-922616

TANGONIGHT
Forum Landsberg, Münchner Str. 32/34
(2nd floor) Sundays 9-11 PM
Tel: 08806-7625

LANDAU
TANGOAVERNE
Hotel Französisches, Reiterstr. 11.
Fridays twice a month 9 PM
Tel: 06341 944120

LEIPZIG
TANGO BAR
Villa Rosental, Liviastr. 8, 04105.
Thursday once a month 9:30 PM
Tel: 0341 980 4059
TANGO in der FABRIK
Baumwollspinnerei, Spinnereistr. 7
Mondays 9 PM and last Friday of month
9 PM Tel: 0341 4808672
MILONGA SIN LUZ
Kreuzstr. 14 / Vorderhaus. Saturdays
9 PM Tel: 0341-9121009

LÜBECK
SALON PARCOUR
Aegidienstr. 29-31 Thursdays 9 PM, last
Saturday of month 9 PM and Sundays 4-
6 PM Tel: 0451-71560

LÜNEBURG
TOLSTEFANZ TANGO
Zentral gelegen: Am Berge 25. Every second and fourth Thursday 8 PM-midnight
Tel: 04138 1375

MANNHEIM
TANGO NIGHT
Opera Buffa, Waldhofstr. 76 Sundays
9:30 PM Tel: 0621-331700

MARBURG
LOS MALDITOS
In Lahngarten, Wehrdaer Strasse 102 in
Wehrda. Wednesdays and Sundays 8.00
PM Tel: 06421 992879

MARZLING (by Freising)
TANGODANCECLUB
Dance School GE-Zwei, Rudlfinger Str.
Second Saturday of month 8 PM-
Tel: 08161 / 62858 or 08161 / 68849

MINDEN
TANGONIGHT
Preussenmuseum, Simeonsplatz 12.
Tuesday once a month 8-10:30 PM
Tel: 0571-3870630

MOERS
TANGONIGHT
CITY-TS in Wall-Zentrum, Neuer Wall 2.
Saturdays once a month at 10 PM
Tel: 02802-7482

MÖNCHENGLADBACH
TANGO ARGENTINO
Stadt-Palais, Wehner Str. 1-7. Thursdays
twice a month 9:30 PM-1 AM
Tel: 02162-580139

MUNICH
PRACTICA IN KHG
Leopoldstrasse 11, 80802. Mondays
8:30 PM-midnight
Tel: 089 30728104
TANGONIGHT
Glockenbachwerkstatt, Baumstr. 8 (1.og)
Mondays 9 PM-midnight.
Tel: 089-20232673
BAILÁ TANGO
Taverna Odysee, Bad-Kreuther-Str. 8
(subway: Innsbrucker Ring) Tuesdays
8 PM-midnight Saturdays twice a month
at 8:30 PM Tel: 089-2013782
TANGO MALDITO (Practica)
Studio Circolo, Rosenheimer Str. 139
Wednesdays 9 PM-1 AM
Tel: 089-4807194
TANGO HANSAPALAST
Hansastr. 41 9 PM Saturdays once a
month

TANGONIGHT
GAP Werkraum, Goethstr. 34
Wednesdays 9 PM, Fridays 10 PM (not during holidays) Tel: 089-776635

EL CHOCLO
Amalienstr. 45/2 (cellar in the back-yard)Tuesdays 9 PM-12:30 AM, Fridays 9 PM, Saturdays 9 PM-3 AM and Sundays 3-7 PM Tel: 089-838497

TANGO BAR
Vollmarhaus, Oberanger 38. Sundays 9 PM-1AM Tel: 089-4807149

TANGO MAX EMANUEL BRAUEREI
Adalbertstr. 33. Tuesdays 8:30 PM-1AM Tel: 089-2715158

BAILAR
Truderingerstr. 9 Thursdays 8:30-11:30 PM Tel: 089-2712134

EL CORAZON
Larchnerstr. 38 Thursday and Friday 9 PM First Sunday of month at 11 AM

EL ANDALUZ
Dachauer Str 36-38 Thursdays 9:30 PM-midnight
Tel: 089-6925367

BEACH BAR TANGO
Kunstpark Ost. Saturday 9 PM
Tel: 089-20232673
For further info. about tango in Munich Tel: CHRISTINA GEBEL (0) 89 2013782 e-mail: BailaTango@gmx.de

MÜNSTER
TANGO APASIONADO
Roter Salon, Schlossgarten Restaurant, Schlossgarten 4 First Sunday of the month 7-12 PM Tel: 0251 274502

CON CORAZON
Friedrich-Ebert-Str. 7. Fridays three times a month, Saturday twice a month 9:30 PM-1:30 AM Tel: 0251-5346234

MURNAU
TANGONIGHT
Westtorhalle, Weilheimerstr. 15. Sundays 9 PM Tel: 08841-5206

NEU-ULM
THEATER NEU-ULM
Silcherstr. 2. Every first, third and fifth Sunday 8 PM Tel: 0731 985670

NÜRNBERG
TANGO ALTERNATIVO
Transit, Karl-Bröger-Str. 9. Thursdays 9 PM-midnight Tel: 911 9455656

TANGO BAR
Tanzgalerie, Rielkestr. 16 Fridays 10PM-1 AM Tel: 911 331445

TANGO 7
Café Salas, Bayernstr. 136. Thursdays 8 PM-12:30 AM
Tel: 0911-9400551

OFFENBACH
TANGO CAFÉ
Ludwigstrasse 129 Tel: 069 813379 (Fabiana Jarma)

OLDENBURG
KULTURETAGE
Bahnhofstrasse 11. Wednesdays 9 PM-12:30 AM Tel: 0441-9572807

OSNABRÜCK
PIESBERGER GESELLSCHAFT-SHAUS
Glückaufstr. 1 Tuesdays 9-12 PM
Tel: 0541 441213

PADERBORN
TANGONIGHT
Grüner Frosch in Lichtenfelde 4. First Friday of month 9 PM-1 AM
Tel: 05251-64992

REGENSBURG
TANGO-WERKSTATT REGENSBURG
Puricellistrasse 40 (Untergeschoss) Fridays once/twice a month 8:30 PM-1 AM Tel: 09404-2176

TANGO NIGHT
Restaurant Vitus, Hinter der Grieb. Wednesdays 8 PM-midnight.
Tel: 0941-53057

TANGO NIGHT
Augustiner, Neupfarrplatz. Sundays
8 PM Tel: 0941-401625

ROSTOCK
BACKSHOP TANGO
Backshop, Wendländer Schilde 5.
Tuesdays 9 PM-midnight
Tel: 0381-2017334 Birgit

SCHNEGA
TANGONIGHT
Seminarhof Proitzer Mühle, 14-
tägig(nachfragen) Sundays 7 PM
Tel: 05842-450

SCHORNDORF
TANGONIGHT
Manufaktur Tanzwerkstatt,
Hammerschlag 8, Sundays 8-11 PM Tel:
07181 65830

STEGEN
TANGONIGHT
Theatre in old Brauhaus, Landsberger
Str,. 57 Tuesdays and Thursdays 9.15
PM-midnight Tel: 08142-5152

STUTTGART
LA REPÚBLICA DEL TANGO
Alarichstr. 18a, Thursdays 9 PM-
12:30 AM
Tel/Fax: (0)711-8560712 Metro U6/13
to Maybachstr.
LA BOCA
Rosensteinstr. 79 / old Postgelände,
Tuesdays 9 PM Tel: 0711-2591949
TANGO-VORSTADT
Christophstr. 40-42, D-70180 Fridays 10
PM-1 AM, Sundays 7-11 PM
Tel/Fax: 0711 649-90-09
TANGONIGHT
Café Marquardt in Schloßplatz,
Königstr.22 Wednesdays 9:30 PM
First Sunday of month 7 PM
Tel: 0711-583411

TANGONIGHT
Naost, Ostendstr. 106a. Wednesdays
8:30-11:30 PM Tel: 0711-606519
SALIDA
Talstr. 41. Saturdays 9:30 PM
Tel: 0711-3166206

SYKE
TANGO SALON
Boschstr. 20 Fridays 10 PM
Tel: 04202-3031

TÜBINGEN
CLUBHAUS
Wilhelmstr. 30 (opposite "Neu Aula"),
First Floor. Tuesdays 7:45-10 PM
Tel: 07121-492106
TANGO WESTBANHOF
Westbahnstr / entrance Schleifmühleweg
Mondays 9 PM and first Saturday of
Month 9 PM Tel: 07071-368863
TANGONIGHT
Trz Tanz and Rock 'n Roll Centre, Lilli-
Zapf-Str. 25 Sundays 8 PM-midnight
Tel: 07073-7717

ULM / NEU-ULM
TANGO EL RUBIO
Lessingstr. 10c. (Neu-Ulm).
Tuesdays 9 PM
Tel: 0731-9806040

VECHTA
TANGOTREFF
Gulf Haus Zitadelle 13. Two Thursdays a
month 8:45 PM Tel: 04442-5471

VELBERT
KOSSMAN TANGO
Tanzhaus Kossman, Küpperstr. 3, 42551.
Every first Friday 9:30 PM
Tel: 02051-251500

WANGEN
TANGONIGHT
Josefshaus, Ratzenried by Wangen.
Sundays 8:30 PM Tel: 07522-20359

TANGONIGHT
Humboldhaus Achberg-Esseratsweiler.
Sundays once/twice a month 4-11 PM
Tel: 07528-7734

WIESBADEN
TANGO IN THE THALHAUS
Thalhaus in Wiesbaden, Nerotal 18,
65193. Two Sundays of month 10 PM-
12:30 AM Tel: 06131-475294
TANGO IN THE TATTERSALL
Tattersal, Saalgasse 34-36. 9-12 PM
Wednesday 9 PM Tel: 06131-475294

WOLGAST
TANGONIGHT
Sportpavillon Wednesdays at 8 PM
e-mail: academia-de-tango@t-online.de

WÜRZBURG
DAS BOOT
Veitshõchheimer Str. 5 Mondays 9 PM-2
AM Tel: 9369 8653
e-mail: werner.ebert@mail.
uni-wuerzburg.de

WUPPERTAL
TANGONIGHT
Café Ada, Wiesenstr. 6 (Eberfeld)
Monday, Tuesday 8:30 PM-1 AM and
Saturdays 8:30 PM-2 AM
Tel: 0202-7489043
TANGO ALLEGRO
Geckersklef 52 Every first and third
Thursday 9 PM Tel: 0202 459 2820
CAFE CENTRAL TANGO
Café Central, Hofaue 59 Sundays 9 PM
Tel: 0202-305857

*For general information about Tango in
Germany contact: James Peace
Rittershausstr. 5, 61231 Bad Nauheim,
Germany
Tel: (0)6032-968492 Fax: (0)6032-968497*

GREECE—0030
Athens
PAVLOS FOTOPOLOS
Tel: 01/ 64-49831 Fax: 01/ 64 22932

LUIS and ELENA NESTRE
Akamantos 14, Thission. Classes and
milonga on Saturdays. Tel: 324 9622 or
e-mail: mestre-tango@hotmail.com

HONG KONG— 00852
TANGOTANG
Helena May's, 35 Garden Road, Central.
(Basement, lower entrance) opp.
American Consulate. Thursdays 7:30-12
PM e-mail: frederic@cafe-charbon.com
THE HONG KONG TANGO ACADE-MY
Scott's Dancing School, 6/F Times Tower,
393 Jaffe Road, Causeway Bay. Practica
10-11:30 PM Classes from 7:30 PM
e-mail: keithandsunshine@aol.com

HUNGARY—0036
BUDAPEST
TANGO Y ALMA
Alkotmaany utca 9-11. Wednesdays 7-
10:30 PM   Tel: 00-267-0600
(Andrea Goetz)
CAFÉ VISTA
Paulai Ede u. Mondays 8 PM-11 PM
Tel: 00-361-339-4978 Budai Laaszio

ISRAEL—00972
TEL AVIV
LIDOR DANCE SCHOOL
Disenchik 9 beit revivim, Shikun dan.
Group classes Saturday and Sunday
Milonga on Saturday nights from 10 PM
Tel/Fax: 3 6497065 Doron Lidor and
Sandomir Liat
e-mail: Lidor1@inter.net.il

ITALY—0039
MILONGAS

ANCONA
"VIVA EL TANGO"
"Thermos", via S. Martino, 10. Mondays
10 PM-12:30 AM

Tel: 071-31759 e-mail: giorpat@libero.it
Web: http://utenti.tripod.it/gio_2html
"VIVA EL TANGO" (Practica)
Salus et Gratia, Viale Della Vittoria 7.
Thursdays 10 PM-12:30 AM Info: Mobile
0339-4038392

BARDOLINO
NUEVO TANGO
Lido Holiday, Punta Cornicello. Fridays
9:30 PM Tel: 045-6211044 / 0338
8445006 (Mobile—Claudia)

BARI
BARI TANGO
OTIUM C, so cavour, 211. Thursdays
Tel: 080-5231406 or
335-6211462 Silvio dello Russo

BELLUNO
DOLOMILONGA
Bar "Al Piave", via S. Ubaldo, 56 (ponte
di S. Felice), Sedico (BL) Fridays
9 PM-midnight Lucio
Tel: 328-136-1402
TANGO QUERIDO
CEIS, Borgo Piave. Sundays 9 PM-
midnight Tel: 437-930489

BERGAMO
CIRCULO "TANGO TAMBIEN"
Tel: 035-24-68-62 Adriana

BOLOGNA
SABATO TANGO CLUB
Cheek to Cheek, via Rocco Stefani 7,
SAN GIOVANNI IN PERSICETO.
Saturdays 10 PM Tel: 0335-6062135
CIRCOLO LA FATTORIA
Via Pirandello 6. 40127. Fridays 10:30
PM-4 AM Tel: 51 505117 / 633 7000 Fax:
633 3781
**GIOVANNI BEGOTTI (Classes and
Practica)**
Circolo della Grada, via della Grada, 10.
Tuesdays andThursdays 10:30 PM-3 AM

Info: 051-244953
Mobile: 0347-8671967 Giovanni
e-mail: giovanbat@interfree.it
TANGO DE ARRABAL
Via Riva del Reno 77/A Sundays 9PM-1
AM Tel: 051-333786 (Patrizio)

BOZEN-BOLZANO
DANCEFORUM
Via Museo 52, Bolzano. Thursdays 10
PM-2 AM Tel: 3483590-1748 Annemarie

BRESCIA
TANGO MI VIDA
"Discoteca Tivoli," Travagliato (BS)
Sundays.
Tel: Lidia 030 348778 / 030 349790
LADY LIDIA TANGO
Stage Lady Lidia Dance di Montirone 9
PM-11 PM Saturdays

CAGLIARI
TANGO
Koala Club, via Mercalli, 29. Weekly
practica Tel: 0338-8442349 (Roberto)

CATANIA (SICILY)
TANGOSUR
Il Capannone, Via del Cimitero 1,
Mascalucia Fridays 10 PM-
Pala CUS, via S. Sofia Saturdays
10:30 PM
12 PM-5 PM Tel: 0349-458-7353

CESENA (RIMINI)
MEDIALUNA
Pizzeria Restaurant "La Pergola,"
Via Cesenatico 918.
Tel: 0547-610141 e-mail: lubas@iol.it

CUNEO
MILONGA A'PRES
Chiusa Pesio CN, via circonvallazione
(per Lurisia)
Wednesdays 9 PM Tel: 0171-734-182
Piero Leli

ISOLA D'ELBA

ASSOCIATION BLU TANGO
Practica Wednesdays. Portoferraio c/o
Noferi G.—Loc. Viticcio—55037
Tel: Giovanni Diversi: 0565 914564
Andrea Palombo 0347-7339115

FIRENZE

CASA DEL RITMO STUD
Via San Giovanni, 28/R Sundays 10 PM
(members only) Tel: 055 220290 Anna
TANGO CLUB CALDINE
Casa del Popolo, "Caldine," Via Faentina
183. Thursdays 10:30-12:30 AM Practica.
Saturdays 10:30 PM- 3 AM milonga
Tel: 0335-390335

GENOVA

ATANEO DELLA DANZA
"Cesanne" via Cecchi 7R. Milonga
Tuesdays 10 PM-1:30 AM
Tel: 010-541607
**MILONGA ASSOCIAZIONE
CULTURALE PandP**
SQUASH di C. So Italia 7a. Saturdays
10 PM Dance on a Terrace facing the sea
Tel: 347-93-59-122 Pasquale

GRASSINI

TANGUETEANDO
near Casa del Popolo di Grassina—
Piazza Umberto 1, 14—Grassina (FI)
Exit Florence south on the autostrada A1
in the direction of Siena for 2km.
Fridays 10:30-3 AM Tel: 055-642639
e-mail: casadelpopolo@fionline.it

MANTOVA

MANTOVA TANGO
For information on practicas
Tel: 0376-220835 Marcello

MARINA DI MASSA

Summer milonga at "Cinquale di Marina
di Massa." Friday evening at the seashore
café "Solcaffe" (Capannina del Cinquale)
Viale IV Novembre 28 Localita
"Cinquale." (Lugomare between Massa
and Forte del Marmi) Tel: 0335-
6164568

MESSINA

TANGOQUERIDO
Amacord, via Panoramica dello Stretto
Thursdays at 10 PM

MILAN

LA MALEVA
via Angera 3. Mondays 9 PM-midnight
MILANOMILONGA
c/o ARCI Bellezza, via Bellezza
10 PM Tuesdays
Also classes with Alberto Colombo
GENTE DE TANGO
c/o ENDAS Acqua Potobile, Piazza
Carbonari 30
Thursdays 10:45 PM and Saturdays 10 PM
Tel: 02-581-10282 / 349-354-0664
LA CONGA
San Giuliano Milanese (Milano), Via
Marcini 17. Thursdays
TANGOMORPHOSI
Piazza Carbonari 30. Saturdays 10 PM
Tel: 02-669-5345
MILONGA IDEAL
La Isla, via Brembo 23. Sundays from 7
PM-12 AM
Tel: 02-53-94-124 / 0339-22-55-305
e-mail: rremon@tiscalinet.it / www.
tiscalinet.it/milongaideal
ASS. CULTURALE TANGOY
Via Monza 140 a Milano. Fridays 10 PM-
2 AM
Tel: Giulia 02-32-72-629 or Roberto
02-2592175
VILLA TANGO
Villa Pallavicini, Meucci 3. Second and
fourth Thursdays 10:30 PM-1:30 AM.
DISFONIA DANCING
Via Massarani 6. Saturdays 9 PM

Tel: 02-539-7347

MILONGADEMISAMORES
Via Moncalieri 5. Fridays 10 PM
Tel: 02-2900-4994 / 333 4442839

MODENA

FLORIDA TANGO
"Florida", via Archirola n° 165-41100
Mondays 9 PM-2 AM Tel: 059-394351

NAPOLI

TANGOANGIOINO
Neagora, via F. Giordano 17 (Mergellina)
Fridays. Tel: 348-2622770
NAPOLI TANGO
Via Goethe 7 Fridays 10:30 PM
Tel: 03336-943231

NAXOS (SICILY)

CANTONE DEL FARO
Via Sirina, Fridays. 0942-56-832

PADOVA

LA MILONGA DEL DOMINGO
Dream, Vicolo Fermi, Strada Battaglia,
Zona Bassanello. Fridays 10 PM-4 AM Tel:
348-4439-776 / 347-5790-061

PALERMO

PALERMOTANGO
"I Candelai," Via dei Candelai, 65.
Tuesdays.

PAVIA

LA MILONGA DE RICARDO and INES
Discoteca "Tabu," Bressana Bottarone.
Sundays 9 PM-2 AM
Tel: 0383-379591 / 0349-8435742

PISA

ASSOCIATION DITANGOINTANGO
Hotel Royal Victoria, Lugarno Pacinotti
12. Sundays 9:30 PM-1:30 AM
Tel: 347-8762057 Michela / 347-

2290247 Beppe

RAVENNA

BLUE TANGO DEMOCRATIC MILONGA
Casa del Popolo di Birisano. Milonga
Sundays 9:30 PM.
e-mail: blutango@artiflex.it

REGGIO EMILIA

ASSOCIAZIONE BARRIO DE TANGO
Castello di Arceto. Thursdays 9:30 PM-
1:30 AM Tel/Fax: 0335 8301763
ASSOCIATION RETANGO
Centro insieme, Via Canalina. Sundays
9:30 PM-12:30 AM

ROME

CENTRO DEL TANGO "ASTOR PIAZZOLLA"
via Macerata 9. (between via Prenestina
and via Casilina) Friday 10 PM
Tel: 70301101
TANGO ARGENTINO CARLOS GARDEL
La Maggiolina, Via Bencivenga 1
(Montesacro). Mondays 10 PM-1 AM Tel:
06-86207352
ROMA TANGO
Riachuelo Via di Monte Testaccio 23,
Testaccio. Tuesdays
Tel: 06-7014517 / 339-7999984
"GIARDINO DEL TANGO" (Open air in Summer)
Via degli Olimpionici, 7. (Flaminio area
near Corso di Francia bridge)
Wednesday, Friday and Saturdays 9 PM-
1:30 AM
EL BANDONEON
Via Degli Angeli 146 Wednesday, Fridays
Tel: 338-4366654 / 335-5286769
CAFE LA PALMA
Via Mirri 35. Wednesdays
Tel: 338-4511593
TANGOPOLIS

Via Degli Ausoni 7, 2nd Floor Milonga
Thursdays, Saturdays 10 PM-1 AM
Tel: 06 701 4517

EL FIRULETE
c/o "Alpheus," Sala Momotombo, Via del
Commercio 36 Sundays In front of
gasometer, Ostiense, Pyramide.
Tel: 347-3778646

MEDIA LUZ TEA TANGO
via di S. Gallicano 8. Sundays 6 PM-9:30
PM Tel: 337-803937

ROVERETO

**CENTRO DIDATTICO MUSICA-
TEATRODANZA**
Bar "Ex Caminetto," Piazza delle Erbe,
Ala (TN) Sundays 5:30-11 PM
Tel: 347-4563-609 / 0464-422-655

SAVONA

**LABORATORIO DI TANGO
ARGENTINO**
C/o ARCA Enel via Cimarosa 29r.
Fridays 11:30 PM-2 AM
Tel: 019-81-33-81 Simonetta Franceschi

SENIGALLIA

TANGO
Milonga at "Gratis,", 20 meters from the
train station. Wednesdays 10 PM
Tel: 348-3808-384 / 333-644-9060

SIENA

TEATRO VERDI
via del Commercio 15,
Poggibonsi/Sienna
Once a month Tel: 0577-345503
(Marina Chiarelotto)

**PATRICIA HILLIGES and MATTEO
PANERO (Classes)**
Corte dei Miracoli, via Roma. Fridays
8:30-11:30 PM
e-mail: philig@tin.it

TODI

TRASNOCHANDO
The Tango Center in Umbria, via
Lorenzo Leoni 21, 06059 Todi.
Saturdays from 10 PM-
Tel: 075-894-2008
e-mail: treitman@giotto.org www.giot-
to.org/vettii/tango_todi.html

TURIN

EL BARRIO TANGUERO (Milonga)
Café Procope (milonga) via Juvarra n.15
10:30 PM-2 AM Fridays
Tel: 011 540 675

DA GIAU
Str. Castello Mirafiori, 346 Tuesdays
from 9:30 PM

GARDEN
Str. Val Salice, 4/A Thursdays from
10 PM

L'ARCA
Via Assarotti 6. Wednesdays 9:30 PM

CAFE BLUE
Via Valprato 68. Sundays 10 PM

HIROSHIMA MON AMOUR
Via Bossoli 83 Sundays 10 PM

SALON DE TANGO
Corso Sicilia 12 Saturdays 9:30 PM-
2 AM

TANGOAPERITIVO ARCA
Via Assarotti 6. Saturdays 5-8 PM

TRIESTE

CIRCULO TANGO ARGENTINO
Riva Nazario Sauro 5/d-Muggia
Thursdays 9-11 PM
Tel: 040 306-996 Michaela

UDINE

TANGHITUDINE
Circolo Sottufficiali, vicolo d'Arcano 5.
Wednesdays 9 PM
Also at: villa Giacomelli in Prademano.
Every other Sunday.

VENICE

TANGO MALENA
S. Marco 2507/A-30124. Thursdays
9 PM-midnight
Tel: 041-5226164 Mobile: 333-2716725

LIBERTANGO VENEZIA
Outdoor dancing in front of the beautiful Salute Church on the Canal Grande every Wednesday night at 9:30 PM-Summertime only, so telephone for confirmation. Tel: 041-5244161 Heribert e-mail: hermaier@bora.iuav.it

VERONA—Lake Garda
MALENATANGO
Bar "Il Glicine", C.so Cavour, 50 near Castel Vecchio (centro storico).
Saturdays. Tel: 0347-0551760 Sofia / 0338 2007087

EL CAFFETIN DE TANGO
Piper, Via Marin Fagliero 100. Thursdays 9:30 PM
Tel: 347-7972507 / 348-7328589

JAPAN—0081

NAGOYA
LA MILONGA TANGO CLUB
1-14, Hirose-Cho, Showa-Ku, Nagoya-Shi, Nagoya 466
Tel: 052 731 6797 / 052 852 1211
Mr. Akira Mizuno

TOKYO
DANCE PUB "CANARO"
37-17, Matubara 1-chome, Setagaya-ku, Tokyo Saturdays 6 PM-12 AM
Tel: 03-3325-5424

MILONGUEROS DE TOKYO
Murakami Dance Culture Public, 2nd Floor Sky View Iogi,
5-19-14 Shimoigusa, Suginami-ku.
Sundays once a month.
Tel: 03 39207245

"CANARO" (Milongueros de Tokyo)
Meeting with dance after organised every second and fourth Thursday of the

month. Tel: 03 3325 5424

SUIYOKAI
Organized every Tuesday 6-9 PM and Saturday 1-4:40 PM Contact:
Mr. Shuichi Yuzawa (President) at:
Kamiochiai 1-20-501 Shinjyuku-ku, Tokyo. 161-0034
Tel/Fax: ++81 3 3360 2151

DANCE PRACTICA "MALENA"
Event Hall Musashino, 2 20-3 Honmachi, Kichijoji, Musashino-shi.
Once a month Sunday 5-8:30 PM
Liliana Nakata Tel: 03 3986 8149

MALENA
4F Yamato Dai-3 bldg. 22-23, Saiwai-cho, Chigasaki-shi, Kanagwa.
Tel: 0467-89-3549
e-mail: malenaraq@aol.com

TANGO XX1
B1F, Roppongi Arts City, 3-4-9, Azabudai, Minatoku. Tuesdays and Thursdays 9-11 PM Saturday 7:30-11:30 PM Tel: 03-3584-5545

For additional information on Tango in Japan contact:
Mr. Kouzou Miura, Milongueros de Tokyo
4-18-13, Shakujii dai, Nerima-ku, Tokyo 177, Japan.
Tel: 03 3920 7245 Fax: 03 3920 7330

KOREA—0082
TANGO CAFÉ
Yangchon-myun, Yuhyun-ri, Kimpo, Kyunggi-do (nr. to capital Seoul).
Contact Mr. Kong, Myung-Kyu.
Tel: 11-286-0454

LEBANON—00961
LIBANTANGO
For details of tango activities, contact:
LibanTango, c/o Diversity Centre Beirut Bureau
Eugene andDima Dabbous-Sensenig
Mohammed el Hout Street, Al Jameel Building
No. 712, 3rd Floor, LB-Ras el Nabe'h,

Beirut, Lebanon.
Tel:1 664505 Fax: 1 705355 e-mail:
sensenig@cyberia.net.lb

LITHUANIA—00370

TANGO CLUB
Café "Zaltvykste." Every Sunday. Juan
Eduardo Gimenez
Classes in both Vilnius and Kaunas
Check
website: www.telenormedia.lt/tango

MALTA—00356

ISLA DEL TANGO
Charlotte Stuart, 15, Sqaq ir-Ruzarju,
Gharghur NXR 07, Malta
Tel: 00356 419370 Fax: 00356 320437
E-mail: paynestuart@waldonet.net.mt

MEXICO—0052

MEXICO CITY

ACADEMIA MEXICANA DEL TANGO
Carril 52, 5ta, Urusia Xitla, 1442 Mexico
DF. Jorge Bartalucci
Tel: 011 525 683 4714
GRACIELA ESCOBEDO
Villa Longin 46-7, Col. Cuauhtemoc,
C.P. 06500, Mexico DF. Tel: 546 5680
MONICA BLANCO
Avenida San Jeronimo 1491, Col San
Jeronimo Lidice, CP 110200 Mexico DF.
Tel: 683 4714 / 622 1797
e-mail: mobla@netservice.com.mx
HOTEL VIENNE
2nd Floor, Friday nights starting 9 PM
"BAR ARRAVALERO"
cnr. of Marsella and Dinamarca on
"Colonia Juarez." Fridays at 9pm

NEPAL—00977

KATHMANDU

ANDREAS LEHRKE
Tango Master—offers private classes,
group training, workshops and Tango
functions. Tel: 1-422033
www.kathmandudancers.net

NETHERLANDS— 0031

ALKMAAR

TANGO CAFÉ
Café de Notaris, Houttil 18 Thirrd
Tuesday of month
Tel: 072-5154235 Fred
DE TANGOSTUDIO
Breedstraat 13a. Fridays 8PM-2 AM /
Sundays 5 PM-8 AM
Tel: 072 5154235

AMERSFOORT

TANGO DE BARRIO
De Lieve Vrouwestraat 13. Tuesdays 8:30
PM-midnight
Tel: 0522-440956

AMSTERDAM

LUNA DE TANGO
1st floor, Royal Cafe de Kroon,
Rembrandtplein 17 (Square).
Every Monday 9 PM—1 AM
Tel: 673-1432
DE BADCUYP (Practica for beginners)
Cultural Café Restaurant, Eerste
Sweelinckstraat 10 / corner Albert Cuyp
St. Tuesdays 10 PM-1 AM
MOEDERS MOOISTE
Marie Heinekenplein 5-8- Tuesdays 9.15
PM-12.45 AM
Tel: 6751568
SCHINKELHAVENTHEATER TANGO
Schinkelhavenstraat 27. Wednesdays
9-11:30 PM
Tel: Roland 020-626-1863
LA ISLA DEL TANGO
AMPStudios, KNSMLaan 13. Most
Thursdays 10:30 PM-1.15 AM
Tel: 020-7704884

ACADEMIA DE TANGO
Studio Korte Leidse, Korte
Leidsedwarsstraat 12. Fridays 9:30 PM-
0.45am Tel: 075-6123700 Arjan Sikking

TANGOSCHOOL AMSTERDAM
Nightclub Panama, Oostelijke
Handelskade 4. Fridays 11 PM-3 AM Tel:
020 6256442 info@tangoschool.nl
www.tangoschool.nl

SALON DE LOS SABADOS
Studio Korte Leidse, Korte
Leidsedwarsstraat 12. Saturdays 9:30 PM-
2:30 AM Tel: 075-6123700 Arjan
Sikking

BOKSSCHOOL ALBERT CUYP
Albert Cuypstraat 241. Every third
Saturday 10 PM- 3AM
Tel: 020 6261863

TANGO NIGHT ARA NOVA
Oudezijds Achterburgwal 237. First
Sunday of month 4 PM-9 PM (in Summer
5 PM-10 PM)
Tel: 020-4182451 / 6933354

EAST OF EDEN
Lineausstraat 11a. Third Sunday of
month 4-9 PM
Info Henk or Miriam Tel: 020 4656994

TANGO IN ARTI
Arti et Amicitae, Rokin 112. Fourth
Sunday of month except July, August
and December 4-11 PM
Tel: 020-6257049 / 6751658

**ACADEMIA DE TANGO CRISTO-
FORI**
Prinsengracht 583. 4-9pm Sometimes
on Sundays with orchestra.
Tel: 075-6123700
www.academiadetango.nl

TANGO
Muiderpoorttheater, Tweede ven
Swindenstraat 26. Occasional tango con-
cert with milonga after. Tel: 6925421

APELDOORN
SAM SAM, TANGO CAFÉ
Van Kinsbergenstraat 17. Every last

Sunday Tel: 0575-510244

ARNHEM
FLOR DE FANGO
Wezenstraat 5a, 6811 CR Second
Saturday 9:30 PM-2 AM Every first and
third Sunday 4-9:30 PM
Tel: 026 4459119

LA ZAPADA
Waalstraat 2. Tel: 026-4434598

TANGO PALET
Vale Poort 8, 6811 BN. Sundays
Tel: 026-4450571

CASTRICUM
**PARTY and DANCECENTRUM
CASTRICUM**
Dorpsstraat 72, 1901 EM

DEN HAAG
CAFÉ HET SYNDICAAT
Nieuwe Molstraat 10. 9.00 PM-1 AM
Every Monday and Wednesday.
Tel: 070 3600053

EL PALACIO DEL TANGO
Westeinde 175-G Thursdays 9:30 PM-
1 AM Tel: 070 364814206

DEVENTER
SALON ABRAZO
De Boze Goudvis, Pothoofd 117
Saturdays Tel: 0570-612403

DE WIJK
TANGO DE BARRIO
Wittenweg 43a. Saturdays 8:30 PM-mid-
night Tel: 0522-440956

EINDHOVEN
TANGO TARRO
Chicano's deSwing Planet, Mauritsstraat
12 Thursdays 9 PM Tel:040-2801800

TANGO CAFÉ
Theatercafé't Rozenknopje, Hoogstraat
59. Mondays 9 PM-1 AM
Tel: 402962903

ENSCHEDE

EL TAMANGO TANGO
Jazz Cafe de Tor, Walstraat 21 Tuesday
9:15-11:30 PM
Tel: 053-4777505 www.eltamango.net

GRONINGEN

OCHO DE MAYO
Hoekstraat 42, 9712 AP. Fridays 9 PM-
1:30 AM Tel: 050 3137668
TANGOCENTRUM LA PASION—
Practica
Nieuwe Boteringestraat 64. Tuesday-
Friday 10 PM-1 AM
Tel: 050 3118888
TANGOCAFÉ
Café Overstag, Zuiderdiep 139. Every
fourth Sunday 8PM-1 AM

HAARLEM

TANGO CAFE
Stadscafe, Zijlstraat 56. Mondays 8PM-
midnight Tel: 023-5338238
EL TREN
Tango at the train station every second
Saturday in the first-class lounge.
8 PM-1am. Tel: 020-4890349 / 023-
5338238

LEIDEN

TANGO POR DOS IN LOS
BAILADORES
Middelstegracht 8. Tel: 020-6698696
TANGO
Zalencentrum Antonius, Lange Mare 43.
Tel: 020-4890340

MAASTRICHT

TANGO
SETH Theatre, Tongerseweg 346 9:30
PM- Mondays

MIDDELBURG

TANGO AL AZAR
De Kloveniersdoelen, Achter de
Houttuinen 30.Tel: 0118-615527

NIJMEGEN

TANGO "EL CORTE"
Graafseweg 108, 6512 CH. First
Saturday of month 10 PM and every
Friday 11 PM-2 AM Tel: 024 3233063
TANGO SALON
De Waagh, Grote Markt 26. Third
Sunday of month. 4 PM-8 PM

ROTTERDAM

CUARTITO AZUL
Theater West, Westzeedijk 513 9.15 PM-
1 AM Info: Marieke 010-452-7377
BARRIO DE TANGO
Meyer et Fils, Henegouwerlaan 53b.
Every second Saturday. 9:30 PM-2 AM
Tel: 10-425-3905
VILLA TANGO
Het Heerenhuys, Euromast Park, Baden
Powellaan 12. Sundays 4-10 PM
Tel: 104253905

s'HERTOGENBOSCH

EL CORAZON DANSCENTRUM
Eindhovenlaan 7, 5224 VG. Last
Saturday of month
Tel/Fax: 73 6238560

TILBURG

TANGO GUAPO
Cafe De Roskam, Heuvel 5. 9 PM-
inf: Tango Guapo, Schoolstraat 14, 6512
Nijmegen. Tel: 024-3888310
Also PRACTICA last Saturday of the
month at 8 PM, but phone to confirm.
EL PORTEÑO
Tango in Theater Zaal 16, Carré 16.
Every third Sunday Tel: 013-5368381

UTRECHT

TANGO SCHOOL EL GANCHO
Van Meursstraat 9, 3532 CH Utrecht
Phone for details of tangosalons and
–parties. Tel: 030 2933608
Fax: 030 2960666

TANGOCAFÉ
Hofman Cafe, Janskerkhof 17A
Tuesdays. 9 PM-late
Tel: 030-2933608 Marjon Reinders

TARDE DE TANGO
Winkel van Sinkel Oudergracht 158.
Second Sunday of month
4-11 PM Tel: 030-2933608

*For additional information on tango
in the Netherlands
contact: Jan Dirk van Abshoven
"La Cadena", Postbus 59054, 1040 KB
Amsterdam*
Tel: 020 682 22 03 / Fax: 020 682 23 39
e-mail: info@cadena.demon.nl

NEW ZEALAND— 0064

AUCKLAND

TANGO IN THE PARK
At various bandstands in the Auckland
Parks during the Summer.
Tel: 025-284-6620 / 356-4389
e-mail: bob.ramsey-turner
@nzl.xerox.com.

FUEGO
5 O'Connell Street in the city.
Wednesdays 7:30 -

EL NINO TANGO
El Nino Bar and Grill, 4 Osborne Street,
Newmarket. Sundays 7:30-late.
Tel: 6520-4304

TANGO UNO
Numero Uno Ristorante, 5/335 Lake
Road, Hauraki Cnr. Takapuna. Irregular
Sundays. Tel: 489-2649

WELLINGTON

TANGO LUNCH
Cuba Mall (Lower End), or outside
Fisheye Discs. Wednesdays lunchtime
12-2 PM
Tel: 567-9406 / 021-254-3891 Alex.

WELLINGTON PERFORMING ARTS

CENTRE
36 Vivian Street Every second Friday
7:30 PM Tel: 04 385 8033

LATIN DANCE CLUB
The Cricketer's Arms, 1st fl., corner Tory
and Vivian Sts. Milongas Friday and
Saturday. Tel: 021-254-3891 / 567-9406
Alex White
e-mail: alex_tangofirulete@xtra.co.nz

BIG TANGO NIGHT
Form Studio, 8 Fifeshire Avenue, off
Cambridge Tce.
Wednesdays 8:30-11pm. Tel: 384 3676
VelthuiC@acc.co.nz

NORWAY—0047

BERGEN

TANGO ABRAZO
Kulterhuset USF, Georgernes verft 3.
Tuesdays and Sundays 7 PM-11 PM Tel:
55-34-00-41 / 55-58-2558 Eero Olli
e-mail: Eero.Olli@isp.uib.no

OSLO

OSLO TANGO CLUB
Cosmopolite, Møllergata 26
Tel: 22 29 7501
Tuesdays 8 PM-11:30 PM Monday classes
by Ramon Gimenez.
e-mail: ramontango@
c2i.net www.oslotangoclub.com

SORIA MORIA
Soria Moria Kulturslott, Vogts gate 64
Mondays Tel: 22 15 2570

THURSDAY PRACTICA
Foss Videregående Skole
Tel: 22 04 6989

SUNDAY PRACTICA
Bärdar Danseinstitutt. Tel: 22 600146
(Erik)

TRONDHEIM

TRONDHEIM TANGO KLUBB
Café "Ni muser," Nidarosdomen.
Mondays 9 PM-midnight

PHILLIPINES

MANILLA

TANGO CANYENGUE

Contact Rogelio Mendoza "Ogie" at e-mail: omen@nsclub.net

POLAND—0048

WARSAW

Saturdays: Stodola, ul. Batorego 10. Tel: Joanna Dabrowska 0-601-335097
Sundays: Ochota Cultural Centre, ul. Grojecka 75
Tel: Darnuta Jampolska 8227436
Wed/Sat: Szkola Baletowa, ul. Moliera 2/4 Tel: 8272 592

For further info. e-mail:
elvagabond@hotmail.com or
tangopolo@hotmail.com
Paulina Policzkiewicz Tel: 22-8311659 / 050-1672273

PORTUGAL—00351

LISBON and PORTO

"CLUBE ESTEFÂNIA"

Rua Alexandre Braga no. 24A, Lisbon
Sundays 11:30 PM

"A BARRACA"

Bar do Teatro "A Barraca," Largo de Santos no. 2, Lisbon. Sundays 9 PM
Tel: 96 516 7431 91 413 1055

TANGO PRACTICA

Casa de Lafoes (Rua da Madalena 199) Practica Fridays 10:15 PM to 1 AM

TANGO NIGHTS

Café Teatro Santiago Alquimista (Rua de Santiago, 19-Lisboa) Once a month.
For lessons in Lisbon and Porto: Guillermo and Elina (Argentina), Esquina Argentina de Tango Tel: 21 815 0913 Mobile: 96 239 4552
Fax: 21-846-52-40
Web: www.portango.com

ART and JAZZ TANGO

Art and Jazz Dance Factory, Rua de Santo Amaro (á Estrela), number 34-1°, 1200-803 Lisbon. Fridays at 10:30 PM
Tel: 1-397-9561

RUSSIA— 007

MOSCOW

PRACTICAS

Every Thursday. Tel: 467-2637
Every Friday. Tel: 420-9744

MILONGAS

Ul. Bol'shaya Dmitrovka 16, Kafe "Kofe Inn". Tuesdays 8 PM
Ascheulov pereulok 9, club "Dzen klub". Sundays 8 PM

More info:
Tel: 7095 4209744 (Valentine) or
7095 931 7923 (Sasha) e-mail:
vistgof@hotmail.com

ST. PETERSBURG

TANGO ARGENTINO

Dancing Centre "Visit", 50 Fontanka emb. Tel: 812 164 3190 or 812 164 3090 e-mail: argentintango@mail.ru

SLOVENIA—0038

LJUBLJANA

TANGO

Club Metropol, Kersnikova 6. Tuesday 8-9:30 PM lesson; milonga after. Tel/Fax: 61 752 254

NINA ORESIC (Classes)

Tomacevo 16 (near Gostilna Kovac) Wed. 9-10:30 PM

SOUTH AFRICA— 0027

CAPE TOWN

MARK HOEBEN

Every Tuesday at The Valve. mark-hoeben@icon.co.za

JOHANNESBURG

TANGO SPEAKEASY
Teacher: Cheryl Borkum. Details contact:
cheryl_borkum@worldonline.co.za
Tel: (011) 447-3482 / (011) 880-8095
Fax: (001) 305-5601
Lessons Mondays 6-8:30 PM Practica
8:30-10pm
GARDELS
Teacher: Ralph Kahn Venue Tanz Cafe.
Tel: 082-4633128

SPAIN—0034

ALBACETE

GOMINA TANGO CLUB
Pub "Commodore", C/Gaona 14.
Last Sunday of month. Tel: 967-604-734

BARCELONA

LA MILONGA DE PATIO DE TANGO
C/Maspons 6 (Graciá)—Esbart Lluis
Millet 11 PM-3 AM
Saturdays 2nd and 4th of month-Tel: 93
412-0165
CASA VALENCIA
C/Corcega 335 (diagonal y Paseo de
Gracia) opposite the metro Diagonal:
Thursdays 10 PM-1 AM
Tel: 93-427-1748
BAILONGU
Pasaje d'Utset 11-13 First Saturday of
month 11 PM-2:30 AM
Tel: 93-2471602 e-mail: bailongu@
nexo.es www.bailongu.com
CLUB 7 TO 9
Pso de Gracia 46. Sundays 10:30 PM-
1 AM Tel: 609-7169-40
BARCELONA PIPA CLUB
Plaza Real 3. Tuesdays 10:30 PM-1 AM
Tel: 93-302-4732
EL DESBANDE
Casa de Murcia, C/Puertaferrisa, 21.
Fridays 11:30 PM-3 AM
Tel: 93-302-6232 / 0659731756
BESOS BRUJOS (Casa de Tamar)
C/Mendez Nuñez 18, 2° 3a.

Fridays/Saturdays 9 PM-12 AM
Tel: 93-315-1965
CAFÉ DE LES ARTES
C/Valencia 234. Wednesdays and
Sundays 8.30 PM-1.30 AM
Tel: 93-213-17-82 / 93-436-90-76
AGUA DE LUNA
C/Villadomat 211 Sundays 8 PM
Tel: 609-716-940 /41

BILBAO

Café BOULEVARD
Paseo de Arenal, 1° planta. First
Saturday of month. 11 PM-

CANARY ISLANDS
LA PALMA

CLUB DE TANGO Y MILONGA
Holiday courses and other activities,
with accommodation
December-March. Fax: 922-408020
Carlos and Nanna

LANZAROTE and FUERTEVEN-TURA

TANGO
Classes, shows and milongas with
Argentine teachers Mariana Leiton and
Mauricio Carlsen.
Tel: +34 6302 13913
www.danzasargentinas.4t.com
e-mail: m_leiton@yahoo.com

TENERIFE

PUERTOS DEL SUR
With teacher Marcos Schulkin. Rotating
milongas every Saturday at 11 PM
www.puertosdelsur.es.fm
e-mail: puertosdelsur@mixmail.com.
Mobile: 686320061 Classes "Stage" La
Higuera, 2. La Laguna. Wednesday-
Friday 8-11 PM, Sundays 6-10 PM Tel:
922-266-176

CASTELLÓN

TANGO BAR
Sala Latino's, Polígono Sur. Sundays
7:30-10 PM

CARTAGENA
CLUB DE LA AUTORIDAD PORTU-ARIA
Plaza de la Isla (junto a la Lonja). Last Friday of month 11 PM-2 AM
Tel: 968-162023

DONOSTIA—SAN SEBASTIAN
LA MILONGA DE ARRABAL
Cafeteria "La Zurriola," Avenida La Zurriola Thursdays 10:30 PM-12:30 AM
LA MILONGA DE AGATA
"Dover latino," c/Loyola 4. Sundays 9:30-midnight

GRANADA
GRANADA TANGO CLUB
Cafe Continental, C/Seminario, 3. Thursdays and Fridays 10:30 PM-
Tel: 649-26-36-54

JEREZ DE LA FRONTERA (Cádiz)
A MEDIA LUZ
C/Avila 19. Third Saturday of month.
Tel: 956-34-9132

MADRID
LA TANGOTECA
Palacio de Gaviria. C/. Arenal, 9. Wednesdays 11PM
Tel: 526 60 69 / 547 69 03 Marcela and Marcelo
LA MILONGA
Sala Cha-3, Plaza de San pol de Mar, s/n. Tel: 541 9090
Thursdays 10:30 PM-3 AM Sundays noon-3 PM
"BUT"
C/Barceló 11. Metro: Tribunal. Mondays 11 PM-2:30 AM (Class ½ hr. before). (Pablo and Beatriz) Tel: 91-448-0698
GOMINA TANGO CLUB
Hotel Meliá Madrid, c/Tutor, 14. Tuesdays 11 PM-3 AM
Tel: 616-815-813

TANGOMANIA
Caché Disco, 24 Orense St. Tuesday 10 PM-2:30 AM
LA ALTERNATIVA
Discoteca Cheyenne, Avnda. Del Brasil 5,4. Sundays 8 PM Tel: 616-815-813
THE SPORTSMAN
Alcalá 65. Saturdays 7-11 PM
Tel: 915-766-908
TARDES DE TANGO EN EL RITZ
Hotel Ritz, Plaza de la Lealtad 5- 28014 Madrid. First two Sundays of month. 7:30-11 PM Tel: 629052251

MAJORCA
TANGO EN CAN PASTILLA
Discoteca "Babalu." 9717-44167

SABADELL
TU Y YO TANGO
Discoteca Concord, C/San Cugat 100. Fridays at 11 PM
Tel: 93 717 98 43 / 696-789-451

SANTANDER (Cantabria)
Café TANGO
C/San Sebastian 5 Fridays 11 PM-12:30 AM Tel: 942-22-14-32

SAN SEBASTIAN
LA MILONGA DEL "ARRABAL"
Cafeteria La Zurriola, Avenida La Zurriola 41. Thursday 10:30 PM-12:30 AM
LA MILONGA DE "AGATA"
Dover Latino, C/Loyola 4. Sundays 9:30 PM-midnight

SEVILLE
MILONGA 2000
Discoteca "Pandau", Avda. de Maria Luisa. Tuesdays (Practica) Wednesdays (Milonga) 10:30 PM Tel: 95 476 1140

TUDELA
LA BODEGUILLA
Calle Concarera, junto a la Plaza Nueva. Sundays 8:30 PM-1 AM

VALENCIA

GLAMOUR
C/Honorato Juan 12. Tuesdays
andSundays 8:30 PM-12 AM
CLUB TANGO VALENCIA
Restaurant Paco Polit, c/Padre Anton
Martin. Sat. 11 PM-3 AM
ASOCIACIÓN ALGIROS
C/Actor Llorens 39. Fridays 11 PM-
2 AM Tel: 96-369-2193
PUB MATISSE
C/Ramon de Campoamor 60. Saturdays
9-11 PM

VALLADOLID

DISCOTECA ASKLEPIOS
C/Torrecilla 14 Wednesdays 10 PM-
2 AM

ZARAGOZA

PRACTICA OF DOMINGO REY
Restaurant Casablanca, via Hispanidad
15-17. Tuesdays and Wednesdays
10 PM-midnight. Tel: 619-25-16-76
MILONGA DEL ARRABAL
Plaza de San Gregorio 2-4. Saturdays 10
PM Sundays 9 PM Tel: 97-659-7132
*MADRID For more information
on tango in Madrid, contact:
Asociacion Amigos del Tango
C/ de los Poetas, 37 4° B, 28032 Madrid
Tel/Fax: (91) 531 38 40
Internet: http://www.esto.es/tango
For more info. on Tango in Barcelona
contact: Patio de Tango, Campo Arriaza,
59 3o, 2a, 08020 Barcelona
Tel:++34 313 19 96 Fax: ++34 302 08 39*

SWEDEN—0046

HELSINGBORG

TANGORAMA
Folkets Hus B-sal, Söderg. 65. Tuesdays
7-11 PM

LUND

KLUBBEN TANGO
Stora Gråbrödersgatan 13. Saturdays
6-10 PM Tel: 046-211-2565
PRACTICA MICHAEL HANSEN
Dag Hammarskjöldsv 4. Tuesdays
6-10 PM

MALMÖ

TANGO ASSOCIATION CAMARIN
Cafi Barbro, Norra Skolgatan 10B.
Every first Saturday of the month.
7 PM-2 AM Fridays 8 PM-midnight
LIBERTANGO—Practica
Vattenverksvägen 44 Thursdays 8-11 PM

STÅNGBY

LA PRADERA—TANGO TRENTAN
Gamla Stationshuset Wednesdays 8:30
PM-12:30 AM

STOCKHOLM

TANGO CLUB
Restaurant "Pelé", Upplandsgatan 18.
Saturday 8 PM-1 AM Tel: 08 319700 to
make sure it is Argentine tango night.
Subway: Odenplan
TANGO PRACTICA
Brunnsgatan 26 Sunday 6-9 PM

UPPSALA

TANGO CAMBALACHE
Tuesdays at: Grand, Trädgårdsgaten 5.
6:30-10:30 PM Fridays at: Drabanten,
Bangårdsgatan 13 7-11 PM
Tel: 018-553895
TANGOCAFE
Ekocaféet, Drottninggaten 5. Sundays
2-5pm

SWITZERLAND— 0041

BADEN

LAVABLE-TANGO IN DER WASCHBAR
Theater am Brennpunkt, Gartenstrasse

11, 5400. Thursdays: 9 PM-midnight
Info: Heinz and Petra Tel: 056 667 11
46

BASEL
TANGO IN RESTAURANT "DREI KÖNIGE"
Kleinhüningeranlage 39. 9:15 PM-
1 AM Fridays Tel: 061-381-1702

BERN
PUBLIC TANGO
Restaurant "Public," Friedheimweg 18,
3007- Wednesdays 8 PM
VIENTO SUR
Club "Viento Sur," Lerchenweg 33,
3000. Fridays 9PM-1am and every first
and third Saturday of month at 9 PM
TANGO-GROOVE
Rägeboge Dance Centre, Laupenstr. 18,
3008. Mondays 9:30 PM (Eric and Jeusa)
VILLA BERNAU
Villa Bernau, Seftigenstr. 243, 3084
Wabern. Wednesdays 9 PM-midnight Tel:
031- 961-6038 / Fax 031-961-6030

BULLE
TANGO
Contact: Mario Tel: 4126 9131858

CHUR
CHUR TANGO
Palace Bar, Masanserstr. 14. Sundays 8
pm.-midnight Tel: 081 2527275

GENEVA
CHEZ ALEJANDRO
"Ecole Mambo Rock," Sunday nights,
8:30 PM-midnight
e-mail: tangogeneve@hotmail.com

KONSTANZ-D
TANGO LIBRE
Gebhardshalle, St. Gebhard-Str. 6
Wednesdays 9 PM Fridays
Tel: 7531 694429

RHEINTERRASSEN-TANGO
Café Rheinterrassen, Spanierstr. 5. Every
other Sunday 10 PM-1 AM

LAUSANNE
TANGOFOLIE
Av. De Severy 1. Thursdays 10 PM-mid-
night Tel: 079-658-64-70
www.tangofolie.ch
LA MILONGA CELESTE
La Factoria, av. Tribunal-Federal 2. First
Sunday of month 7-9 PM
Tel: (0)21-321-3835 / (0)79 708 6829
www.carte-blanche.ch
e-mail: bluelezard@carte-blanche.ch or
annamarie@gotan.ch
LA MILONGA DE ALEGRIA
"Club Chilien", Avenue Jean Jacques
Mercier 6 (next to Flon metro)) Tuesdays
8:30-midnight Shawn and Cathy de
Mandrot Tel: 079-637-64-54
e-mail: alegria@gotan.ch / www.gotan.ch

LOCARNO
TANGO LOCARNO
Grand Hotel Locarno, Via Sempione,
6600 Locarno-Muralto. Last Tuesday of
month at 8:30 PM- Tel: 091-743-2418
Associazione Amici del Tango.

LUGANO
LUGANO TANGO
Sala Topo Rosso (ex-Birelli), first and
third Saturday of month Tel: 079-413-
6585 (Benito) 078-6060257 (Vincenzo)

LUZERN
LA LUZ DEL TANGO
Bar 57, Haldenstr. 57. Last Sunday of
month. 8PM-2:30 AM
Tel: 041 2101163

NIEDERLENZ
TANGENTE
Mühlestr 6. Monday practica 8 PM
Second and fourth Saturday
milonga Tel: 62 892 14 98/56 442 13 43

SOLOTHURN

TANGO CLUB SCHWEIZ

Classes, weekends, intensive courses, holiday courses and milongas. Carlos E. Matheos and Nanna Zernack Tel/Fax: ++41 32 392 1541

ST. LEGIER

TANGO

Every Sunday 7-10pm. Tel: 021 9225974 Philippe

WETZIKON

EVITA BAR

Zurcherstr.27 Wednesday 9-12 PM Tel:+41 01 3212772

WINTERTHUR

HOT-POT

Technikumstrasse 60. First Saturday of month 8 PM Tel: 052 2336494

ZURICH

CLUB SILBANDO

Geroldstrasse 5, CH-8005. Monday: 9 PM-midnight, Friday: 10 PM-2 AM Tel: (1) 271 6264 (Daniel Ferro) or (1) 493 4732 (Rolf Schneider)

A MEDIA LUZ (at Garufa)

Pfingstweidstrasse 10, 8005. Wednesday 10 PM Tel: (0) 1 241 4961 (Daniel Montangero)

MILONGA TANGOTRA

Pfingstweidstr. 12, 8005. Saturday 9 PM-2 AM Tel: 01 273 11 36 (Fabio Valeri)

For details about tango in Zurich contact ift—Tango, Albertstrasse 11, 8005 ZurichTel: 0041 (1) 271 6264 Fax: 0041 (1) 271 6364 E-mail: ift@tango.ch www.tango.ch For details about some tango events/classes etc in Switzerland and nearby France, SHAWN KOPPENHOEFER of Lausanne can help. Tel (41)79-637-64-54 e-mail: shawn@gotan.ch

TURKEY—0090

ISTANBUL

HOTEL ARMADA

Ahirkapi—sahilyolu Sunday evenings with Umit Iris and Monday evenings with Serdar Sungar. Tel: 532-664-8836

TANGUISIMO WITH MR. TANJU YILDIRIM

Milonga in Tanguisimo: Wednesdays 9 PM-1 AM Milonga in Grand Hotel Halic: Fridays 9 PM-3 AM Tel: 216-336-0022 Mobile: 0532 2518381 www.tanguisino.com

ISTANBUL SANAT MARKEZI

Milongas with Aysegul Betil on Sunday afternoons. Tel: 532-371-7989

MÜHENDISHANE

Taskisla—ITU Alumni Association. Milonga Monday evenings

TANGONEON

Milongas on Saturdays with Cetin Cengiz Tel: 532-291-9982

ANKARA

Contact: Merih Maraplyoolu Tel: 3124460136 Fax: 3124462961 e-mail: merihc@aydiner.com.tr

BAILA TANGO CONTACT DETAILS (Metin Yazir)

Istanbul: Tel: 212-211-11-41 e-mail: Istanbul@bailatango.com Eskisehir: Tel: 532-683-73-06 e-mail: Eskisehir@bailatango.com Ankara: Tel: 532-357-67-49 e-mail: ankara@bailatango.com

UNITED KING-DOM—0044

MILONGAS

BELFAST

Contact Rory O'Connor, Clarke's Dance Studios, Donegall Street Tel: (0)1232 241949

BRISTOL

TANGO AZUL
Oddfellows Hall, 20 West Park, (nr.
BBC), Clifton. First three Fridays of
month 7:30-11:30 PM Tel: Janet 0117-
9622710 Andrew 01225-423008 Iwona
0117-3774129

CAMBRIDGE

TANGO BAR
Centre at St. Paul's, corner of Hills Rd.
and St. Paul's Rd. Tuesdays 9 PM-11 PM
(Classes at 7 PM and 8 PM)
Tel: 01223 572 795 (Stephanie) /
522 214 (Mike)
e-mail: esor_ekim@hotmail.com
TANGAMENTE
Unitarian Church Hall, corner of
Emmanuel Rd. and Victoria St.
Every second and fourth Saturday of
month. 7-11:15 PM Class followed by
dancing. Tel: 01223 721344 Sam
e-mail: sw5@mrc-lmb.cam.ac.uk

CARDIFF

**TANGO Y NADA MAS (Cardiff
Argentinian Tango Club)**
The Village Hall, Heol Syr Lewis,
Morganstown, nr. Cardiff Thursdays
7:30-11 PM Beginners and Intermediates.
Tel: 01633-440706 Mike

CHICHESTER

Adriana—Murray Hall, University
College Tel: 0958-277462

DEVON

TANGO OBLIVION
Salons once a month. Contact Ruth for
details: Tel: 01803 868302
e-mail: z.ruth@members.shines.net

DUBLIN

**DUBLIN ARGENTINE TANGO
SOCIETY**

Turks Head, Temple Bar, Parliament
Street, Dublin 2. Sundays 7:30 PM
(except Bank Holidays). Tel: see below.
**DUBLIN ARGENTINE TANGO
SOCIETY**
Mother Redcaps Tavern, Back Lane,
opposite Christchurch Cathedral, Dublin
2. Tuesdays Salon 9-11 PM
Tel: 00353 86 316 6333
*Info: Dublin Argentine Tango Society
c/o 136 Tongelee Road, Raheny, Dublin 5,
Ireland Tel: 00353 86 316 6333
DURSLEY (Gloucestershire)*
**DURSLEY GLOUCESTERSHIRE
TANGO CLUB**
Dursley Community Centre, Rednock
Drive. 1st and 3rd Saturday of month. 7-
10 PM Tel:01594 826 354 /
07971 513 639 (Laurie)

EAST KENT

KENTANGO
St. Nicholas-at-Wade, Classes, practicas,
milongas. Tel: 01843 861066

EDINBURGH

OUTHOUSE TANGO
The Outhouse, Broughton Street Lane.
Wednesdays 9 PM-12 PM
Tel: 557-5217 Steve. (Class before
salon)
EL PORTEÑO
Club Java, Commercial Street, Leith.
Thursdays 9 PM-12 PM
Class beforehand Tel: 557-5217 Steve
BARACOA
Victoria Street, Sundays 5 PM-10 PM
(Intro. Class 5:30-6 PM free)
THE COUNTING HOUSE
The Counting House, West Nicholson
Street, 6-14 New Street Milonga and
Practica Tuesdays 8 PM-11 PM
Tel: 070070-82646
DANCE FOR ALL STUDIOS
106 St. Stevens Street, Stockbridge.

Thursdays 10 PM-midnight
(Classes 7:45 and 9 PM)
LA SALIDA (Salon)
Last Saturday of the month. Dance for all
Studios. Phone for details.
Tel: 0700-7082-2646 (Toby Morris)
More information from:
Edinburgh Tango Society
e-mail: info@edinburghtango.org.uk
web: http://www.edinburghtango.org.uk
Toby Morris, 20 South Lauder Road,
Edinburgh, EH9 2NA
Tel: 070070-82646

ENFIELD
TANGO BAR
The Townhouse, 48 London Road.
Thursdays 8:30-11 PM
Tel: 0208-372-8150
e-mail: tango@dancematrix.com

FAREHAM (Hants)
SALON TANGO
Catisfield Memorial Hall, Catisfield Lane,
(Junction 9 M27 direction Fareham)
Monthly on Saturdays. Please ring for
dates. Contact Brian and Jackie 01329
280530
e-mail: salontango@cwcom.net

GLASGOW
TANGOGLASGOW
St. Francis Centre, 405 Cumberland
Street. Class and practica.
Tel: 0141 942 1484
e-mail: tangoglasgow@ukonline.co.uk

HARROW
TANGO ARGENTINO
Harrow Regal Dance Centre, Top Floor,
314 Station Road. Tuesdays 10:30 PM-
midnight. Class before
Tel: 01923 210016 Paul and Annette

KINGSTON UPON THAMES
TANGO ARGENTINO
Kingston Dance Studio, Richmond Road
(over Gala Social Club). One Sunday
and Last Saturday of the month and
every Thursday. Alfredo for details.
Tel/Fax: 020 8394 1610

LANCASTER
LANCASTER TANGO
Polish Centre, Nelson Street, after
monthly workshop, first Sunday of the
month. Also practicas Wednesday
evenings. For details: Jessica Abrahams
e-mail: j.abrahams@lancaster.ac.uk

LEEDS
TANGO CAMINITO LEEDS
The Liberal Club, Woodhouse Street,
Hyde Park. Tuesdays 8 PM-11 PM
(Practica followed by dance)
Info: Sven/Jutta: 0113-2611096
e-mail: sven.plein@leedsth.nhs.uk
www.tangoforfun.co.uk

LEICESTER
TANGO PRACTICE GROUP
Friends Meeting House, Clarendon Park.
Every other Wednesday at 7:30 PM
Visiting tangueros most welcome.
Contact Pablo 0116 2702572
e-mail: kin@le.ac.uk
CLUB DE TANGO CAMINITO
29/31 New Bond Street. Sunday 25th
June. 9-11 PM Regular dates to follow.
Phone for details Tel: 0116-2511084 /
2693618 John Crewe

LONDON
SUNDAY
THE FACTORY DANCE CENTRE
407 Hornsey Road, N19. 8:30-11:30 PM
Tel: 020 7272 1122
FOREVER PIAZZOLLA TANGO
Sunday tango soirée last Sunday of the
month. Contact Tel: 020 8291 4977

Mobile: 07703 942 690
Fax: 020 8291 1628
e-mail: federico@tango-federico.co.uk /
www.tango-federico.co.uk

TUESDAY

FUNKYMONKEY TANGO
Funky Munky, 25 Camberwell Church
Street, SE5. 7:30 PM-9.45 PM plus practi-
ca/milonga 'til after midnight
Tel: 020 7733 0262 / 07944 128 739

CHRISTINE'S
The Museum Wine Bar, 2, Montague
Street, WC1. (Under the White Hall
Hotel, by British Museum) 8-11 PM free.
Tel: 020 7837-9720

"LAS ESTRELLAS"
2-3 Inverness Mews, W2. 9:30 PM-midnight Tel: 020 7221 8170 / 5038

TANGOTROIKA CLUB
Phoenix Pub, Cavendish Square. W1 9
PM-11.15 PM Classes before from 7:30 PM
Tel: 020-8368-3358 Dave 07710-
179.174 Kevin

WEDNESDAY

ZERO HOUR
The Dome, Boston Arms, Dartmouth
Park Hill, N19. 9 PM-midnight
Tel: Mobile: 07966 457 863
e-mail: biljana@ftech.co.uk

FOREVER PIAZZOLLA TANGO
Chiswick Town Hall, Chiswick High
Road, Chiswick. 9-11pm Class beforehand. Tel: 020 8291 4977 Mobile:
07703 942 690 Fax: 020 8291 1628
e-mail: federico@tango-federico.co.uk /
www.tango-federico.co.uk

THURSDAY

THE TANGO CLUB
Bilongo, 56 Bondway, SW8. 9 PM until
late. Tel: 0207 407-8027
e-mail: info@TheTangoClub.com
www.TheTangoClub.com

FOREVER PIAZZOLLA TANGO
Quintin Kynaston School, Marleborough
Hill, St. Johns Wood. 9:30-11:30 PM

Class beforehand. Tel: 020 8291 4977
Mobile: 07703 942 690
Fax: 020 8291 1628
e-mail: federico@tango-federico.co.uk /
www.tango-federico.co.uk

TANGO CULTURE
The Dimson Hall, 141 Battersea Church
Road, SW11. (near Battersea Bridge)
Bus: 239 9:30 PM 'til late
Tel: 0870 723 0040 tangoculture@
hotmail.com

FRIDAY

TANGO THE ARGENTINO WAY
The London Welsh Centre, 157, Grays
Inn Road, London, WC1. 8-10:30 PM
Tel: 020 7720 7608

**SPIRIT OF THE SOUTH (Closed until
April 2002)**
The Dimson Hall, 141, Battersea Church
Road, SW1. 10:30 PM-3 AM
Tel: 0792 9550924 / 020 7585 2773
Anthony or Lorna. Buses: 19, 49, 239,
319 or 345 to Battersea Bridge

SATURDAY

EL ONCE CLUB DE TANGO
The Crypt, St. James Church,
Clerkenwell Close, Clerkenwell Green,
EC1. (Tube: Farringdon) Second and
fourth Saturday of each month
Tel: 020 7582 0910
e-mail: elonce@dircon.co.uk
www.elonce.dircon.co.uk

"LAS ESTRELLAS"
2-3 Inverness Mews, W2. 9:30 PM-midnight Tel: 020 7221 8170

JONET'S TANGO SALON
Upstairs at Joice's Irish Bar, Connell
Crescent, Park Royal, W5. First and
third Saturday of month. 9 PM-late. Tube:
Park Royal.

CORRIENTES
Mary Ward Hall, 5 Tavistock Place, WC1
8:45 PM-1 AM Tube: Russell Square Tel:
020 77384 404/ 07957 160521 danza-
latina.uk@virgin.net

MANCHESTER
ZUMBAR MEXICAN RESTAURANT
14 Oxford Road (Upstairs), opposite
BBC. Practica on Wednesday nights
Tel: 01706 641177 Frank Smith.
TANGO SALON
Brevent, 201 Urmston Lane, Stretford.
Contact Charmaine for details:
Tel/Fax: 0161-865-3070 / 07885-
476462
e-mail: charmaine@brevent.fsnet.co.uk

NEWCASTLE
TANGO
The National Glass Centre, Liberty Way,
Sunderland, SR6 0GL. Intro class 8-9 PM
and milonga. 9-11 PM Contact Chie
Nakatani
e-mail: nakatani@onetel.net.uk

NORWICH
TANGO NORWICH
Kier Hardie Hall, St. Gregory's Alley (off
Pottergate). Wednesdays 8 PM
Tel: 01603 443559 John Groves
e-mail: Norrdance@aol.com

OXFORD
OXFORD TANGO GROUP
The Meeting House, 43 St. Giles Fridays
7-10:30 PM Beg./Int/Practica
Tel: 01491-681484 (Roger) / 01865-
202100 (Gael) /
07968-397347 (Peter-OU Dancesport
Club)
TANGOSCENE OXFORD
Sunningwell Village Hall (opp. Church),
Sunningwell. Saturdays once a month—
16/9, 7/10, 18/11, 16/12, 20/1 Tel:
01865-391672 Brian

PORTSMOUTH
TANGO PARA TODOS
Friendship House, Elm Grove, Southsea,
Hants. PO5 1JE Alternate Tuesdays :
milonga 9:30-10:30 PM (classes before)
Brian/Fiona Tel: 01703 693026 or

Margaret/Neil 02392 610269
e-mail: tango@freechariot.co.uk /
www.TangoUK.co.uk
**HEATHER KEAL SCHOOL OF
DANCING**
11b, Alliance House, 14 St. Mary's Rd.,
Second. Saturday of each month 8-10 PM
Tel: 023 9229 6069

READING
TANGO AT THE RISING SUN
The Rising Sun Arts Centre, 30 Silver
Street, RG1 2ST. (Close to junction of
London Rd. and London Street)
Thursdays after class at 8:45pm Sunday
TANGO TEA DANCE every third
Sunday.
Tel: Larry Watson 0118 9866788

SOUTHAMPTON
TANGOUK@TLC
Ex-servicemen's Club, Archers Road,
Southampton. Every Tuesday Milonga
9:30-11 PM (classes before)
Tel: Tracie Gooch 07889 288368 or
Steve and Debbie 01962 881576
e-mail: tango@grafix.co.uk /
www.TangoUK.co.uk

TOTNES
TANGO TOTNES
St. Mary's Church Hall. Thursday
evenings or Sundays.Tel: 01803-868302
e-mail: z.ruth@members.shines.net

YORK
TANGO YORK
Guppy's, 17 Nunnery Lane. All Fridays
except first of month. 8 PM
Tel: 01904 622879
john@johnbakeronline.co.uk

URUGUAY—00598
MONTEVIDEO
JOVENTANGO
Rio Branco # Soriano 956. 6-9 PM

LA VIEJA CUMPARSITA
Carlos Gardel 1181
OMAR CORREA
Tel: (2) 902 5039 (teacher)

USA—001

ALASKA
ANCHORAGE
LA MILONGA MARIPOSA
Pioneer School House, 437 West 3rd
Avenue. Every third Saturday of month.

ARIZONA
TUCSON
Call John Dahlstrand for activities in
TUCSON Tel: 602-622-5095 or
602-940-6432 x214 Bruss Bowman
TANGO ZONE
1517 West Prince Avenue. Friday and
Saturday
TANGO
Sheraton El Conquistador Hotel, 10000
N. Oracle Rd., N. Tucson. Thursdays
Tel: 520-498-1573

CALIFORNIA
LOS ANGELES
CLUB DANZARIN
Londance Studio, 3625 W. MacArthur
Blvd., #307-308, Santa Ana, Orange
County. Sundays 8 PM-midnight
Tel: 714-837-0440
**ARGENTINE ASSN. OF LOS ANGE-
LES**
2100 N. Glenoaks Blvd. Burbank.
Sundays 7-11 PM
Practica Wednesdays 7:30-9:30 PM
Tel: 818-567-0901
TANGO PASIÓN
12215 Ventura Bl., Studio City Tuesdays
8:30 PM-midnight Tel: 818-752-7333
TANGO HOLLYWOOD
Hollywood Dance Studio, 817 N.
Highland (1¹/₂ blk. N. of Melrose),

Hollywood. Wednesdays 9-11 PM
Tel: 818-752-7333
NORAH'S PLACE
5667, Lankershim Bl., No. Hollywood
dance. Fridays 6 PM-1 AM and show and
classes on Saturdays from 7:30 PM Tel:
818-980-6900
**YOLANDA and MICHAEL'S BAILON-
GO**
1941 Westwood Blvd. (LA Dance
Experience), Westwood. Fridays 9 PM-1
AM First and third Friday and first and
last Saturday of month
Tel: 818-244-2136
EL ENCUENTRO
4633 Van Nuys Blvd. (1 blk. South
Ventura fwy), Sherman Oaks. Saturdays
9 PM-1 AM Tel: 818-252-3320
e-mail: latango@hotmail.com
SALON RECUERDO
Culver City Masonic Lodge, 9635 Venice
Blvd. (between Overland and Main).
Thursdays 8 PM-midnight
Tel: 310-666-9280 Hector Zeballos.
OLD PASADENA
Romanesque Room, Green Hotel, Old
Pasadena. Mondays: Class 6:30-7:30 PM
Milonga 7:30 PM-
Tel: 626-794-8713 Jorge Gonzales-
Becerra
ORANGE COUNTY
ORANGE COUNTY TANGO
The Dance Partner Dance Studio, 347 E.
Grove Avenue, Orange. 9 PM- Classes
from 7 PM Tel: 714-901-4007
NOCHE DEL TANGO
DanScene Studio in Orange County,
2980 McClintock way, Costa Mesa. First
and second Saturday of month. 8 PM-
12:30 AM Tel: 949-833-1844
SAN DIEGO
LA ACADEMIA, 6904 Miramar Road,
Suites 109/110, CA 92121.
Tel: 619 689 2422

SAN FRANCISCO

SUNDAY

TANGO ON BROADWAY
Broadway Studios, Studio 435, 435
Broadway, San Francisco. 9 PM-midnight
Tel: 415-468-7777

TUESDAY

RAMILONGA
El Valenciano, 1153 Valencia St. San
Francisco. 8 PM-midnight
Tel: 415-978-0878

TANGO ALLEGRO
Allegro Ballroom, 5855 Christie Ave.
Emeryville. Every second and fourth
Tuesday. Tel: 510-655-2888

WEDNESDAY

ROBERTO and JOCELYNE'S TANGO
Italian Athletic Club, 1630 Stockton.
6-9 PM Tel: 415-681-4402

THURSDAY

LA MARIPOSA
2424 Mariposa Street, San Francisco.
Class and Milonga 8:30-midnight.
Tel: 415 239 7002 (Victor)
415 824 7006 (Christy)

FRIDAY

THE FRIDAY MILONGA
Monte Cristo Club, 136 Missouri
Str.(@17th), San Francisco. (Excl. fourth
Friday) 7 PM-midnight (Class and Salon)
Tel: 415-641-0703

LA TANGUERIA
FairFax Women's Club, 46 Park (Marin
County), 9-midnight fourth Friday each
month. Tel: 415-456-4373

LOS ALTOS MILONGA
American Legion, 347 1st St. off San
Antonio Rd. Los Altos. 8:30 PM-
midnight Tel: 510-889-1672

MISSION BLUE MILONGA
Mission Blue Centre, Brisbane 9 PM-midnight

MILONGA IN FRESNO
Dance Works Studio. Third Friday
8-10 PM Tel: 559-226-8010

SATURDAY

MISSION BLUE MILONGA
Mission Blue Centre, Brisbane 9 PM-midnight. Every first Saturday

LA MILONGA DE NORA
Second Saturday each month: San
Francisco International Centre, 50 Oak
Street (between VanNess and Franklin)
3rd floor. 9 PM-2 AM
Tel: 510-482-2524

LA MILONGA DE LOS RIOS
Young Ladies Institute, 1400 27th St. @
N, Sacramento 8 PM-midnight. every fifth
Saturday Tel: 916-991-3193

THE DANCEASY MILONGA
The Danceasy, 9951 San Pablo Ave. El
Cerrito First, third and fifth Sat. 8 PM-
midnight Class and milonga
Tel: 510-524-9100

MILONGA AT THE MASONIC
Masonic Lodge, 890 Church St.
Mountain View. 9 PM-1 AM Every fourth
Saturday Tel: 650-368-3114

LA MILONGA DE JEANNE
La Fayette Veterans Hall, 3491 Mt.
Diablo Blvd. Every second Saturday 8:30
PM-1 AM Class and salon
Tel: 510-283-0191

LA RAYUELA—HOPSCOTCH
The Beat, 2560 9th Street, Berkeley.
Every fourth Saturday All-night milonga
10:30 PM-dawn.

MILONGA DE CARMEL
Sunset Center Scout House, Mission and
8th, Carmel. Second Saturday 8:30 PM
Tel: 831-372-4062

EL 2 POR 4
The Dance Spectrum, 1707 So. Bascom
Av., Campbell. Fourth Saturday of
month. 9 PM-1 AM Tel: 408-920-0975

MILONGA BY THE RIVER
128 J Street (upstairs), Old Sacramento.
Second and fourth Saturday
Tel: 916-443-7008

GOLDEN GATE MILONGA

Golden Gate Yacht Club, 1 Yacht Rd. on the Marina. First, third and fifth Saturdays 9 PM-1 AM
Tel: 415-332-0935
SATURDAY MATINEE MILONGA
Golden Gate Yacht Club, 1 yacht Rd. on the Marina. Fourth Saturday 5 PM-9 PM

The information regarding tango in North California has been taken from the LA MILONGUITA TANGO ACTIVITIES LIST compiled and distributed by POLO TALNIR. Many thanks go to Polo, who can be reached at Tel: 415-326-1060. e-mail: polo@informix.com Web:http://bdsweb.ballroom.com/polo.htm

CAROLINA
MI-PALS ARGENTINE TANGO
Knights of Columbus, New Hope Road, Raleigh, North Carolina. Saturdays 8:30 PM Tel: 919-365-7837

COLORADO
BOULDER
KAKES TANGO
KAKES STUDIO, 2115 Pearl Street, Boulder. Class and Practica 5:30-8 PM
Contact: Gabriela Carone
Tel: 303-492-8267 Fax: 303-492-8386
TANGO PRACTICA
Thursdays 7:30-10 PM Fridays 7-9 PM Contact: Francisco Quiroz. (303) 616-8371
DENVER
MILONGA MERCURIO
Mercury Café, 22nd and California. Fridays 9:30 PM-2 am. Workshops, milongas. Tel: 303-294-9281 / 294-9258
TANGO COLORADO (Practica)
Denver Turnverein, 1570, Clarkson. Tuesdays 7-10:30 PM
Tel: 303-745-7679 Delmer Johnson
FORT COLLINS
SUNSET MILONGA
Sunset Nightclub, 242 Linden, Ft.

Collins. Fourth Fridays 6-8 PM
Tel: 970-484-9121 Carly Martin
TANGO PRACTICA
Masonic Temple, 225 West Oak. Fridays 7-9 PM Carly Martin

DISTRICT OF COLUMBIA
(WASHINGTON, D.C.)
DIVERSITE NIGHT CLUB
1526 14th Street NW. Mondays 7:30-midnight Tel: 202-234-5740
SUNDAY MILONGA
DC Jewish Community Centre, 1529 16th Street, NW (Corner of Q street) Every third Sunday 5-8 PM
Tel: 202-256-6288
LEON'S HOUSE TANGO (Practica)
Leon's, 1250 New Jersey Ave., NW DC. Tuesdays andWednesdays 9-11 PM
Tel: 202-638-3589
LATIN DANCER TANGO
Latin Dancer, 2052-B North Albermarle, Arlington, VA. Thursdays 9-11 PM
Tel: 703-841-9375
LatinDancer@aol.com
TAP ROOM TANGO
Vienna Tap Room, Maple Avenue, by the side of White Tiger Restaurant, 146 Maple Avenue. Thursdays 8:30-11:30 PM
Tel: 703-698-9811
TANGO MILONGA
Old Stone House at Rock Creek Park, Meadowbrook Lane, Chevy Chase, MD Second and last Fridays 8:30-11:30 PM
Tel: 202-244-2787 / 301-299-8728
TANGO MILONGA
Chevy Chase Ballroom, 5207 Wisconsin Avenue NW. Third and fourth Saturdays. 9 PM-2 AM Class at 8 PM
Tel: 301-890-4869
TANGO OPEN-AIR
Sunday afternoon milonga on the Washington Waterfront, overlooking the Rosslyn Skyline, Watergate, Kennedy Centre.

BAILATANGO
Basement of the White Tiger Restaurant,
146 Maple Avenue East, Vienna VA.
Every third Thursday 8:30-11:30 PM

B.A. TANGO LOUNGE
B.A.Restaurante, 1512-B 14th Streeet,
NW. 7:30-10:45 pm
Tel: 202-234-0886
*24-hour tango hotline for all details
in Washington DC
Tel: 202-546-2228.*

CONNECTICUT

TANGO
100 Arch Street (I-95, exit 3), Greenwich
Class 5:30 Milonga 7-11 PM
Tel: 203-406-4387

TANGO PRACTICA
Rhythms in Motion Studio, 60 Access
Road, Stratford. Sundays 2-4 PM
Tel: 203-874-2102 Judith Phelps
e-mail: http://home.att.net/~phelpstango/
index.htm

TANGO SALON
Rhythms in Motion Studio, 60 Access
Road, Stratford. First Saturday of month
8 PM-midnight. Judith Phelps
Tel: 203-874-2102 or
e-mail: john.grasso@snet.net

TANGO BAR
Metro Club, 492 Pleasant Street,
Northampton. Sunday. 6-9 PM
Tel: 413 585 9695

TANGO PARTY
Spontaneous Celebrations, 45 Danforth
Street, Jamaica Plain. Every last Friday. 6
PM-1 AM Tel: 617-524-6373

SUNDAY PRACTICA
Dance Gallery, 817 Chapel Street, New
Haven, 2-4 PM Tel: 203-874-2102 Judith
Phelps

STUDIO 440 PRACTICA
Studio 440, 440 Somerville Avenue,
Somerville. First and third Friday 8-10
PM Tel: 617-776-0329

**THE DOME ROOM at DCA PRACTI-
CA**
55 Audubon Street, New Haven
Thursday 7-9 PM Tel: 860-346-2210
Willie Feuer

FLORIDA
GAINESVILLE

MILONGA
The Karate Centre, 809 West University
Ave. Saturdays and Wednesdays 8:30 PM-
midnight.

HOLLYWOOD

DANCE MORE TANGO
The Rotary Club, 2349 Taylor Street,
east of 95. Fridays 9 PM-2 AM
Tel: 305-891-9992 / 954-921-4500

MIAMI

EL BIG 5
Elks Lodge, Coral Gables Wednesdays
8PM-1 AM Tel: 305-446-9444

ROBERTO'S MILONGA
Knights of Columbus Hall, Catalonia
270, Coral Gables Fridays Milonga 8 PM-
2 AM Tel: 305-441-0204

INT. CLUB OF ARGENTINE TANGO
Hallandale Cultural Community Centre,
410 SE 3rd St., Hallandale. Sundays
8:30 PM-midnight Tel: 305-864-5785
Juan

SUNDAY MILONGA
Arther Murray Ocean Ballroom, 18100
Collins Avenue (RK Plaza), Sunny Isle
Beach. Sundays 8 PM-midnight

SUNDAY MILONGA
Miami Concorde Supper Club, 3201 SW
32 Avenue, Miami (Close to Coral Way).
Sundays Tel: 305-759-1224

LAS COPAS TANGO
Las Copas on the Beach, Hotel Versailles,
3415 Collins Avenue. Thursdays. Class
from 7:30 PM and milonga all night long.
e-mail: Stellamilano@earthlink.net

THE MILONGA
8300SW Flagler Street #165 (La Roma

Plaza). Saturdays 10 PM-1 AM—class before. Tel: 954-894-7703 Oscar

ORLANDO
TANGO ATLANTIC
Atlantic Dance Hall. Monthly milonga.
Tel: 407-355-7778

POMPANO BEACH
MILONGUEROS OF POMPANO
2309 E. Atlantic Boulevard. Saturdays 8 PM-midnight Tel: 305 891-9992

MR. DANCE'S BALLROOM
4695 N.State Rd 7, Lauderdale Lakes, Fl 33319. Sundays 8 PM-midnight Class/Milonga Tel: 954-733-2623

LAKE WORTH
ROBERTO'S MILONGA
American-Finnish Community Centre, 908 Lehto Lane. Sundays Class: 7-8 PM Salon 8 PM-midnight

SARASOTA
SARASOTA DANCE CENTER
7222 Tamiami Tr.S (US 41) Friday class 7:30 before milonga. Tel: 941-924-5215

TANGO PLUS
Elks Lodge 5680 Rosin Way. Sundays 2-5 PM Wednesday Practica 8:30-9:30 PM Saturday workshop once a month Tel: 941-922-7900 Nicole

TAMPA BAY (WEST COAST)
SATURDAY MILONGA
Continental Ballroom, (Sherry's) Park Boulevard (between 65th and 66th Streets), Pinellas Park (pinellas County). First and fourth Saturday of month 9 PM-midnight. Tel: 727-541-5485

DUNEDIN MILONGA
Starlight Dance Club (Judy's), 1401 Main Street, Dunedin. Second Saturday of month. 9 PM-midnight
Tel: 727-733-5779

CLUB MILONGA (Tampa Bay Tango Club)
Ballroom and Latin Dance Centre, 1969 Sunset Point Rd., Clearwater. Third Saturday of month. 9 PM-midnight
Tel: Jana 813-960-8871 / 813-222-5040

ABCTANGO
ABC (JDpanguin), 6943 W. Hillsborough av., Tampa. Fridays 6-7:15 PM
Tel: 813 8142010 / 813 2058801

WEST PALM BEACH
ROBERTO MAIOLO (Class)
Organizacion Cultural de Argentina de Palm Beach, 6295 Lake WorthRd. Pine Brook Sq. Shopping Centre, Palm Beach. Wednesday 7-11 p,m. Tel: 561-966-7640

For Tango in Florida also contact:
Daniel Lapadula
Tel: (305) 631 9180
e-mail: Tangomio@aol.com or
DaniTango@aol.com

GEORGIA
TANGO RIOPLATENSE
Manuel and Ronda Patino Tel: 404-377-5822 Website: www.tango-rio.com
Tel: Stephen Rose 373-0341 for info.

HAWAII—001
HAWAII
TANGO ARGENTINO ASSOCIATION DE HAWAII
98-857 Laelua Place, Aiea, Hawaii 96701
Tel: ++1 808 488 9610
Fax: ++1 808 484 4084
e-mail: aurora-maria@webtv.net

HONOLULU
PUERTA AL TANGO
Contact Rosa and Alberto Archilla
Tel: 808-484-0664
e-mail: alapaki@aol.com

ILLINOIS
CHICAGO TANGO CLUB
Club 720, 720 North Wells at Superior. Tuesdays 7-10 PM

TANGO...NADA MAS
6137 Northwest Highway, Chicago. Classes/practicas Monday and Thursday. Milonga Saturday 9-2 AM

CHICAGO TANGO CLUB
Chicago Dance Studio, 3660 West Irving
Park. Every first Sunday 6:30-9:30 PM.
LAKE STREET MILONGA
942 W. Lake Street, three blocks west of
Halstead. Second and third Thursdays
8PM-midnight. Tel: 312-258-6137 / 773-
505-1577
e-mail: tangojan@hotmail.com or
tango@argentinamail.com

IOWA
TANGO SALON
Starlite Village Motel, 2601 E. 13th St.,
AMES, IA 50010. Usually last Thursday
in month. Weekly classes in summer,
occasionally during year. Class 7-8 PM,
dance 8-10 PM Info: Valerie Williams Tel:
515 232 7374
TANGO SALON
Café Diem, 323 Main Street, Ames,
50010. Alternate Thursdays Class 7-8 PM
Salon 8-10 PM Contact Valerie Wiiliams.
Tel: 515-232-7374
e-mail: valeriejwilliams@yahoo.com

LOUISIANA
NEW ORLEANS
**PLANET TANGO STUDIO and
SALON**
Alberto Paz and Valorie Hart
Publishers of El Firulete, The Argentine
Tango Magazine
1000 Bourbon Street, #202
New Orleans, LA 70116
Tel: 504-894-1718
e-mail: info@planet-tango.com
On-line: http//www.planet-tango.com

MAINE
PORTLAND
Casco Bay Movers Dance Studio,
151 Saint John St. Portland, Maine.
Sunday practica 7-8:30 PM
Tel: 207-729-8214

MASSACHUSETTS
THE BOSTON TANGO SCHOOL
Sharna Fabiano/Daniel Trenner
Tel: 617-623-5532
sfabiano@hotmail.com or
dtango7@aol.com
**TANGO ARGENTINO IN THE
BERKSHIRES**
River Front Grill Housatonic. Fourth
Saturday of Month. Tel: 413-528-5600
e-mail: dutango@hotmail.com
**WEDNESDAY TANGO DANCE
BREAK**
The VFW Mount Auburn Post, 688
Huron Ave., Cambridge, off Fresh Pond
Parkway. Class: 7:30-8:30 PM Milonga:
8:30-11 PM
**TANGO PRACTICE (POLLY and
STEVE)**
First Baptist Church, 5 Magazine St.
Central Sq. Cambridge. Fridays 8-11 PM
Tel: 781 396 8469
**MOONLIGHT TANGO ON THE
FOOTBRIDGE**
Weeks Pedestrian Footbridge over the
Charles River near Harvard Square.
TANGO RIALTO
Rialto, 1, Bennett Street, The Charles
Hotel, Harvard Square, Cambridge
Fridays 10:30 PM-1:30 AM Class 9-
10 PM
MILONGA ARMENONVILLE
Brazilian Cultural Centre, 310 Webster
Avenue, Cambridge.
Bimonthly, 1st and 4th Sundays 8-11 PM
Tel: 877-937-3399
TANGO
Lady Maidana Studio (Jacqueline
Maidana), 41 Union Street Easthampton.
First and third Fridays 8 PM Second
Saturdays Tel: 413-529-9070
BERKSHIRE TANGO
At the Bandstand behind the Great
Barrington Town Hall. Fridays at 7:30 PM
Check before with TangoLine at:
617-699-6246 or 617-699-6246

MICHIGAN
DETROIT

TANGO SUAVE
7758 Auburn Road, Downtown Utica.
Fridays and Saturdays 9 PM-midnight.
Tel: 810-254-0560

BRICKHOUSE TANGO
The Brickhouse, Auburn Rd. (One block
west of Van Dyke) Sundays 7 PM-

TANGO NIGHT CLUB
Arriva Restaurant, E.12 Mile Rd.,
Warren. Saturdays 9 PM
e-mail: LnBrtn@compserv.net

SANGRIA
411 S. Lafayette (4th and Lafayette),
Royal Oak Thursdays
10:30 PM-2 AM Tel: 248-543-1964

**THE LATIN and ARGENTINE
TANGO CLUB OF DETROIT**
1860 Telegraph, Dearborn. Saturdays
8 PM-1 AM Classes most days of the
week. Tel: 313-561-3236 Fax: 313-561
4505 Amy Calio and Ray Hogan
e-mail: rhogan1@ford.com
More info. available from Lori Burton at:
Tel: 810 254-0560
e-mail: LnBrtn@compserv.net
http://www.argentinetangodetroit.com

MINNESOTA
MINNEAPOLIS AND ST. PAUL

REBECCA TROST
The Quest, 110 5th St. North,
Minneapolis. Mondays Class 7 PM
Practica 8-8:45 PM Also at: 1637
Hennepin Avenue South, Nr. Loring
Park. Practica Tuesdays 9 PM
Tel: 612-342-0902

STEVE LEE
Tel: 612-729-5306
e-mail: twin-cities-tango@juno.com

TANGO LAB
1940 Hennepin Avenue. Practica
Wednesdays 8-10 PM
Tel: 612 927 7039 Frank Williams

For more information contact:
Tango Society of Minnesota.
Tel: 612-930-9221
Hotline 612-930-0929

MISSOURI
ST. LOUIS

Call Roxanne 314-490-2430 or Carter
314-579-6880

NEW JERSEY

El Mirador (Tango Salon once a month)
Info: 201-440-2290

NEW MEXICO
ALBUQUERQUE

Paul Garcia Tel: 505 823 9725
SANTA FE

**MICHAEL WALKER and LUREN
BELLUCCI**
1704-B Llano #287, NM 87505 Practica
Mondays: 7:30-9:30 PM l Milonga
Tel: 505-820-2064
Tel: Kris Hotvedt 505-465-0434
for Santa Fe.

NEW YORK
ALBANY

TANGO ALBANY
69 Fuller Road. 12205 NY
Tel: 518-459-2623
www.lorrainemichaelsdance.com
HUDSON VALLEY

Various events. For details contact: Rob
Clarke from Poughkeepsie at
e-mail: rob@cdc.com
ITHACA

SUNDAY MILONGA
Chanticleer Loft, cnr. of State and
Cayuga St. 8:30 PM-midnight

COMMON GROUND MILONGA
Common Ground, 1230 W. Danby Rd.
(south on route 96B past Ithaca College)
8-9 PM Class, practica, dance every first
and third Wednesday of month

TANGO PRACTICA
North Room, Willard Straight Hall. 7-9 PM Wednesdays when no other special events occur.

PRACTICA WITH MATEJ (Thursdays)
Courtside Fitness and Racquet Club, 380 Pine Tree Rd. Tuesdays 8.15-9:30 PM Thursdays 8:30-10 PM (workshops)

LONG ISLAND

LONG ISLAND DANCE CONNECTION
Club 56, 56th Fighter Group Restaurant (at Rupublic Airport), Rt. 110 (between Conklin St. and Route 109), East Farmingdale. Tuesdays 8-10:30 PM Tel: 516-694-8280

NEW YORK CITY AND OTHERS

SUNDAY

"EL RECODO"
Dancesport, 1845 Broadway, 2nd Floor (@ 61st St), 9 PM-12:30 AM Tel: 212-307-1111

TANGO BRUNCH
Sandra Cameron Dance Centre, 199 Lafayette Street. 2-5 PM Tel: 212-674-0505

TANGO PORTEÑO
(Outdoors—resumes in spring) Pier 16 between the Ambrose and Peking—one block south of the South Street Seaport 6 PM-9:30 PM

PRACTICA "EL RUSO"
Stepping Out, 37 W. 26th Street, (between 6th Ave. and Broadway). 3:30 PM-5:30 PM. Tel: 646-742-9400

LA MILONGA DOMINGUERA
Stepping Out, 37 W. 26th Street, (between 6th Ave. and Broadway). 5:30-10 PM Tel: 646-742-9400

MONDAY

DANCE MANHATTAN
39 West Nineteenth Street, 5th floor, NY 10010. Salon 9:30 PM-12:30 AM Rebecca and Fabienne Tel: 212-807-0802

TUESDAY

LA BOCA
Il Campanello Restaurant, 136 West 31 Street (between 6th and 7th Aves.). 8:30 PM 'til late. (No milongas in December except New Year's Eve). Tel: 212-725-1078 Gayatri Martin

TRIANGULO
675 Hudson Street, Apt. 3N 9.15 PM-1 AM Tel: 212-633-6445 e-mail: carina@tangonyc.com

TANGO ELEGANTE
Pierre Dulaine Dance Club, 25 West 31st Street (5th Ave. and Broadway) 10PM-12:30 AM Tel: 212-244-8400

WEDNESDAY

DANCESPORT
1845 Broadway (at 60th Street), 2nd Floor, NY 10023 Classes 7:30-9:30 PM and Milonga 9:30-11:30 PM Tel: 212-307-1111

DANCE MANHATTAN
39 West Nineteenth Street, 5th floor, NY 10010. 9 -11 PM Practica

LA ESTACIÓN (YOU SHOULD BE DANCING)
412 8th Avenue (31st Street). 9PM-1 AM Tel: 212-252-3753
Resumes in the fall.

SPICE SUMMER FESTIVAL
Pier 63 just north of the Chelsea Piers Equestrian Centre. 8PM-2 AM Until Sept. 29th—summer only

THURSDAY

SANDRA CAMERON DANCE CENTER
199 Lafayette Street. Classes: 7:30 PM-9:30 PM Salon: 9:30 PM-midnight Live music every first Thursday of the month.Tel: 212-674-0505 or 718-325-6579

STEPPING OUT
Stepping Out, 37 West 26th St. (between 6th Ave. and Broadway). Practica 9:30-11 PM

TANGO LA NACIONAL
Centro Español, 239 West 14th St. Class
7-8:30 PM Salon from 9:30 PM-1:30 AM
Tel: 212-385-9698 / 917-385-9698
FRIDAY
HOUSE OF LATIN DANCE
SAVA Arts, 25th Street (between
Broadway and 6th Ave.) 9 PM-2 AM
DANCE MANHATTAN
39 West Nineteenth Street, 5th floor.
NY10011 9:30 PM-12:30 AM Second
Friday of month Tel: 212-769-9559 /
212-807-0802
LA BELLE EPOQUE
827 Broadway (between 12th and 13th
Sts.), 2nd floor 9:30 PM-2:30 AM
Tel: 212-254-6436
MILONGUITA
Triangulo, 675 Hudson Street, Apt. 3N
8.30 PM Tel: 212-633-6445
e-mail: carina@tangonyc.com
SATURDAY
CHELSEA MARKET TANGO
(Resumes in the fall)
Chelsea Market, 9th Avenue (between
15th and 16th Streets,) 4-7 PM
DANCESPORT
1845 Broadway, 2nd floor (at 60th
Street), NY 10023
Second and fifth Saturday of month
7:30-2 AM 212-750-5892 / 307-1111
(Danel and Maria)
BAILEMOS TANGO (Danel and Maria)
Every first Saturday of month. 92nd
Street and Lexington at the "Y." Every
second and fifth Saturday of the month:
DanceSport, 1845 Broadway, 2nd Floor.
7:30 PM class and salon
Every third an fourth Saturday of the
month: Pierre Dulaine Dance Club,
25 W. 31st St. 4th Floor. Live music.
Tel: 718-325-6579 or 212-674-0505.
Live music at every milonga by The New
York Tango Trio.
TANGO IN THE PARK

Tango by the Shakespeare Statue,
Central Park at around 6-8:30 PM June-
October. Phone Lucille Krasne 212-777-
6053 for starting date and details. Bring
music, food drink, candles.
LAFAYETTE TANGO
Lafayette Grill, 54 Franklin Street, nr.
Broadway. Beg. lessons at 7:30 PM, then
salon 9:30 PM 'til late.
Tel: 212-732-5600
LA PRACTICA
Dance Manhattan, 39 West 19th Street,
5th floor, NY 10010. 11 AM-2 PM Tel:
212-807-0802
HOUSE OF LATIN DANCE
SAVA Arts, 25th Street (between
Broadway and 6th Ave.) 9 PM-2 AM
MILONGA MATINEE
Dance Times Square, 156 W. 44th Street
(between 6th and 7th Aves.)
3 PM-5 PM Tel: 212-799-5712 Kana
NEW YORK TANGO HOTLINE
Tel: 718-35TANGO 718-358-2646)
ROCHESTER
ROCHESTER TANGO
Paradigm Supper Club, 3400 Monroe
Avenue. Wednesdays Class: 8 PM
Milonga 9 PM-midnight
TANGO DANCE-ENCOUNTER
DanceEncounters Studio, 28 Atlantic
Avenue. 14607. Sundays 8-10 PM
Tel: 716-739-3120
e-mail: de@rpa.net
TANGO DANCE-ENCOUNTER
RJ's Pub, 140 Alexander Street. Dinner,
dance, show from 7 PM
Tel: 716-739-3120
TANGO RED
Red Social Lounge, 171 Saint Paul Street.
NY 14604 Saturdays 7-10:30 PM
Tel: 716-546-3580
e-mail: red@fnmail.com
WESTCHESTER
TANGO
Conga Restaurant and Lounge, 615 Main

Street, New Rochelle. Fridays 7 PM-midnight. Tel: 914-235-2922

OHIO
CLEVELAND
TIMMY TANGO
Belinda's Night Club, 9613 Madison Ave. Saturdays 8-10 PM (class at 7:30 PM) Info: Tim Pogros Tel: 440-327-8211 Classes also available.
E-mail: TimmyTango@aol.com
TIMMY TANGO
Club Isabella, 2025 University Hospitals Drive. Tuesdays 7:30 PM
Tel: 216-229-1177
CINCINNATI
CINCINNATI TANGO SOC.
Larry and Tina Gutierres
Tel: 513-681-8008
COLUMBUS
TANGOHIO
Jon Devlin-Tel: 614-898-9119

OKLAHOMA
OKLAHOMA CITY
Community Dance Centre. Details
Tel: 918-241-9713 Tonya Smith and Bob Menhart.
*Info. Tel: 528 2737 Louie Macias
(Dance Centre)*
OREGON
PORTLAND
CLAY'S DANCE STUDIO
6959 SW Multnomah Blvd. Every Monday Classes 6:30-9:30 PM Practica to 11:30 PM.
Tel: Clay Nelson 1-503-244 8699

PENNYSYLVANIA
PHILADELPHIA
JEAN'S PRACTICA
Tokio Ballroom, 2nd fl., La Champignon Restaurant, 122-124 Lombard Street. Wednesdays Class: 7:30 PM Practica: 8-10:30 PM Tel: 215-628-3524 / 609-869- 0010

TANGO TEA
Trocadero Dance Studio, 2030 Sansom St., 2nd fl., Adrienne Theatre. Every 2nd Sunday 7:45-10:30 PM
SUNDAY CLASS
Philly-Total Fitness and Dance, 7140 Germantown Ave. Sundays 3-5 PM More info. in Philadelphia contact: Philly-Tango Grapevine (Jean Fung).
Tel: 215-628-3524 Fax: 215-242-9625. PO Box 466, Ambler, PA 19002-0466
NOCHES DE PHILLY-TANGO
Tokio Ballroom, 2nd fl., Le Champignon Restaurant, 122-124 Lombard Street. First and third Saturdays. 8:30 PM to 1:30 AM Tel: 215-922-2515
e-mail: phillytango@hotmail.com
PITTSBURGH
**PITTSBURGH TANGO
(Class/Practica)**
Wilkins Centre, Regent Square. Sundays Class 4:30-6:30 PM Practica 6:30-8:30 PM
PITTSBURGH TANGO (Dancing)
Brickhouse Bar and Grill, 563 Greenfield Avenue. Thursdays 9-11 PM (Lessons from 8:30 PM)
PITTSBURGH TANGO (Milongas)
Wilkins Centre, Regent Square. 9 PM-midnight. Tel: 242-6335 / 244-9661
RHODE ISLAND
RHODE ISLAND TANGO SOCIETY
Providence Ballet Studio, 107 Eddy Street, Providence. Class and Practica Fridays 7-9 PM

TEXAS
DALLAS/FORT WORTH
LA MILONGA
Dallas Opera Rehearsal Facility, 4301 S. Fitzhugh Ave. Every third Friday 7-11 PM Tel: 214-520-0244 Carlos
SALON PAVADITA
2714¹/₂ Greenville Avenue. First and last Sunday of month 8-11 PM
Tel: 214-288-5412 Lisa Ellison

HOUSTON
HOUSTON ARGENTINE TANGO ASSOCIATION
Stevens of Hollywood Dance Studio, 2143, Westheimer, Houston. Practica and lesson every Tuesday 8-10 PM
Teacher: Joe MacLaughlin
Contact: A. Lester Buck
713-665-3812 (Tango Hotline).

AUSTIN
AUSTIN TANGO CONNECTION
Tapestry Dance Studio, 507B Pressler.
Tel: Chris Humphrey at 512-480--9899
Fax: 512 471 0616
e-mail: atc@mods.com

UTAH
THE WASATCH TANGO CLUB
YWCA, 333 South, 200 East Street, Salt Lake City
Tel: 801-463-7992 Theresa

VIRGINIA
Tango in Arlington. Info: 703 841 9375

WASHINGTON
SEATTLE
Weekly Milongas
SALON DE TANGO
Velocity Dance Studio, 915-E Pine Street (@10th Ave), 2nd Floor. Fridays 9 PM-1 AM Tel: Larry Martin 206-632-6570
SATURDAY NIGHT MILONGA
Freehold Theater Lab Studio, 1525 10th Ave (@ E. Pine). 9 PM-midnight every Saturday excl. second Sat.
Tel: 206-781-9553 (Ilana Rubin)
206-325-5198 (Janeen Field)

SUNDAY TANGO SOIREE
Ballard Firehouse Studio, 5429 Russell Ave. NW (@ NW Market), 3rd floor.
Sundays 7:30-11 PM Tel: 206-325-5198 Janeen Field or 206-323-4858 Patricia Malillo

Weekly Practicas
DANCE ON CAPITOL HILL
340-15th East. (@ E. Harrison), downstairs. Thursdays 9:30 PM-1 AM
For info on dancing in Seattle, contact: Andre Samson. Tel: 206-528-8141
TANGO CLUB OF SEATTLE
(non-dancing info) Tel: 206-323-2143 (Art Hemingway)

For further information on tango in the U.S.A., please contact: Danel and Maria P.O.Box 260, Woodlawn Hts., NY 10470 Tel/Fax: 718 325 6579 Danel and Maria publish The Tango Times. The Tango Times is the official publication of the Argentinean Tango Dancers Association. It comes out 3 times a year, Jan.-May-Sept.

VENEZUELA—0058

CARACAS
LA TERRAZZA ATENEO DE CARACAS
Tuesdays 9 PM-1 AM
CLUB URUGUAYO (LOS CHORROS)
Wednesdays 8 PM-1 AM
CIRCULO MILITAR
Fridays twice a month 9 PM-4 AM
e-mail: TangoCaracas@egroups.com

For additional information on tango call DanceSport at 212-307-1111 or visit www.dancesport.com

Acknowledgements

In the desire to make this book as comprehensive as possible, I was fortunate to have the cooperation and contribution of many people without whom the result would not be nearly as complete. I'd like to thank those whose work you find throughout these pages. They are all stars, and the order that follows in no way indicates what role they played. They are listed in alphabetical order.

PABLO ASLAN, who wrote "The Music of Tango" for this book, is an Argentine-born bassist and composer. He is a founder and co-director of New York Buenos Connection and New York Tango Trio. He has toured the world, recently with cellist Yo-Yo Ma and members of the Astor Piazzola Quintet. His list of recordings is vast and includes working on soundtracks for Dave Grusin's *Random Hearts* and *Flawless* featuring Robert De Niro to name just two.

He is also a scholar and teacher of tango music and has lectured on the history of tango at many universities. He teaches tango musical techniques throughout the country.

KEITH ELSHAW, whose expertise is seen in our "Tango: The Music" is a broadcast voice artist and producer who surrendered to the tango obsession in 1990. He publishes articles and assorted information about tango on his website which you can visit at www.ToTANGO.net. Linda Valentino, who contributes to Keith's website, provided the basic information for the interview with Gloria and Eduardo.

JEANETTE JONES is a talented photographer whose work you will find throughout this volume. Her photos were taken in New York and in Buenos Aires and do much to enhance the spirit of this book. She lives in England and is in demand as a portrait, reportage and advertising photographer. In addition, she has published her own book, *Walk on the Wild Side* (also by Barricade Books) a collection of provocative photographs of cross-dressers, drag artists and transsexuals.

KATHARINE JONES wrote about the history of tango for this book, and her editing skills are to be found throughout the pages. She worked with me over many months to help make the reading as smooth as possible. She is a New York writer, screenwriter and author of the soon to be published documentary book *New York Stories: City of Strangers*. She has a long relationship with contemporary dance, which includes writing text pieces used in the performances of American choreographer Meg Stuart and Canadian choreographer Benoit LaChambre. She was first introduced to tango in 1987 and has since become an avid tango dancer.

PAUL LANGE & MICHIKO OKAZAKI, editors of *El Once Tango News*, very generously provided the exhaustive listing of tango venues throughout the world. *El Once Tango News* is a quarterly publication devoted to Argentinean tango, with articles, photos, news and much more, including the world-wide listing of tango venues. For more information about them please see their website at www.elonce.dircon.co.uk

DONNA D. LEES, whose photo is used on the cover of this book, has been the studio photographer for DanceSport since 1985.

MARILYN COLE LOWNES in no small way is responsible for this book being published since she introduced my publisher, Carole

Stuart, to tango several years ago. Marilyn is a good friend and one of my pupils and visits milongas in London, New York, Paris, Aspen and Buenos. Aires. When not tangoing, Marilyn writes for *British Esquire*, *The Times of London*, *Irish America Magazine* and *Boxing Digest*.

CARLOS QUIROGA is publisher and editor of *ReporTango* magazine as well as a tango disk jockey in much demand at New York City milongas. His music recommendations are an important part of this book. He is often disk jockey at my DanceSport studio. A number of the interviews in this book were contributed by *ReporTango*. The website for *ReporTango* is www.reportango.com

PAMELA SAICHANN has been a vital part of the process of putting this book together. She has worked as my assistant and her organizational skills are to be admired. She corresponded with many of the artists who are included in the book and also worked in the layout and design of the instruction section. When she is not working with me she is contributing editor to *ReporTango* magazine.

CAROLE STUART, my publisher, is also one of my students. Tango became a passion for her and on several occasions she was part of our group when we partied in Buenos Aires. Her suggestion that I write this book turned into a journey that we traveled together with many twists, laughs, and surprises along the way.

LESLIE WHITESELL comes last on this list, but her contribution is certainly not small. Her help in providing the phonetics in the tango section should help readers decipher the Spanish terms.

I would also like to thank my DanceSport teachers, colleagues and students for their generous cooperation as this book took shape. They offered themselves up as willing and trusting guinea pigs and enabled me to have a laboratory from which to research and develop my often unorthodox teaching techniques which are reflected in these pages. I also want to thank all of the coaches who were so elpful in sharing their knowledge and experience of dance with me.

Acknowledgements

Finally, I'd like to mention that if this book has piqued readers' curiosity about tango and they'd like to learn even more—please look at the website for my studio, DanceSport at www.dancesport.com. We'll be happy to provide you with information on how to obtain the instruction section on CD, video or CD-ROM.